The Translingual Verse
Migration, Rhythm, and Resistance in Contemporary Italophone Poetry

LEGENDA

LEGENDA is the Modern Humanities Research Association's book imprint for new research in the Humanities. Founded in 1995 by Malcolm Bowie and others within the University of Oxford, Legenda has always been a collaborative publishing enterprise, directly governed by scholars. The Modern Humanities Research Association (MHRA) joined this collaboration in 1998, became half-owner in 2004, in partnership with Maney Publishing and then Routledge, and has since 2016 been sole owner. Titles range from medieval texts to contemporary cinema and form a widely comparative view of the modern humanities, including works on Arabic, Catalan, English, French, German, Greek, Italian, Portuguese, Russian, Spanish, and Yiddish literature. Editorial boards and committees of more than 60 leading academic specialists work in collaboration with bodies such as the Society for French Studies, the British Comparative Literature Association and the Association of Hispanists of Great Britain & Ireland.

The MHRA encourages and promotes advanced study and research in the field of the modern humanities, especially modern European languages and literature, including English, and also cinema. It aims to break down the barriers between scholars working in different disciplines and to maintain the unity of humanistic scholarship. The Association fulfils this purpose through the publication of journals, bibliographies, monographs, critical editions, and the MHRA Style Guide, and by making grants in support of research. Membership is open to all who work in the Humanities, whether independent or in a University post, and the participation of younger colleagues entering the field is especially welcomed.

ALSO PUBLISHED BY THE ASSOCIATION

Critical Texts
Tudor and Stuart Translations • *New Translations* • *European Translations*
MHRA Library of Medieval Welsh Literature

MHRA Bibliographies
Publications of the Modern Humanities Research Association

The Annual Bibliography of English Language & Literature
Austrian Studies
Modern Language Review
Portuguese Studies
The Slavonic and East European Review
Working Papers in the Humanities
The Yearbook of English Studies

www.mhra.org.uk
www.legendabooks.com

TRANSCRIPT

Transcript publishes books about all kinds of imagining across languages, media and cultures: translations and versions, inter-cultural and multi-lingual writing, illustrations and musical settings, adaptation for theatre, film, TV and new media, creative and critical responses. We are open to studies of any combination of languages and media, in any historical moments, and are keen to reach beyond Legenda's traditional focus on modern European languages to embrace anglophone and world cultures and the classics. We are interested in innovative critical approaches: we welcome not only the most rigorous scholarship and sharpest theory, but also modes of writing that stretch or cross the boundaries of those discourses.

Editorial Committee
Chair: Matthew Reynolds (Oxford)
Robin Kirkpatrick (Cambridge)
Laura Marcus (Oxford)
Patrick McGuinness (Oxford)
Ben Morgan (Oxford)
Mohamed-Salah Omri (Oxford)
Tanya Pollard (CUNY)
Yopie Prins (Michigan)

Advisory Board
Jason Gaiger (Oxford)
Alessandro Grilli (Pisa)
Marina Grishakova (Tartu)
Martyn Harry (Oxford)
Linda Hutcheon (Toronto)
Calin-Andrei Mihailescu (London, Ontario)
Wen-Chin Ouyang (SOAS)
Clive Scott (UEA)
Ali Smith
Marina Warner (Birkbeck)
Shane Weller (Kent)
Stefan Willer (Berlin)

Managing Editor
Dr Graham Nelson
41 Wellington Square, Oxford OX1 2JF, UK

www.legendabooks.com/series/transcript

TRANSCRIPT

1. *Adapting the Canon: Mediation, Visualization, Interpretation*, edited by Ann Lewis and Silke Arnold-de Simine
2. *Adapted Voices: Transpositions of Céline's Voyage au bout de la nuit and Queneau's Zazie dans le métro*, by Armelle Blin-Rolland
3. *Zola and the Art of Television: Adaptation, Recreation, Translation*, by Kate Griffiths
4. *Comparative Encounters between Artaud, Michaux and the Zhuangzi: Rationality, Cosmology and Ethics*, by Xiaofan Amy Li
5. *Minding Borders: Resilient Divisions in Literature, the Body and the Academy*, edited by Nicola Gardini, Adriana Jacobs, Ben Morgan, Mohamed-Salah Omri and Matthew Reynolds
6. *Memory Across Borders: Nabokov, Perec, Chamoiseau*, by Sara-Louise Cooper
7. *Erotic Literature in Adaptation and Translation*, edited by Johannes D. Kaminski
8. *Translating Petrarch's Poetry: L'Aura del Petrarca from the Quattrocento to the 21st Century*, edited by Carole Birkan-Berz, Guillaume Coatalen and Thomas Vuong
9. *Making Masud Khan: Psychoanalysis, Empire and Modernist Culture*, by Benjamin Poore
10. *Prismatic Translation*, edited by Matthew Reynolds
11. *The Patient, the Impostor and the Seducer: Medieval European Literature in Hebrew*, by Tovi Bibring
12. *Reading Dante and Proust by Analogy*, by Julia Caterina Hartley
13. *The First English Translations of Molière: Drama in Flux 1663-1732*, by Suzanne Jones
14. *After Clarice: Reading Lispector's Legacy in the Twenty-First Century*, edited by Adriana X. Jacobs and Claire Williams
15. *Uruguayan Theatre in Translation: Theory and Practice*, by Sophie Stevens
16. *Hamlet Translations: Prisms of Cultural Encounters across the Globe*, edited by Márta Minier and Lily Kahn
17. *The Foreign Connection: Writings on Poetry, Art and Translation*, by Jamie McKendrick
18. *Poetics, Performance and Politics in French and Italian Renaissance Comedy*, by Lucy Rayfield

The Translingual Verse

Migration, Rhythm, and Resistance in Contemporary Italophone Poetry

Alice Loda

Transcript 21
Modern Humanities Research Association
2021

Published by Legenda
an imprint of the Modern Humanities Research Association
Salisbury House, Station Road, Cambridge CB1 2LA

ISBN 978-1-78188-592-5 (HB)
ISBN 978-1-78188-596-3 (PB)

First published 2021

All rights reserved. No part of this publication may be reproduced or disseminated or transmitted in any form or by any means, electronic, mechanical, photocopying, recording or otherwise, or stored in any retrieval system, or otherwise used in any manner whatsoever without written permission of the copyright owner, except in accordance with the provisions of the Copyright, Designs and Patents Act 1988, or under the terms of a licence permitting restricted copying issued in the UK by the Copyright Licensing Agency Ltd, Saffron House, 6–10 Kirby Street, London EC1N 8TS, England, or in the USA by the Copyright Clearance Center, 222 Rosewood Drive, Danvers MA 01923. Application for the written permission of the copyright owner to reproduce any part of this publication must be made by email to legenda@mhra.org.uk.

Disclaimer: Statements of fact and opinion contained in this book are those of the author and not of the editors or the Modern Humanities Research Association. The publisher makes no representation, express or implied, in respect of the accuracy of the material in this book and cannot accept any legal responsibility or liability for any errors or omissions that may be made.

Trademark notice: Product or corporate names may be trademarks or registered trademarks, and are used only for identification and explanation without intent to infringe.

© Modern Humanities Research Association 2021

Copy-Editor: Richard Correll

CONTENTS
❖

	Acknowledgements	ix
	List of Abbreviations	xi
	Introduction	1
1	Trajectories: Translingual Migrant Poetics in Contemporary Italy	9
	Migration Literature and Italy: From Contexts to Texts	9
	Travelling Concepts: Reorienting Italophone	13
	Translingualism: *Within* and *Beyond*	15
	Mobilizing Paradigms: Post-Monolingualism and Resistance	19
	Rupture: Linguistic Distance and Transformation	22
	The Translingual Verse: Rhythm and Movement	24
	Translingual Migrant Poetics in Contemporary Italy	26
	Corpus	28
	Methodology	29
2	Gëzim Hajdari's Poetics between Italy and Albania	37
	Proximity and Distance: A Transmediterranean Poetics	37
	Poesie scelte (1990–2007): The Self-Anthology as Long Form	42
	Poetic Forms: Circularity and Transformation	44
	Hajdari's Metres: Between Syllabic and Accentual Verse	60
	Double Language: Translingualism, Space, and Movement	72
3	Dissolving Boundaries: Mobilization and Transformation in Barbara Pumhösel's Poetry	83
	Translingualism, Ecopoetics, Ecofeminism	83
	A More-Than-Human Book: *prugni*	88
	Poetic Forms: A Semantics of Brevity and Contact	91
	A Transient Rhythm: Pumhösel's Metres	100
	Touching, Glancing, Hearing, Feeling: A Transitional Language	107
4	Hybridity and Dynamism in Hasan Atiya Al Nassar's Verse	117
	Al Nassar's Iraqi-Italian Poetic Journey	117
	Fire, Water, Stone: Hasan Al Nassar's *Roghi sull'acqua babilonese*	121
	Poetic Forms: Passage and Hybridity in Al Nassar's Long Poems	123
	Metre and Hidden Metre	131
	Linguistic Deformation and Mobile Trajectories	145
	Conclusion	153
	Bibliography	159
	Appendix	167
	Index	181

*To the memory of my father
and to Elsa, Lisa and Nina*

ACKNOWLEDGEMENTS

The Translingual Verse has been written on the unceded land of the Gadigal People of the Eora Nation. I would like to pay my respect to their Elders past, present, and emerging.

This book is based on my doctoral dissertation, completed at the University of Sydney in 2017. I would like to express my gratitude to the University of Sydney for supporting my doctoral studies with a University of Sydney International Scholarship, and to the University of Technology Sydney for providing financial support for this research project.

I wish to thank Assoc. Prof. Francesco Borghesi, Dr Maria Cristina Mauceri, Prof. Gianfranca Lavezzi, and Dr Lucia Sorbera for their support during my doctoral studies and beyond. I am grateful to Prof. Sonia Gentili, Assoc. Prof. Ombretta Frau, and Assoc. Prof. Marco Sonzogni for the attention they have dedicated to my work and their important suggestions towards improving it. I acknowledge the work of Dr Francesco Bailo and Dr Francesco Possemato, who helped me in designing and refining the concordances. Many thanks go to Dr Emma Barlow, who professionally edited this book with outstanding care, accuracy, and dedication. I am grateful to Silvana Grippi, Director of DEA press and to Dr Ian Seed for their care and warm support to this project. I also wish to thank Olivia Hamilton for her outstanding commitment to editing the translations of poetry.

This book has benefitted from discussions with a number of scholars and friends. I wish to thank in particular Dr Mia Lecomte, Edoardo Olmi, Dr Rosanna Morace, Dr Matteo Fadini, Dr Valentina Seffer, Dr Emilio Sciarrino, Dr Fabrizio Miliucci, and Dr Elena Carletti for providing me with materials and sources. My gratitude goes to Assoc. Prof. Ilaria Vanni, Assoc. Prof. Paul Allatson, Prof. Maryanne Dever, Dr Valentina Gosetti, Assoc. Prof. Julie Robert, and Assoc. Prof. Giorgia Alù, who have mentored me and encouraged me all the way through. Many thanks also go to Dr Beate Mueller, Dr Nicholas Manganas, Dr Angela Giovanangeli, Dr Emi Otsuji, Dr Carlo Tirinanzi de Medici, Dr Sabina Groeneveld, Assoc. Prof. Antonia Rubino, and Assoc. Prof. Susan Oguro, for their suggestions and friendship. An important moment in my career was my participation in the Institute for World Literature seminars, organized by Harvard University at the City University of Hong Kong in 2014; I wish to thank Prof. David Damrosch and Assoc. Prof. Delia Ungureanu for making that experience possible. I am grateful to Prof. Matthew Reynolds and Dr Graham Nelson of Legenda who believed in this project, and provided invaluable guidance, and to Richard Correll, copy-editor, for his thoroughness and his support.

I wish to thank my family, in particular Dr Agnese Loda, Dr Friedeman Loos, Rita Berruti, and Nina for their care and support. I am immensely grateful to Dr Francesco Bailo, Elsa and Lisa for being by my side every day.

Finally my heartfelt gratitude goes to the authors, Gëzim Hajdari, Barbara Pumhösel, and Hasan Atiya Al Nassar, for the attention they have dedicated to my studies, for their words, and for their suggestions. Most of all, I wish to thank them for their poetry and for what their translingual verse has taught me.

I acknowledge that some background data and analysis have been used in the following publication:

LODA, ALICE, '"Dolce era la notte." Iraqi and Iranian Poets in Italy: Metrical-Stylistic Implications of Translingual Versification', Italian Culture, 33.2 (2015), 105–25

And that parts of the Introduction and Chapter 4 have been used in:

LODA, ALICE, 'Corpo e tempo: Eros and Melancholy in Gëzim Hajdari's Transmediterranean Poetics', Ticontre. Teoria Testo Traduzione, 10 (2018), 137–67

All translations throughout the book are mine, unless otherwise stated. Poems and excerpts of poetry have been translated by myself and edited by Olivia Hamilton, unless otherwise stated

A.L., June 2021

LIST OF ABBREVIATIONS

Poetry collections, sections and poems (in excerpts):

PS   Gëzim Hajdari, *Poesie scelte (1990–2007)* [Selected poems (1990–2007)] (Nardò: Controluce, 2008).

Sections of PS:

EM   *Erbamara* [Bitter grass]
AP   *Antologia della pioggia* [Anthology of the rain]
OC   *Ombra di cane* [The dog's shadow]
SC   *Sassi contro vento* [Stones upwind]
CP   *Corpo presente* [The present body]
STG   *Stigmate* [Stigmata]
SN   *Spine nere* [Black thorns]
MD   *Maldiluna* [Maldiluna]
PG   *Peligòrga* [Peligòrga]
PN   Barbara Pumhösel, *prugni* [plum trees] (Isernia: Cosmo Iannone, 2008)

Sections of PN:

BL   *bioluminescenze* [bioluminescence]
LP   *lezioni di poesia* [poetry lessons]
PN   *prugni* [plum trees]
GD   *guadare* [fording]
SM   *simmetrie mancine* [left-handed symmetries]
MG   *la maniglia di ghiaccio* [the ice handle]
PS   *poesie sparse* [scattered poems]
HK   *haiku* [haiku]
RG   Hasan Atiya Al Nassar, *Roghi sull'acqua babilonese* [Fires on the waters of Babylon] (Florence: DEA, 2003; 2nd edn, 2004)

Poems are identified with a progressive numeral which follows the order of their appearance in the respective collection. Numbers are preceded by the abbreviated form of the collection (and the section for *PS* and *PN*), and followed by the line numbers where relevant.

Metres:

BS   *bisillabo* [disyllabic line]
TS   *trisillabo* [trisyllabic line]
QS   *quadrisillabo* [quadrisyllabic line]

QN	*quinario* [pentasyllabic line]
SN	*senario* [hexasyllabic line]
ST	*settenario* [heptasyllabic line]
OT	*ottonario* [octosyllabic line]
NO	*novenario* [nonasyllabic line]
DS	*decasillabo* [decasyllabic line]
ED	*endecasillabo* [hendecasyllabic line]
VL	*verso lungo* [long line]

You cannot explain everything by counting, but if you can count, count.
FRANCESCA TRIVELLATO

Some etymologists speculate that the word 'canon' (as in 'canonical') is related to the Arabic word 'qanun', or law in the binding, legalistic sense of that word. But that is only one rather restrictive meaning. The other is a musical one, canon as a contrapuntal form employing numerous voices in usually strict imitation of each other, a form, in other words, expressing motion, playfulness, discovery, and, in the rhetorical sense, invention.
EDWARD SAID

We fall in love with languages like we do with people.
I'm a polygamous poet.
GËZIM HAJDARI

INTRODUCTION

Bie shi vazhdimisht
në këtë
vend
ndoshta ngaqë jam
i huaj.

Piove sempre
in questo
paese
forse perché sono
straniero.

[It always rains
in this
country
maybe because I am
a stranger.]¹

The Albanian-Italian poet Gëzim Hajdari wrote the above verse in 1993. One year earlier, he had arrived in Italy in self-exile, as his life was being threatened due to his intellectual and political activity in his city, Lushnjë, in central Albania. Hajdari had been one of the founders of the Democratic and Republican Party and had begun to develop a solid journalistic and literary career. In his works, which had always been foregrounded by an irresistible search for the truth and a *civile* commitment, Hajdari had denounced the atmosphere of violence and corruption that characterized the communist regime and the troubled years following its fall. As Graziella Parati pointed out, Hajdari's short verse was destined to become a manifesto for an entire generation of authors, especially those who had arrived in Italy from many different places over the last three decades of the twentieth century.² In fact, it is within this crucial timeframe that Italy experienced increasing migratory influxes, a novel phase in its history.³ As an effect of these dynamics, the critical discourse on postcolonial, transcultural and fluid identities began to assert itself within the Italophone context. As many scholars have argued, the composite realm of migrant, translingual, postcolonial and post-ethnic writings that arose played a pivotal role in the process of recovering the trajectories of movement that profoundly marked Italy's history since before its unification, but which had been substantially removed from the country's official narratives and self-representations.⁴ This dialogic generative role of translingual migrant writing is still central today.

Leaving aside for the moment the socio-cultural and historical discourses, I would like to return to Hajdari's short verse above and elaborate on a series of interesting aspects that are, in general, useful for a preliminary discussion of the main trajectories I explore in this book. First, Hajdari's short verse presents itself on the page in a double and parallel unfolding, with the Albanian version on the left and the Italian on the right. This configuration characterizes the majority of

Hajdari's translingual works and is a distinctive way in which the author inflects the experience of linguistic movement that is entailed in his displacement. In a persuasive study on translational dynamics in Somali-Italian literature, Simone Brioni demonstrated that linguistic choices are extremely significant in the context of postcolonial, migrant and translingual writing.[5] In this context, the configuration of languages on the page can reveal important insights regarding the authors' positionings in terms of the complex and fluid experience of physical and linguistic movement. In the case of Hajdari, as I shall discuss, the presence of parallel texts alludes to the inseparability of the two languages across which the author's moves: his first or 'native' one, Albanian, and his second one, Italian, which Hajdari acquires in adulthood in extremely challenging conditions and after the trauma of a forced migration. Hajdari develops a particular relationship with his two languages. Instead of being separated or alternated, the two languages are, in fact, employed as indivisible tools on his page, and their entanglement creates, as per the author's words, a novel and unique 'lingua doppia' [double language].[6] Notably, Hajdari's double language reflects an instinctive translingual rhythmical surfacing, and it is configured as a syntonic pulsation that connects the languages and is then transitively transcribed on the page. As I shall discuss in this book, other translingual authors experience moving across languages differently, and yet the presence of this rhythmical encounter, which occurs even before the agglomeration of words on the page, appears to be constitutive in the unfolding of the translingual verse.

A second important aspect emerges from a detailed reading of the above poem, one that is, again, a central focus of this book. In fact, in transcribing his verse on the page, the poet demonstrates a sensing of the words that is, first, physical and material. The words that foreground his verse are chosen for their rhythmical and sensual qualities, and they sharply adhere to the reality that they embody. As such, they appear on the page as stones, as materials for construction and as bodies that take shape in parallel in the two languages. The verse is moulded through a radical process of subtraction, which supports signifiers to provide a novel relief on the page. The development of this material relation with words is an experience that many translingual authors have in common and which in Hajdari's case significantly impacts the early development of the double verse. This is a quality that allows, among other things, the profoundly transformative power of translingualism to emerge, a process that mobilizes the perception of signifiers, and produces important reverberations in the authors' use of their mother tongue, as I shall discuss in the body chapters.

A third and final aspect that emerges from the analysis of the poem pertains to the relationship between the subject and outer reality. An evident perception of alterity foregrounds more-than-human entanglements in the verse. The binding between subject and world is compromised. Non-human actors, such as the rain, participate in a process of radical isolation of the subject, while the poem foregrounds a path towards separation. Significantly, the perception of alterity which permeates the text is inscribed in an ambivalent formal-semantic configuration. In fact, Hajdari anchors the central subject to the landscapes of exile through a powerful expressive use of spatial indexicality (*in questo paese* [in this country]), and then he proceeds to reveal, through his portrayal of missed or impossible encounters, the irrelevance of the same subject to the reality in which it is nonetheless immersed. The complexity of this unfulfilled trajectory of belonging points, of course, to the contrapuntal nature of the experience of exile, which performs a central function in the articulation of Hajdari's translingual verse. Here, as in the works of many displaced translingual migrant authors, exile generates a constant oscillation between inside and outside, past and present. At the same time, translingual verse makes visible a radical mobilization of the way in which the subject senses their outer reality, which is perceived and written differently as an effect of linguistic and physical movement.

Analysing Hajdari's poem has allowed me to enter into some of the fundamental themes that I will explore in this book, particularly the ways in which linguistic movement is configured on the page, the mobilization in the perception of words and matter that the experience of travelling languages and cultures enacts, as well as the use of indexicality to foreground contrapuntal and fluid spaces and positions of the subject. I maintain that the discussion of all these aspects is central for deepening the critical discourse on translingual migrant poetics.

On the whole, in this study I foreground what happens when poetry emerges from the encounter of different languages and cultures within one sole authorial voice and as an effect of migration. In order to illuminate these complex and multi-layered trajectories, I enter into the poetic laboratories of three Italophone translingual migrant authors: Gëzim Hajdari, Barbara Pumhösel and Hasan Al Nassar. These authors arrived in Italy from three very different countries: Albania, Austria and Iraq, respectively. Their experience of movement and their positioning with respect to the Italian language are extremely diverse. Nonetheless, their translingual and migratory paths present a series of important intersections, which allow me to develop a comparative discourse. These intersections will be explored in detail in the following chapters, but it is important to introduce some of them here. First, all the poets arrived in Italy over the last decades of the past century. As such, they all played a significant role in the process of affirmation of translingual migrant voices in this context, a process that I intend to capture. Second, all the authors learned Italian as adults and began to employ it after their migration. This aspect allows me to observe closely the generative effects of linguistic distance within their translingual verses. Linguistic distance, a concept I will elaborate on further, has long been associated with the ideas of limit, boundary and barrier and, as such, has been mostly conceptualized as an impeding factor, something that prevents the full articulation of a literary discourse. However, recent studies and interventions have challenged this idea, framing linguistic distance as a tool that may, on the contrary, generate novel and powerful textual ecologies.[7] These latter originate precisely from the fluid ways of perceiving and inhabiting languages that are entailed in the experience of physical and linguistic movement. As I shall illustrate, there is not one sole effect of linguistic distance, and each translingual author inflects this distance differently, but always significantly. A final point the authors have in common is that while they developed a significant Italophone literary trajectory, they also wrote poetry in their first language, often before their migration. As I have explained,

Hajdari continued to employ Albanian in the construction of his double verse after his displacement. Meanwhile, the other two authors alternated between their first and second language and developed parallel bilingual literary paths. Some of them self-translate their works, while others write directly in one language or another. In any case, the rhythmical action of the mother tongue, and its prosodic qualities, surface within the innermost components of their translingual verse, and mostly in the form of metrical or linguistic-semantic encounters. As I shall discuss, Vered Shemtov described the dialogic effects that contrapuntal rhythmical configurations may foreground in poetry by employing the notion of metrical hybridization and tracing the socio-cultural implication of this process.[8] In this book, I further her discourse, intersecting it with the one on contrapuntal dynamics, which emerge from the analysis of translingual migrant poetics.

This book focuses exclusively on the genre of poetry. While cultural theory, particularly generative travelling notions such as counterpoint, minor literature and hybridity,[9] inform the conceptualization of this study from a theoretical point of view, the translingual verse is analysed mostly through methodologies that belong to the field of stylistics. This is a specific choice of field. As I shall explain, within the panorama of studies on Italophone translingual and migrant poetics, few works have dealt exclusively with the realm of poetry, and practically none has been dedicated to foregrounding the formal qualities of the translingual verse. Nonetheless, maintaining Roland Barthes's assumption of the inseparability of form and ideology in poetry,[10] and acknowledging more generally the central semantic role that the material articulation of verse plays within the genre, I argue that a stylistic investigation can add important insights to the critical discourse on translingual and migrant literature. Moving across these scholarly trajectories, I read forms, metres and rhythms as the fluid product of the continuous dialogic process of translation and contacts across languages and cultures, which the translingual practice always foregrounds. As such, I intend not only to contribute to filling a significant gap within the scholarship on Italophone literature but also to propose a path of approximation to the text that has significant potential to complement and further the socio-cultural and historical discourses within the fields of translingual and migrant literature.

As the title suggests, this book deals with a series of critical notions. While I leave the discussion of the majority of them — such as rhythm, resistance and movement — to the first chapter, a few preliminary words on my use of the term translingualism will be useful at this point. If we adopt the generative terminology introduced by Mieke Bal, translingualism can be considered as a travelling concept,[11] and a very contested one as well. In the literary field, and mostly following a study authored by Steven Kellman,[12] the term translingualism has come to indicate the ability of authors to write in a language other than their mother tongue. This definition has since been extensively challenged,[13] but it has proved to be an important point of departure for a critical debate that is now extensive and insightful. Notably, the introduction of the notion of translingualism has allowed scholars to trace a critical line between multilingualism, that is, the occurrence of different languages in a single text, and translingual practice, which, as I shall discuss, does not necessarily entail the explicit surfacing of different languages on the page. Despite being extremely common in the literary field, historically this practice has been relegated to a shadowy corner of the critical landscape. With this book, I aim to further the theoretical and critical exploration of translingualism in literature, expanding and complicating the boundaries of the term. In order to do so, and given the constitutive fluidity that foregrounds translingualism as a practice, I conceptualize it as a trajectory, one that has generated a series of intersections. Italophone translingual migrant poetics, which are the specific object of my analysis, represent only one of these many intersections. Finally, in my discussion of the term, I allow it to interact with two other critical notions: translanguaging and translation. While a conceptual link with the first term, drawn from sociolinguistics, was introduced by Natalie Edwards in a persuasive study on francophone life writing,[14] the maintaining of this triple entanglement represents one of the original contributions that I wish to offer to the present debate on translingual and migrant literature.

In terms of structure, the book is organized into four chapters. Chapter 1 builds the theoretical basis and the context of the study. First, it explores the positioning of translingual and migrant literature in contemporary Italy and the relevant scholarly discourse. Within this discourse, analyses oriented towards sociocultural aspects have prevailed, although a number of recent studies have proposed a closer approximation to the text. It is within this latter specific scholarly realm that my study is positioned. Second, the chapter discusses the use of the term Italophone, which was proposed and then partly retracted within the field. I propose to employ a reoriented version of the term, which I maintain is important to foreground the disentanglement of any rigid coupling of language–nation and to break any residual hierarchical separation within the relevant literary field. Third, the chapter deals with the notion of translingualism. Through a critical discussion and complication of the boundaries of the term, I identify a translingualism from *within* and a translingualism from *beyond* and illuminate the transformative nature of both practices. Fourth, the chapter engages with two other terms that characterize the translingual literary field: post-monolingualism and resistance. The first was famously introduced by Yasemin Yildiz in an important study on Germanophone non-monolingual writings.[15] In my discussion, both terms are employed to allude to the radical role that translingual and migrant writings play in resisting any monolingual paradigm and monologic understanding of languages and cultures and, as such, in generating social change. Fifth, the chapter discusses the notions of rhythm and movement and asserts their profound interrelation in the realm of poetry writing. Finally, the last part of the chapter explores the specific context of the rise of translingual migrant poetics in Italy, builds the corpus, and unpacks the methodology that informs the ensuing textual analysis.

The book then proceeds with a series of three monographs, each dedicated to one author. Chapter 2 is dedicated to an exploration of Hajdari's verse, with a focus on the collection *Poesie scelte (1990–2007)*.[16] This work is fundamental for the poet, as it collects almost twenty years of translingual poetic activity. First, the chapter locates Hajdari's work within a transmediterranean discourse, positioning it in the landscape of complex entanglements and colonial influences that, historically, have foregrounded Italian–Albanian relationships. Second, the chapter explores the significance of Hajdari's experience with the double language and the specific unfolding of his first self-anthology in the broader context of his literary path. Third, the chapter maps the diachronic evolution of Hajdari's translingual verse at the intersection of his use of poetic forms and the progression of his investigation of displacement, which develops in parallel to the evolution of the double language. Third, the chapter expands on Hajdari's use of metres and discusses the progressive rhetoricizing of his diction as an effect of the erosion of linguistic distance that occurs with time. Finally, the closing section is dedicated to an examination of lexical values, including an evaluation of the progressive morphological encounter of Albanian and Italian, which is substantiated in the mature phase of Hajdari's translingual verse.

The third chapter analyses Barbara Pumhösel's translingual works, particularly expanding on the collection *prugni*.[17] This latter is at once a debut and retrospective for the author, as it is her first poetry book, and yet it collects verses from around two decades of translingual practice. The chapter engages first with Pumhösel's distinctive interpretation of the translingual experience and with her use of linguistic distance as a tool to open novel perceptive and epistemological spaces. Moreover, the first section identifies the entanglements between translingual practice and the development of an ecopoetic and ecofeminist trajectory within Pumhösel's poetry. This development is mostly based on the very frequent occurrence of what I call transitional imagery in her verse. Second, the chapter explores *prugni*'s forms and elaborates on the semantics of brevity and subtraction, which foregrounds the articulation of Pumhösel's translingual verse and also enacts a series of reverberations in her employment of the mother tongue. Third, the chapter explores the metrical profile of the book, mapping the progressive construction of what I define as a transient rhythm in her Italophone diction. Finally, the chapter analyses the dynamics of linguistic mobility in *prugni*, with a focus on their significance in the broader context of her translingual practice.

The fourth chapter investigates the poetry of Hasan Atiya Al Nassar, with a focus on his second and major poetry collection *Roghi sull'acqua babilonese*.[18] First, it contextualizes the author's work and expands upon his empirical and poetic experience of exile, which leads him to express what I define as a language of pain, a characteristic that is consistent in his translingual works. Second, the chapter examines the poetic forms of *Roghi* and expands on Al Nassar's distinctive use of the long poem and its intersections with the Arabic long song *qasīda*. On the whole, Al Nassar's long poems constitute an example of the creation of a powerfully hybrid and resistant diction, which articulates through the fluid means offered by the translingual verse. Third, it explores the revisiting of Italian conventional metres in his works, identifying the role of rhythm and iterations in creating contrapuntal dynamics. The chapter closes with a discussion on language and movement, which takes into account multilingual inserts, linguistic rupture, and radical metaphorization in Al Nassar as signs of an underlying expressionist vocation.

Finally, the conclusion elaborates upon the main findings of the study, summarizing the theoretical discourse and comparatively discussing the metrical, rhythmical and linguistic considerations that emerged in each chapter.

The Translingual Verse has been written in my second language, English, from my house in Alexandria, Sydney, on the land of the Gadigal people of the Eora nation, in the midst of a global pandemic. The poems that I have analysed here have helped me in these challenging times. I hope that, in these pages and through these translingual verses, the reader will find the same sense of hope, light, and home.

Notes to the Introduction

1. Gëzim Hajdari, *Ombra di cane* (Frosinone: Dismisura, 1993), p. 47.
2. See Graziella Parati, *Migration Italy: The Art of Talking Back in a Destination Culture* (Toronto: University of Toronto Press, 2005), p. 62.
3. For an overview see Asher Colombo and Giuseppe Sciortino, *Gli immigrati in Italia* (Bologna: Mulino, 2004); Maria Immacolata Macioti and Enrico Pugliese, *L'esperienza migratoria: immigrati e rifugiati in Italia* (Roma-Bari: Laterza, 2010).
4. See for instance Norma Bouchard, 'Reading the Discourse of Multicultural Italy: Promises and Challenges of Transnational Italy in an Era of Global Migration', *Italian Culture*, 28.2 (2010), 104–20.
5. Simone Brioni, *The Somali Within: Language, Race and Belonging in Minor Italian Literature* (Oxford: Legenda, 2015).
6. Gëzim Hajdari and Giulia Inverardi, 'Il poeta epico delle montagne maledette. Intervista a Gëzim Hajdari', *Comunicare letterature lingue*, 7 (2007), 299–312 (p. 302).
7. See for instance Yoko Tawada, 'From Mother Tongue to Linguistic Mother', trans. by Rachel McNichol, *Manoa*, 18.1 (2006), 139–43 <https://doi.org/10.1353/man.2006.0039>.
8. Vered Shemtov, 'Metrical Hybridization: Prosodic Ambiguities as a Form of Social Dialogue', *Poetics Today*, 22.1 (2001), 65–87.
9. For an introduction to these critical notions see the three following fundamental studies: Edward W. Said, *Reflections on Exile and Other Essays* (Cambridge, MA: Harvard University Press, 2000); Homi K. Bhabha, *The Location of Culture* (London: Routledge, 1994); Gilles Deleuze and Félix Guattari, *Kafka: pour une littérature mineure* (Paris: Minuit, 1975).
10. See for example Roland Barthes, *Mythologies* (Paris: Seuil, 1957), pp. 179–233.
11. Mieke Bal, *Travelling Concepts in the Humanities: A Rough Guide* (Toronto: University of Toronto Press, 2012).
12. Steven G. Kellman, *The Translingual Imagination* (Lincoln: University of Nebraska Press, 2000).
13. See, for example, Sarah Dowling, *Translingual Poetics: Writing Personhood under Settler Colonialism* (Iowa City: University of Iowa Press, 2018).
14. Natalie Edwards, *Multilingual Life Writing by French and Francophone Women: Translingual Selves* (New York: Routledge, 2020)
15. Yasemin Yildiz, *Beyond the Mother Tongue: The Postmonolingual Condition* (New York: Fordham University Press, 2011).
16. Gëzim Hajdari, *Poesie scelte (1990 — 2007)* (Nardò: Controluce, 2008).
17. Barbara Pumhösel, *prugni* (Isernia: Cosmo Iannone, 2008).
18. Hasan Atiya Al Nassar, *Roghi sull'acqua babilonese* (Florence: DEA, 2003; second edition 2004).

CHAPTER 1

Trajectories: Translingual Migrant Poetics in Contemporary Italy

Migration Literature and Italy: From Contexts to Texts

In this work, I engage with a series of critical notions that deserve a preliminary exploration. The first is the highly contested and non-transparent one of migration literature. Among the scholars who have expanded upon migration literature at the intersection with Italophone expression are Loredana Polezzi and Jennifer Burns.[1] Polezzi, in an essay that explores relevant critical trajectories, refers to *scritture migranti* [migrant writings] as 'scritture che portano il marchio (i marchi) della mobilità (linguistica, culturale, geografica)' [writings that hold the sign (signs) of mobility (linguistic, cultural, geographical)].[2] Polezzi's notion of migrant writings is highly fluid, and it may contain, within Italophone landscapes, writings by authors who migrated to and from Italy, authors who were born in Italy to non-Italian parents, and — albeit with important distinctions — postcolonial, post-ethnic, and post-migrant authors. In her study, Polezzi identifies three key aspects for the analysis of works foregrounded by linguistic, cultural, and geographical mobility. The first relates the use of critical tools provided by the field of postcolonial studies, a field of inquiry that intersected the Italophone realm relatively late compared to Francophone and Anglophone contexts. The second is the profound and radical significance of linguistic choices in migrant writings. The last aspect pertains to the centrality of translation processes, and of translation itself as both concept and metaphor, in understanding the dynamics that guide the conceptualization and the material creation of migrant writings.[3] I will return specifically to this latter aspect within this work, but I will retain for now Polezzi's resistance to encapsulating the notion of migrant writings in rigid taxonomies. Burns maintains a similar position in a monograph that investigates recurrent tropes in the narratives of authors who have migrated recently to Italy, tropes that co-occur to configure what Burns defines as a 'migrant imaginary'.[4] In her monograph, Burns rejects the notion of immigration literature, as the term immigration is tied to 'governmental or intergovernmental policy, border controls, alarmist public discourse',[5] and implies a linear understanding of the migratory experience as a path from an origin to a supposed destination. Instead, Burns insists on the term migration literature, clarifying that 'arguably, it encompasses too much'.[6] Similarly, I resist binary taxonomies and boundaries in approaching writings that are marked by linguistic, cultural, and geographical mobility, embracing migration literature and migrant writers as two open and mobile concepts that are traversed by a complex set of trajectories. The object of my study, translingual migrant poetics in contemporary Italy, represents one of the possible trajectories — or, better, an intersection of numerous trajectories — which crisscross the fluid landscape of migration literature. The poetics studied herein dwell in the 'too much', which, rather than being coterminous with a literary category or genre, represents a radically non-linear and intrinsically open realm of textualizations.

The discourse on migration literature permeated the landscape of Italian studies with increasing intensity during the 1990s, when the number of works by migrant authors in Italy began to grow exponentially,[7] as a consequence of an unprecedented surge in influxes into the country which had begun over the previous two decades.[8] These works emerged rapidly and enjoyed a polycentric circulation that I define below as occurring *at different intensities*. Their role within the socio-cultural and literary landscapes of Italy has been a pivotal one. In fact, these writings contributed, among other things, to increasing the visibility of trajectories of movement — including emigration, colonialism, the controversial process of unification, the position of minor languages in respect to the monolingual paradigm arising from the nation-state, and so on[9] — that had been substantially removed from the country's self-representation. As such, works authored by migrant writers in these crucial years provided an impetus for the emergence of a composite realm of acts of talking back, foregrounded by mobility. The variegated landscape of postcolonial Italophone literature, which includes internationally recognized voices such as Igiaba Scego, Ubah Cristina Ali Farah, and Gabriella Ghermandi, contemporaneously acquired critical space.[10] This is also the context in which the poetics of Hajdari, Pumhösel, and Al Nassar emerged, and as such its exploration is of central significance for the critical positioning of my study.

In analysing this composite realm of migrant writings that emerged in the Italophone scene at the crossroads between the past and the present century, scholars have pursued a prominent sociological and cultural angle of inquiry, positioning themselves at quite a distance from the texts, particularly during an initial phase.[11] This approach has been productive in discussing the broad processes of social and cultural change that are foregrounded by migration literature in contemporary Italy. An insightful mapping of this scholarly landscape has already been provided by Chiara Mengozzi, and so there is no need to reproduce it here.[12] I do, however, intend to recall some trajectories that informed the early debates so as to provide grounds for the process of reorientation to which my work intends to contribute. Over three decades, Graziella Parati, whose work belongs to the field of cultural studies, authored a series of critical studies that are merited with advocating for the radical mobilization of a transitive identification between culture, language, and nation within the realm of Italophone writings.[13] Parati introduced three main nodes that will be retained in this study. First is the conceptualization of Italy as an intersection of complex geographical and socio-historical landscapes, an angle that has also animated recent studies.[14] Second is the resistance to understandings of Italian culture that profile it as homogeneous and static.[15] Third is the function of talking back as an act that migrant writings have performed in the contemporary space, and the contribution of those writings to the construction of what Parati calls 'a destination culture',[16] a critical space in which difference is visible and valued, rather than challenged.

Even earlier than Parati, Armando Gnisci conducted an important critical reframing in this field, this time combining critical theory with tools that belong to the field of comparative literature. Focusing largely on works written in Italian by authors who had migrated to Italy during the last three decades of the twentieth century, Gnisci maintained what Burns has defined as 'a globally comparative approach'.[17] In his numerous works, he generally read the experience of Italophone migrant writers through the lens of the planetary state of creolization proposed by Éduard Glissant.[18] Gnisci accomplished an in-depth reframing which relied on two main aspects. First, he insisted on the component of innovation and transformation that migrant writings have the potential to inject into the realm of contemporary literature in Italy, a realm that he read as being otherwise extremely static.[19] Second, Gnisci evaluated the transformations brought about by migration literature in terms of their ability to generate social change, and advocated for scholarly perspectives that were able to decolonize critical discourses and epistemological categories.[20] In so doing, he identified comparative literature as a productive space in which to explore contact outside of the tight boundaries of 'national' literatures. In order to resist trapping migrant writings within linear developments, Gnisci also expanded on the idea of what he calls 'Italian migration literature' as a literary zone, thereby pointing to a geographical angle famously elaborated by Carlo Dionisotti.[21] While Gnisci's transitive application of the Glissantian concept of *toute-monde* to the Italophone realm has been extensively questioned,[22] his works foregrounded the transformative nature of the experience of migration, translated through the act of writing to the collective social sphere, and provided a first critical gaze on the emergence of these dynamics within the Italophone realm. The current work retains, from Gnisci's early reflections, a focus on transformation and translation as two central aspects in the shaping of migration literature.

Both perspectives, and Parati's in particular, maintain an important degree of validity today, and have been extremely productive in stimulating the growing interest in the study of migration literature in Italophone contexts. However, they both invoke a distant approach to texts that generates a series of epistemological risks, all of which, for the purposes of the present study, need in turn to be identified and counteracted. The first of these is that socio-cultural and global comparative approaches to Italophone migration literature often entail a consideration of the text as a direct, unmediated, and in some ways realistic representation of the empirical act of migration. It is to this issue that Polezzi points when she argues that a text is not 'un semplice documento linguistico rispecchiante una realtà autenticabile' [a simple linguistic document that mirrors an attestable reality].[23] On the contrary, she argues that linguistic and translational choices in migrant writings deserve to be read well beyond a mimetic, realistic, or testimonial function. Similarly, Burns resists perspectives that establish transitive connections between migration literature and the empirical event of migration.[24] Burns turns instead to the conceptual weight of the term *literature* in the syntagma *migration literature*, rejecting the separation that had arisen in the field between migrants who write and writers who migrate, and reorienting her analysis of migrant texts towards the 'aesthetic and affective capital that they produce'.[25] A similar operation has been conducted in a series of recent studies, among which I shall refer to Simone Brioni's important monograph on Somali-Italian literature and Christiane Kiemle's text-centred work on multilingualism in Italophone migration literature.[26] These scholars conduct a persuasive operation that can be identified as a critical reorientation towards the text, one that my study enthusiastically embraces.

A second complex aspect resides in the fact that the discussion on the potential of texts for social and cultural change, if traced beyond a discussion of aesthetic capital, risks overlooking the nexus between form and ideology. This nexus, among many others, has been persuasively identified by Roland Barthes,[27] and is maintained as a conceptual pillar of this study. To consider form as a neutral, or worse, as a subordinate component in the realm of textualization leads to perilous critical territories. The controversial withdrawal from close analysis of migrant writings within the Italophone realm, though challenged by some scholars, has largely been claimed as a response to the need to decolonize methods.[28] It is perhaps also indicative of the difficulties scholars face in mastering the critical tools necessary to approach the multi-layered mobility that complicates migration literature, especially in the realm of poetics. Yet the discourse on textualization, and in particular on style, form, and genre, can be performed at the intersection with cultural and critical theory, rather than in tension with it, as long as style, form, and genre are themselves understood not as rigid compartments but instead as mobile trajectories. In their natures as trajectories, they maintain both tension and crossing as constitutive elements, and are subject to a constant reorientation that is significant per se. In this sense, text can be read as a process, a dimension of crossing in and of itself, and the discourse on style, forms, and genre can thus uncover some foundational elements of that process. These are precisely the issues that are closely observed in my study.

Finally, a rapprochement with the text means refocusing on the validity of individual experiences over and above their abstract, uncritical, or non-text-based inclusion in a collective intention. In other words, it brings about the ability of individual experiences to embody the collective — to build a chorus, as Guido Mazzoni would say[29] — but it also upholds as fundamental the exploration and acknowledgment of their unique positioning. This operation resists the conceptually opposed exercise of enclosing individual experiences within collective trajectories of social and cultural change only on the basis of their immediate engagement with linguistic and cultural mobility or, once again, on the basis of the empirical act of migration experienced by authors. This reorientation may seem obvious, and yet it is still crucial, as it first foregrounds unicity without neglecting multiplicity, and then resists the transitive essentialized emanation of the first from the second. Moreover, this reorientation notably intertwines with one of the most cited concepts within the contemporary literary space, that is, Deleuze and Guattari's notion of minor literature.[30] Reading textualization as a process crisscrossed by multiple trajectories, while retaining a focus on multiplicity embedded in the unicity of the voices that compose it, generates a complication of the non-linear path from individual to collective which confirms, at large, the critical validity of the category of *minor*. These concepts and metaphors are maintained at the centre of my critical discourse.

Travelling Concepts: Reorienting Italophone

A second, albeit essential, reorientation must be performed on another term that I employ extensively in this study: the much-contested *Italophone*. This term was first introduced into the specific field by Parati, in a work that examined early texts authored by contemporary migrant writers in Italy,[31] but was then rapidly retracted. Parati initially left the semantic boundaries of the notion wide open, yet she employed the term primarily to refer to so-called collaborative autobiographies, narratives that were published in Italy by migrant authors such as Salah Methnani, Pap Khouma, and Mohamed Bouchane in collaboration with Italian native speaker journalists and authors,[32] and that underwent a process of textual manipulation that Caterina Romeo rightfully approximates to linguistic normalization and even censorship.[33] Together with these, Parati also drew into her discourse on Italophone literature other migrant authors who had recently begun to publish in Italy, such as Ribka Sibhatu, Christiana de Caldas Brito, and Shirin Ramzanali Fazel. Three main critiques were levelled against Parati, some of which were validated by the scholar herself when discussing in retrospect her use of terminology.[34] First, she had identified the term *Italophone* as stemming directly from French contexts, where the homologue *Francophone* had been used in substantially non-neutral ways, foregrounding an element of subordination that excluded migrant and postcolonial writings from a canonized, or official, French tradition. Lucia Quaquarelli, for one, claimed that the evident bias that was attached to the homologue would affect the validity of its use in the context of Italy as well.[35] Second, and as a consequence of this, the term *Italophone* was deemed highly divisive, inasmuch as it traced a line of demarcation between a supposed Italian literature, noble and canonized, and an Italophone production, that did not, or did not yet, qualify for ascension to that realm.[36] Third, Parati herself returned to the term, clarifying that it was useful in emphasizing the acquisition of Italian as a new language and hence in defining migrant writings that emerged in Italy in the early 1990s, but noting that the term lost its validity in the face of the increased complexity of texts that characterized the subsequent phases of production.[37] By so doing, Parati brought about a considerable restriction of the semantic fluidity of her first formulation, and hence greatly reduced its productivity within the relevant literary context.

I maintain that the terms of this question could be turned upside down if we read the issue *à rebours*, focusing on the other pole of the discussion, that is, on the implications of using the qualifier *Italian* as an umbrella term. If we advocate for an uncritical inclusion of texts foregrounded by mobility within the realm of Italian literature, we must first of all ask ourselves what Italian literature actually is. In light of critical notions such as counterpoint, minor literature, and hybridity,[38] which stem from critical theory and which have had time to become abundantly productive within the literary and linguistic fields, can we still confidently maintain that even canonized authors such as Pier Paolo Pasolini and Carlo Emilio Gadda inhabit a quintessential realm of Italian literature? And if so, to what aspects of their empirical and literary experience does the qualifier *Italian* point? To their nationality or birthplace? Or rather to their use of language, which indisputably far transcends the boundaries of any national language? To what extent can the work of even the most established author of the 'national' tradition, and one of the earliest debaters of the well-known *questione della lingua*, Dante Alighieri, be constrained unequivocally to the descriptor *Italian*? The issue is evidently a complex one, and one which deserves further reflection.

Scholarship has made a plethora of attempts to react to these questions, creating a definitory *furor*, as Ugo Fracassa has poignantly depicted it,[39] but the question still lay largely unresolved. However, the discourse above supports me in maintaining that any uncomplicated use of the term Italian points, more or less explicitly, to a reinforcement of the identification between literature, nation, and a somewhat standard emanation of its language. The fictitious nature of this juncture brings me to question its validity as an umbrella term. This is an evident tension which the most sensitive studies that have recently emerged in the field have substantially addressed, primarily through a reorientation of the term Italian in a dialogic and non-binary direction. This is the position maintained by Simone Brioni, for instance, who explains at length, and persuasively, the reasons for which he does not renounce the use of the construct Somali-Italian literature when analysing the work of authors such as Scego, Ali Farah, and Ghermandi.[40] A similar reorientation informs Burns's use of the notion of Italian migration literature and that of transnational Italian writers.[41] My position is ideally in dialogue, yet terminologically in tension, with Brioni and Burns. In fact, while they conduct the mobilization of the term Italian from the inside, I decide instead to step aside and project my reorientation towards the term Italophone instead. In so doing, I maintain that a reoriented use of Italophone, which has been too rapidly dismissed, allows the non-homogeneous and mobile textualities that have for centuries inhabited the composite realm of the Italian language, placing more or less pressure on its boundaries, to emerge outside of any rigid nation-language identification.

Having delineated the rationale that brings me to use the term Italophone in this study, I still need to explain what my reorientation consists of, and why it merits inclusion in the current scholarly landscape. First of all, I conceptualize the term herein not as a compartment but, again, as a trajectory that brings together all writings that intersect the realm of literary expression in the Italian language, with different degrees of heterogeneity. This includes a relative minority of writings that align with a canonized and normative use of the language, as well as a relative majority of writings that challenge this use with varied degrees of intensity. This trajectory also ideally intersects with the realm of literary translations into Italian, not only in order to acknowledge translational dynamics as a foregrounding element of the articulation of most Italophone expression, grounded as it is in polycentric and plurilingual dynamics, but also to acknowledge the authorial status and positioning of translators, whose work performs significant mobilization within the language itself. In this inflection, Italophone, extricated from any specific descriptive desire, would thus embrace a polycentric realm of textualizations that inhabit the Italian language with different degrees of continuity and of rupture with respect to its more central or standard embodiments.

On the whole, this procedure qualifies as a radical reframing of Parati's conceptualization of the term, and especially of her retrospectively restricted version, insofar as it maintains a programmatically fluid nature and resists specificity. Moreover, the idea of trajectory entails the positioning of the many individual experiences as intersections, each one unique in nature, yet all dialogically related. This approach has many advantages. For one, it challenges isolation and facilitates non-linear crossings. The latter function is particularly important in analysing how non-normative works and acts of talking back have functioned across the centuries in performing resistance and in liberating the language from the nation. As such, this approach will allow an investigation of translingual and migrant contemporary poetics in light of a complex set of disruptive and dialogic processes.

Translingualism: *Within* and *Beyond*

A third important reorientation must be performed on the critical notion of translingualism. The notion was introduced into the literary field by Steven Kellman in 2000.[42] Kellman identified literary translingualism as the authors' ability to write literature in a language other than their mother tongue.[43] This definition is specific yet intrinsically broad, needing as such a further critical exploration. In his work, which builds on pioneering studies in literary multilingualism such as *The Poet's Tongue* by Leonard Forster,[44] Kellman conducts a mapping of translingual voices, mostly traced towards Anglophone trajectories, and carries out a series of critical operations. First, he identifies the pervasiveness of literary translingualism across history, while also delineating the contemporary as a locus of translingual acceleration. As such, he challenges the commonplace according to which monolingualism is the norm, in both communities and in literatures. Second, Kellman creates a field of tension between translingualism and multilingualism, reorienting the translingual experience towards the multilingual imagination of the authors, rather than towards the explicit multilingual nature of texts, and explaining that 'texts by translinguals usually reveal traces of other tongues, but most are written entirely in one language or another'.[45] This element is relevant as it inscribes to the translingual realm writings that do not show a marked multilingual or plurilingual *effect*, as Stefano Colangelo would call it.[46] Third, Kellman foregrounds literary translingualism as a process of radical transformation, which engages with complex categories such as resistance, freedom, becoming, interference, opaqueness, and distance, albeit without fully grounding his claims.[47] All these aspects deserve critical attention, and inform to different degrees the reorientation of the notion of translingualism that I conduct in this section.

Kellman navigates literary translingualism in his work by first of all proposing a bipartite taxonomy.[48] On the one hand, he identifies authors who have written literary works in more than one language, usually their mother tongue and one additional language, such as Francesco Petrarca, Vladimir Nabokov, Samuel Beckett, Giuseppe Ungaretti, and Elsa Triolet, as 'ambilingual translinguals'. On the other hand, he employs the term 'monolingual translinguals' to refer to authors who have written in a single language but one other than their mother tongue, that is, 'authors who jumped a tongue and stuck with it'.[49] In this group he includes authors such as Joseph Conrad, Elena Poniatowska, Tristan Tzara, and Salman Rushdie. If we apply this taxonomy to the Italophone context, Hajdari, Pumhösel, and Al Nassar, who authored creative works in both their mother tongues (Albanian, German, and Arabic respectively) and in their adopted language or stepmother tongue (Italian) would as such belong to the first category.

Kellman's bipartite taxonomy might be useful for a partial descriptive purpose, but it must also be questioned on a conceptual level, for two main reasons. First, the adoption of the terms 'ambilingual' and 'monolingual' in these constructs runs the risk of domesticating the plurality of translingual writings into binary patterns. This non-fluid understanding of translingualism constitutes the backbone of critical approaches that operate within what Yasemin Yildiz has identified as a 'monolingual paradigm', rather than in tension with it.[50] The word ambilingual also recalls the notion of bilingualism, a notion that applied linguistics, for instance, has long since abandoned in favour of a more inclusive and fluid terminology, such as *translanguaging*.[51] Moreover, the inclusion of the term 'monolingual' in the second construct, performed without a solid critical reorientation, threatens to attach to these experiences an element of linguistic homogeneity, which any conceptualization of translingualism must resist. Second, the taxonomy does not clarify the position of a variegated set of authors who in part escape its strictures, and who, I contend, are nonetheless amenable to the realm of translingualism, albeit with different degrees of intensity. Here I allude to authors who do not have one sole mother tongue or who live and speak multilingually but write only or prevalently in their first language or languages; authors who write their works in more than two languages; and authors who combine different languages in their texts, while generally maintaining a production oriented towards their first one.[52] Moreover, the taxonomy does not account for authors who adopt different language varieties such as regional varieties and dialects in their works. This is a critical territory that intersects the Italophone landscape extensively, and is traceable for instance in the plurilingual works of Carlo Emilio Gadda.[53] If we maintain that one of the functions of literary translingualism — perhaps the most significant one, as I will explain — is that of talking back to homogenous, linear, or transitive language-nation identifications, a discussion of the positioning of these latter writings becomes all the more crucial. Finally, the taxonomy excludes writings that deal with an alternation of technical, sectorial, and specific languages, which are nonetheless informed by pervasive dynamics of linguistic mobility and are often permeated by the distancing effect that Kellman observes to be one of the most productive tensions arising from literary translingualism.[54] On the whole, all of these forms of literary expression develop across the porous boundaries that articulate *between* and *within* languages, and are, I maintain, essential in giving nuance to the notion of translingualism.

In this study I open up the notion of literary translingualism to writings that are permeated (to different degrees) by dynamics of linguistic mobility, and that entertain a complex yet dialogic relationship with two critical categories: translation and translanguaging. With the term translation, I allude herein not to the prototypical 'notion of translation as something that happens to an original',[55] but instead to the complex set of translatorial dynamics that, as Polezzi has demonstrated within the realm of migration literature, are highly pertinent to translingual writing and that are in place even when a material translation does not exist at all.[56] On the whole, translation provides not only a set of theoretical and methodological tools that can be used to approach translingual writing, as Brioni proved with his analysis of Somali-Italian literature,[57] but also a space to think translationally; that is, to think beyond homogeneous views of languages, and across the porous spaces that both connect and foreground them. In fact, as Polezzi sustains, 'translation takes place not only when words move on their own, but also when people move into new social and linguistic settings', a notion that is all the more meaningful when one considers that 'people have a tendency to keep moving, to occupy multiple places and spaces at once, to be part of different yet connected communities'.[58] In order to acknowledge the pervasiveness of these dynamics in literary history, I maintain in this work the centrality of translation as a metaphor and a practice in informing literary translingualism. In fact, it is not by chance that this centrality has been pointed out extensively by translingual writers themselves.[59]

On the other hand, the notion of translanguaging, borrowed from applied linguistics,[60] provides further grounds for complicating and expanding the concept of literary translingualism. In a recent monograph, Nathalie Edwards employed translanguaging as a framework to approach multilingual life writing by French and Francophone women.[61] Her research established a transdisciplinary connection that I consider to be a significant one. Edwards recalled that in the field of applied linguistics, the theory of translanguaging had progressively replaced studies oriented towards more linear categories of bilingualism and code-switching.[62] This passage was crucial, not least because it foregrounded a shift from binary views of language interaction (languages understood to varying degrees as sets of separate resources) to the idea of integrated language systems (languages understood as integrated resources foregrounding a common repertoire). The shift is embodied in the term itself, which marks a passage from noun (language) to verb (languaging), thus acquiring dynamicity. Building on the works of Catherine Mazak, Kevin Carroll, and Suresh Canagarajah, among others, Edwards retained three critical aspects brought about by the theory of translanguaging. First is a shift in focus from languages to practices. Second is the idea of a transformative potential associated with the movement across languages, that is, 'the ability of multilingual people to create new forms of language, new ways of understanding and new patterns of expression'.[63] Third is the potential for mobilizing language–culture–nation identifications brought about by the concept of translanguaging. All these aspects are maintained as fundamental ones in the experience of literary translingualism as well.

In this work, I propose two other aspects that the theory of translanguaging has the power to foreground, and that have the potential to broaden the trajectory of literary translingualism. On the one hand, it provides grounds for closely considering the *within*, and as such for discussing the positioning of those authors who use different language varieties, as well as those who alternate between different sets of technical and specific discourses in their writings within the porous boundaries of a sole language. To refer to these cases, Mike Baynham and Tong King Lee speak of intralingual and interdiscursive translanguaging,[64] two practices that are visited by the transformative and performative tensions that are of great interest to the translingual discourse. On the other hand, engagement with translanguaging allows me to further corroborate the connections between translingualism and translation. In fact, if we accept the scalar approach proposed by Baynham and Lee,[65] translation, in its more material connotation, could be read as the product or — better — the residue of multiple dynamic acts of translanguaging. Conversely, translanguaging could then be read as a process foregrounded by multiple and dynamic acts of non-material translation. This juncture suggests the need for reflection on the positioning of literary translations within the realm of literary translingualism — a task that is beyond the scope of this study, but that I put forward for future explorations. For now, reading translation and translanguaging as processes that foreground translingual literature allows me to retain what Edwards would define as a focus on the trans;[66] that is, on the transformative and generative power of languaging beyond a monolingual paradigm, and on the novel textual ecologies that this practice has the potential to bring about. In this sense, translingualism comes to represent a further trajectory of the literary field, and one that has the potential to produce a variegated set of powerful intersections.

Having performed this further critical reorientation, I may now turn to three concepts that foreground the specific intersection that I examine in this study, and that generate a series of operative tools that I employ in my analysis: resistance, distance, and rhythm.

Mobilizing Paradigms: Post-Monolingualism and Resistance

Mobilizing the boundaries of the notion of literary translingualism means acknowledging its continuity and pervasiveness, and confirming with Polezzi that 'once we renounce the assumption of monolingualism as the linguistic norm of human communities, more dynamic processes come to light'.[67] In order to comprehensively address the intersection that is of interest to this study, I must now expand on the specificity of translingual migrant literature, and single out its positioning in respect to the discourse on national languages. I will do so, first of all, by engaging with the critical notion of resistance. In a monograph that focuses on linguistic mobility in the context of Germany, Yasemin Yildiz provided an attempt to historicize non-monolingual literature in Europe, engaging in particular with the works of Franz Kafka, Theodor W. Adorno, Yoko Tawada, Emine Sevgi Özdamar, and Feridun Zaimoğlu.[68] In order to contextualize her discourse, Yildiz argued that a 'monolingual paradigm', which has roots in pre-Romantic and Romantic thought, had asserted itself in Europe in parallel to the consolidation of the nation-states.[69] The paradigm is a programmatic emanation of the nation-states themselves, and a structuring principle that strives for the homology of language, culture, ethnicity, and nationality. Moreover, Yildiz observed, the paradigm 'has functioned to obscure from view the widespread nature of multilingualism, both in the present and in the past'.[70] The notion of monolingual paradigm has been an extremely generative one within the literary field, and it maintains a central significance in this study.

According to Yildiz, the various crises of the nation-states and the increase in translingual and transnational contact that have occurred during recent decades enacted a weakening pressure on the monolingual paradigm, thus allowing non-monolingual cultural productions to gain space and transaction contextually. Yildiz maintains that while it is weakened, the paradigm is far from being defeated. Moreover, she notes that it was in fact able to assimilate non-disruptive and superficial forms of multilingualism, successfully modifying its narrative in order to adapt to the present globalized context.[71] This is an adaptive mutation that Sarah Dowling frames within the boundaries of 'neoliberal multiculturalism',[72] and that is highly relevant to this discourse. On these bases, both Yildiz and Dowling assert that not all cultural productions that visibly engage with more than one language necessarily operate in tension with the monolingual paradigm. This assertion is confirmed by the work of Simone Brioni, which demonstrated that the function of talking back that permeates Somali-Italian literature is not directly related to a performative or marked use of multilingualism.[73] On the contrary, Brioni proved that radical transformative and disruptive dynamics foreground even those texts in which language alternation is extremely limited.

In her study, Yildiz then proceeded to conceptualize the term post-monolingual, which encompasses writings that actively resist the monolingual paradigm and represent 'the incipient moves to overcome it'.[74] The use of *post-* in this construct signals the distinctive positioning of non-monolingual writings that emerged *after* the establishment of the paradigm. But *post-* also presages the disruptive element introduced by these writings; that is, the resistance that they perform with respect to the paradigm, and as such the act of talking back that they execute in the face of a linear language–culture–nation identification.

In Yildiz's view, post-monolingual writings, despite their distinctiveness, entertain dialogic relations with the non-monolingual writings that preceded them. More specifically, the scholar argues that post-monolingual writings have in fact enabled non-monolingual practices which had been historically obscured to gain crucial visibility.[75] As mentioned above, since the first appearance of migration literature on the Italophone scene, scholars have attributed to it the radical function of recovering trajectories of movement. If we merge the two discourses, and we maintain the idea that migration literature performs a series of assaults on linear identifications of language-culture-nation, it becomes clear that the poetics of Hajdari, Pumhösel, and Al Nassar can be positioned at the crucial intersection between translingualism and post-monolingualism.

In order to be fully productive in the specific case of Italy, Yildiz's historicization requires a series of contextual inflections. The first must account for the specific status and development of a national language in this context. In a famous study belonging to the field of linguistics, Tullio De Mauro illustrated the radical polycentrism that foregrounded the linguistic landscape of the peninsula before the rise of the nation-state.[76] This polycentrism continued to assert itself in large part for decades following unification. As De Mauro explains, the consolidation of a common language in Italy was significantly impacted by dynamics of internal and external migration, the troubled growth of institutions, the actions of the media, and the vitality and pervasiveness of dialects and regional varieties of language. The resilience of the latter in particular must be placed at the centre of any discourse that involves the development of the Italian language, and the positioning of both the monolingual paradigm and literary writing in respect to it.

Another distinctive element that foregrounds the linguistic landscapes of Italy in respect to other European contexts, as explored by Yildiz, is that the discussion regarding a common language to be employed roughly within the present borders of the country had been initiated there well before the eighteenth century and the subsequent affirmation of the nation-state.[77] The historical articulation of this discussion in Italy sparked a centuries-long *questione della lingua* [language question], considered to have been initiated by Dante Alighieri at the beginning of the fourteenth century.[78] The *questione* mostly involved intellectuals who were committed to legitimizing (and in many cases codifying) the use of different inflections of vernacular language for literary expression, in an attempt to challenge the cultural hegemony of Latin. The emergence of a series of linguistic centres as a result of the *questione*, and the affirmation of the nation-state's monolingual paradigm, are evidently not coterminous. For one, the former is a discourse rooted in the literary sphere, and is attached to technical notions such as that of genre; the second operates according to a narrative that is grounded in the political-ideological prerogatives of the nation-state itself, and is attached to its bureaucratic apparatus. While both of them deal with power, they do so through substantially different ideological orientations and to different extents. Although some aspects of the *questione* have been appropriated by the monolingual paradigm in the Italian context, the substantial conceptual distinction between the two must be maintained.

On the whole, the position of literary language in respect to the consolidation of a monolingual paradigm in Italy was historically quite an idiosyncratic one. In fact, De Mauro states that in post-unification Italy from the end of the nineteenth century, the literary language developed largely in tension with monolingualizing and standardizing pressures emanating from the nation-state.[79] Providing grounds and evidence for Pier Paolo Pasolini's intuitions of a linguistic rupture enacted by literary language, articulated by the author through an engagement with Antonio Gramsci's thought, De Mauro delineates the ways in which the Italophone literary language (and the poetic one in particular) performed multiple assaults on the monolingual paradigm from *within*.[80] In so doing, De Mauro demonstrated that the centripetal drives towards monolingualization (intended as nation-culture-language identification) that originated from the nation-state were substantially challenged in the realm of literature, even in works that, given a superficial reading, would appear to align with the paradigm. This is an important aspect, because it allows a resistance from *within* to emerge in the Italophone tradition, a resistance that can further complicate the trajectory of continuity and rupture foregrounded by translingual migrant writings, and increase their dialogic potential.

As a result of these dynamics, the presence of non-monolingual productions and of writings that resist the monolingual paradigm is particularly pervasive across the history of Italophone literature. As Christiane Kiemle argues, placing these trajectories in dialogue with the realm of migration literature is productive on many levels.[81] The qualities of writings marked by what Kiemle calls 'linguistic heterogeneity',[82] and more generally of those that engage historically with resistance to monolingualization within an Italophone trajectory, have been analysed by numerous scholars, in studies that provide critical tools to be tested in the field of translingual migrant writing. Among these scholars are Cesare Segre and Gianfranco Contini, whose works deal substantially with style, and are thus of close interest to this research. Segre, for instance, identified a series of powerful sixteenth-century responses to linguistic centres, and in particular to Pietro Bembo's successful codification of the *volgare*, responses which were articulated through engagement of the authors with living, popular, and local inflections of the vernacular.[83] The merit of Segre's analysis lies in its reading of these responses not as a turn towards spontaneity or a mimesis of spoken varieties, but as an intellectual choice made by the authors on the basis of an aesthetic desire that he calls 'linguistic hedonism'.[84] In its most powerful trajectories, the latter, which permeates the spirit of the century, entails a favouring of the rhythmical, tangible, and mobile qualities of language. These are qualities that clearly escape normative strictures, and that the authors aim to reaffirm with their creative practice. Segre identifies as such a trajectory of resistance that is articulated towards the material qualities of language itself, and towards its performative use.

A focus on non-monolingual and post-monolingual tensions from *within* also animates Gianfranco Contini's famous work on literary expressionism.[85] In this work, Contini maintains a distinction between expressionism and expressivity, and separates the historical notion of expressionism from the metaphorical one, which he then proceeds to theorize.[86] Contini ascribes to the field of metaphorical expressionism a composite realm of writings that are visited by a radical transformative tension in their use of language. The authors who engage with this field within an Italophone trajectory include Giovanni Boine, Clemente Rebora, Carlo Dossi, and Carlo Emilio Gadda.[87] Contini's work is useful from a methodological point of view, in that it traces the textual embodiments of this tension: programmatic violations of the linguistic norm; predominance of action in the diction (achieved through the multiplication of verbal forms); focus on the sensuality and corporeality of language; taste for plastic deformation; frequent anthropomorphizations; tendency to coin neologisms or to experiment in other unprecedented ways with lexical forms; construction of new words through composition; hyperbolic suffixation and prefixation; and finally courageous and even outrageous metaphorization. Furthermore, Contini, recalling Leo Spitzer's words on the works of Jules Romain, connects these aesthetic qualities and related metaphysics of language to the emergence in these works of a perception of the world that is equally mobile, resistant, and fluid, and as such reinforcing the bridge between form and ideology that constitutes one of the theoretical bases of this study.[88] As I shall demonstrate, these kinds of dynamics are frequently found in the works of translingual and migrant poets, where they are often radicalized by the effect of what I refer to below as linguistic distance. The emergence of these intersections allows me to appropriate some of the tools that Contini designed to theorize and analyse metaphorical expressionism, and furthermore allows me to use this critical category to begin historicizing textual resistance at the junction with translingualism and migration.

Rupture: Linguistic Distance and Transformation

In this contextual discourse, I have begun to foreground the distinctiveness of translingual migrant writings, while simultaneously immersing them in horizontal and vertical trajectories of continuity. At this point, however, a further element of rupture must emerge, one that is related to the critical notion of linguistic distance. The idea of linguistic distance as a powerful force permeates Kellman's study on literary translingualism, albeit primarily as an intuition. In this study, the scholar framed distance as 'the emancipatory detachment of writing in another tongue'.[89] Kellman contended that this process can be a painful one, yet he also argued that it can entail trajectories of liberation. In recent scholarship, the idea of linguistic distance has been investigated mostly through the concept of exophony, a critical notion that was introduced into the literary field in a 2007 collection of essays edited by Susan Arndt, Dirk Naguschewski, and Robert Stockhammer.[90] Within its own morphology, the word exophony points directly to the idea of speaking from outside of a language. This alludes to a distant positioning that, as maintained by exophonic theory, is distinctive to the act of writing creatively in a language other than one's mother tongue.[91] In this sense, the critical reflection on exophony both foregrounds and nuances the main intersection that animated Kellman's early conceptualization of translingualism. In respect to my reoriented idea of translingualism, exophony is therefore a much more specific term, in that, rather than expanding on the *trans* — that is, on the trajectories that connect languages — it instead builds on the effects that occur due to a change of language in the author's imagination. While the two perspectives may exist in tension with one another,[92] I would argue that an engagement with exophony is productive in foregrounding a number of constitutional aspects of the translingual verse.

Among the scholars who have tested the semantic potential of exophony are Marjorie Perloff and Chantal Wright.[93] Through their works, and through Wright's especially, exophony has quickly come to pinpoint the intersection between allophonic expression and migratory dynamics, pointing to the effects of the use of a second language on authors who have experienced migration and who have acquired a language contextually. Wright explains that in this specific case 'the adopted language is typically acquired as an adult' and that, as such, 'exophonic writers are not bilingual in the sense that they grew up speaking two languages'.[94] This is exactly the case for Hajdari, Pumhösel, and Al Nassar, who all migrated to Italy as adults, learned the Italian language contextually, and began quite rapidly to employ their second language in their creative works.

The idea of writing creatively beyond the mother tongue, and from a distance, is a very powerful one. For one, it radicalizes the process of resistance to the monolingual paradigm, insofar as the practice itself is located beyond monologic identifications of language-culture-nation. It also challenges the commonplace notion that poets may possess only one *true* language, a belief with deep historical roots.[95] As such, this practice has proved to be possessed of a radical potential in the literary field, a potential that is further amplified in the realm of poetry, in which the idea of distance brings about a further important conceptual rupture. In fact, poetry is historically associated with a metaphorical return to an original language, the language of childhood.[96] To adopt a second language is thus to materially break that bridge to childhood. This process of rupture is illustrated by Ornela Vorpsi, a writer born in Albania who regularly publishes in Italian:

> Per scrivere avevo bisogno di una lingua che non portasse in sé l'infanzia e per me l'italiano è una lingua senza infanzia. [...] Un'altra lingua vuol dire un'altra cultura, un altro paese, un oceano di distanza con il tuo popolo, con il tuo vissuto e io per ragioni personali avevo bisogno di questa distanza.
>
> [In order to write I needed a language that did not bring with it a childhood, and for me Italian is a language without a childhood. [...] Another language means another culture, another country, an ocean of distance from your people, from your lived experience, and for personal reasons I needed that distance.][97]

Vorpi's reflection is significant on many levels. For one, she identifies exophony not as an impediment to her creative practice, but rather as a resource, a path to be taken towards a process of linguistic liberation, which occurs through distance. This effect is also described in detail by Yoko Tawada, who has authored creative works in Japanese, her mother tongue, and in German, a language that she learned as a result of her migration to Hamburg in 1982. In her famous narrative *From Mother Tongue to Linguistic Mother*, Tawada speaks of the second language as a 'staple-remover', a tool that allows her to liberate her words from the weight of semantic complication, and that as such enables her to reappropriate a material, sensual, and bodily relation with language itself.[98] In other words, exophony enacts a profound mobilization of the relationship between signifier and signified, and allows the establishment of a novel relationship between subject and word. The epistemological spaces opened by this practice can be connected, on a theoretical level, to Mikhail Bakhtin's trope of *outsideness*, which he considers 'a most powerful factor in understanding'.[99] In the case of translingual authors, novel ways of understanding permeate the use and manipulation of language, which in turn, and through distance, gain novel trajectories.

On the whole, an engagement with exophonic frameworks also allows me to reflect deeply on a number of common dynamics generated on a textual level by linguistic distance. These include the mobilization of the relationship between signifier and signified; morphological and semantic word play; extensive metalinguistic inserts; syntactic simplification; visual sensitivity; and abundant transitional imagery. These elements have brought me to preserve exophony as a productive angle from which to analyse Hajdari, Pumhösel, and Al Nassar's verse and to assess the potential of distance to generate novel poetic ecologies within the Italophone trajectory.

The Translingual Verse: Rhythm and Movement

My study engages with the realm of poetry specifically, and with the dynamics that govern versification on a formal level in the context of translingual migrant poetics. Further theoretical and methodological tools may be acquired through engagement with the notion of rhythm, which I employ as a guiding point in my analysis. Studies on poetry translation, especially since post-formalist developments, provide instruments that can be used to complicate the notion of rhythm. In scholarship, rhythm has come progressively to be defined not only in the narrow sense of intralinear accentual development, but also as a more ample notion involving any aspect of the agglomeration of meaning in verse.[100] Henry Meschonnic is among the scholars who have provided insightful contributions to this discussion. Through a series of theoretical studies,[101] Meschonnic builds an anti-semiological definition of rhythm, which he considers to be the main agent of the configuration of sense in poetic discourse: the movement of a specific subjectivity within a history-language. Meschonnic writes:

> [...] je prends le rythme comme l'organisation et la démarche même du sens dans le discours. C'est-à-dire l'organisation (de la prosodie à l'intonation) de la subjectivité et la spécificité d'un discours: son historicité. Non plus un opposé du sens, mais la signifiance généralisée d'un discours.
>
> [[...] I take rhythm as the organization and the very movement of meaning in discourse. That is to say, the organization (from prosody to intonation) of the

subjectivity and specificity of a discourse: its historicity. No longer an opposite of meaning, but the general meaning of a discourse.][102]

On the whole, Meschonnic reads poetry translation as a passage of rhythm across histories-languages, a syntonic vibration of two specifically located subjectivities. This passage unfolds in two stages. An initial phase of decentring is followed by one of recomposition of rhythm within a second subjectivity and in a second language-history. The translator, whose full authorial status is firmly advocated for by Meschonnic, is the protagonist of both of these phases. Meschonnic's conceptualization allows me to point simultaneously to the semantic-ideological value of rhythm and to the potential of translatorial dynamics in analysing the translingual verse. Moreover, it allows me to foreground the rhythmical distinctiveness of translingual migrant poetics. In this latter case, in fact, the decentring and reconfiguring of rhythm described above happens within one sole subjectivity: a subjectivity in movement. The formal and rhythmical analysis that I dedicate to each author's work in the following three chapters aims to explore and historicize the specificities and qualities of this process.

The evaluation of this rhythmical in-betweenness is a complex one; yet I contend that the tools of stylistics can open productive spaces in which to analyse it. An important support is offered by Vered Shemtov's studies on poetic dialogism.[103] Shemtov has worked extensively on the relation between rhythm and ideology in poetic writing, making substantial use of Bakhtinian theories and also building on the works of Barthes and Meschonnic. For instance, in an article authored in 2001, she identified, through a rhythmical analysis, the function of resistance embedded in the alternation of a masculine and a feminine voice in the verse of Emily Dickinson.[104] In this study, Shemtov demonstrated that this alternation is rooted in prosodic choices that allowed Dickinson to juxtapose and contrast different social contexts, performing the function of talking back to authority. Shemtov refers to this process as 'metrical hybridization', describing it as an affect that 'can occur in poetry through rhythm and prosody when one considers these as ideological concepts. A mixture of two, or more, prosodic structures, each referring to a different set of poetic and ideologic conventions can and does create double voice'.[105] In other studies, Shemtov connects these theories to translingualism, introducing the notion of 'hidden metre', a prosodic memory of the mother tongue active beneath the surface of a second language on a prosodic level in works of displaced authors, and possessing the ability to perform a similar function of resistance.[106] In the current study, both of these notions inform the conceptualization of the contrapuntal nature of translingual verse, presenting an opportunity to complicate the space occupied by the *trans* through an engagement with rhythm, and to begin observing its action within versification practices.

Another notion that I identify as productive within the specificity of poetry is that of movement. According to the semiotician Patrizia Violi, movement can be understood as 'spazio più soggetto e temporalità' [space plus subject and temporality].[107] In analysing translingual migrant poetics, I am interested in addressing their engagement with spatiality, and specifically in individuating how movement through space is configured in these verses on a figurative and a semantic level. The relation between poetry writing and movement has famously been described by Amelia Rosselli in *Spazi metrici*, a self-reflective piece that deals with the material practice of versification and its intersection with the body's mobility.[108] In this work, Rosselli explains how the writing of poetry can condense dynamic perceptions, through a process that she came to closely observe in her own poetry practice. More specifically, Rosselli writes:

> Tentai di osservare ogni materialità esterna con la più completa minuziosità possibile entro un immediato lasso di tempo e di spazio sperimentale. Ad ogni spostamento del mio corpo aggiungevo tentando, un completo 'quadro' dell'esistenza circondantemi; la mente doveva assimilare l'intero significato del quadro entro il tempo in cui essa vi permaneva, e fondervi la sua propria dinamicità interiore.

> [I tried to observe every external materiality with the most absolute meticulousness possible within an immediate period of experimental time and space. With each additional movement of my body, I would attempt a complete 'picture' [*quadro*] of surrounding existence; my mind had to assimilate the picture's entire meaning within the period of time in which it remained there, merging with its own interior dynamism.][109]

As the essay progresses, Rosselli indicates a correspondence between movement through space and the material profiling of words on the page, intensifying the idea of verse as a structure that can dynamically embed the body's movement within it. She also explains how her transition to metrical and rhythmical regularity corresponded to a refinement of this process.

As such, on the whole, investigating movement and spatiality in poetry means engaging with its semantic-material unfolding within the verse, in light of the specific entanglements with dynamic perception that the genre foregrounds. This is why a conventional application of spatial theory is not as fruitful in poetry as it is, for instance, in narrative works. The unique positioning of poetry in its engagement with spatiality is confirmed by Nicola Gardini, who stresses that spatial referents, which capture the coordinates of movement, are never to be considered in their empirical nature in verse, but rather as a substitution of the referential world: that is, a subjectively located model or idea of the world.[110] In responding to the need to trace movement within and not beyond the innermost levels of textuality in verse, I develop in my analysis a focus on spatial deixis and verbs of movement, which constitute some of the indicators of the positioning of the translingual verse, and the fluid idea of the world that it comes to embody.

Translingual Migrant Poetics in Contemporary Italy

Having set the theoretical coordinates within which my work operates, I move now to the specific socio-historical context in which the verses of Hajdari, Pumhösel, and Al Nassar emerged. I have mentioned above that, since the 1990s, migration literature written in Italian has experienced dissemination at different intensities. After the initial phase of attention caused by the first collaborative autobiographies, the interest of major publishers in Italophone migration literature decreased significantly. In the years that followed, minor publishers and cultural associations played a pivotal role in collecting and making available a composite realm of migrant writings, which began to occupy a peripheral space within the Italophone tradition.[111] Gnisci speaks of this process as the alternation of two subsequent phases: *una fase esotica* [an exotic phase], wherein major publishers responded to the curiosity of audiences towards migrants' journeys to Italy, and their life therein; and *una fase carsica* [a karstic phase], wherein writings emerged through more subterranean paths, yet increasingly affirmed themselves.[112] Many authors whose works were published for the first time during this period, and as part of the karstic phase, are now internationally renowned. Among them are for instance Amara Lakhous, Gëzim Hajdari, Hamid Ziarati, and Igiaba Scego. Yet the substantial separation of these works from the most canonized intersections of the Italophone tradition still persists, and is visible in the development of university curricula within the country.[113] When placed in dialogue with my previous considerations, this separation indicates the flexibility of the tradition (in its more conventional, linear and 'national' embodiments) to accept non-monolingualism from *within*, and reject instead post-monolingualism from *beyond*. This is a position that many studies have attempted to challenge, and that my work also firmly resists.

The idea of a dissemination of the works of translingual and migrant authors at different intensities applies more so to the realm of prose, and less so to that of poetry. On the whole, the poetic works of authors who began to be published in the early 1990s emerged almost unequivocally through karstic and troubled paths. An important means of initial dissemination were the anthologies of literary prizes dedicated to migrant writers, which included poetry sections.[114] Towards the end of the 1990s, the scholars Mia Lecomte and Francesco Stella began to edit a series of volumes that collected works in Italian by migrant poets originating from a common country or area, contributing to the emergence of a number of new voices.[115] These volumes are possessed of a unique value, as they record and memorialize the early works of translingual migrant poets in Italy, some of whom have not been published since. As a translingual poet and scholar herself, Lecomte's pioneer work involved editing *Ai confini del verso*,[116] the first organic anthology of translingual migrant poetry in contemporary Italy. This anthology contains the works of Hajdari, who at the time was the only substantially affirmed author in the anthology, as well as a collection of poems by Pumhösel and Al Nassar. The collection was translated into English with a few changes, and re-edited by Lecomte herself in collaboration with Luigi Bonaffini.[117] These volumes still represent a crucial instrument in accessing the production of Italophone translingual and migrant poets, and, through their rich paratextual materials, in gaining critical tools to approach them.

The process of isolation which I have indicated above as foregrounding the emerging of Italophone migration literature is radicalized in the case of poetry. Over the years, with the exception of Hajdari's work, which was recognized with the Premio Montale in 1997,[118] and of a few other sporadic acknowledgements, the works of translingual migrant poets continued to primarily occupy an autonomous zone with respect to the rest of the Italophone poetry tradition.[119] This occurred despite a very solid poetic production in Italian developed by authors such as Vera Lucia de Oliveira, Arnold de Vos, Božidar Stanišić and Gladys Basagoitia Dazza, to name but a few. Other authors, who had published less extensively but still notably, were emerging in parallel: not only Barbara Pumhösel and Hasan Al Nassar, but also Ndjock Ngana Yogo, Natalia Bondarenko, Barbara Serdakowski, Eva Taylor and Anila Hanxhari. At the same time, a project on oral, performative, and collective poetry conducted by a transnational group of female authors, *La compagnia delle poete*, was attracting increasing attention worldwide.[120] This group still constitutes a unicum in the realm of Italophone poetry, and perhaps also in the transnational one. On the whole, these experiences have contributed to introducing novel elements into the contemporary poetry scene in Italy, and they are only now beginning to receive the attention that they deserve.

As mentioned above, dynamics of isolation did impact heavily on the dissemination of works of translingual migrant poets. This also meant, however, that in respect to narrative works, translingual migrant poetics had the opportunity to develop outside of dynamics of linguistic normalization and exoticization from a very early phase, and largely as a part of inclusive editorial practices. Moreover, as poetry remained outside of mainstream market dynamics, it suffered less, when compared to narratives, from the pressure to act as testimony of an author's empirical migration and life circumstances.

The landscape of scholarly studies on translingual migrant poetics in contemporary Italy is still a relatively narrow one. When I began my research, the anthological works edited by Lecomte were the principal means of first contact with translingual migrant poetics. Aside from those, there were few publications: one monographic volume on the poetry of Gëzim Hajdari,[121] one volume of interviews,[122] and a small number of articles, reviews, interviews, and dissertations.[123] Since then, the situation has changed rapidly, and the field is increasingly witness to the emergence of new relevant scholarly works.[124] Among these I make particular note of Lecomte's monograph *Di un poetico altrove*, which provides an historical account of the emergence of translingual migrant poetics in contemporary Italy, and to Flaviano Pisanelli and Laura Toppan's *Confini di-versi*, which explores the poetics of twelve authors from a thematic point of view and in light of dynamics of the creolization of languages and literatures.[125] My research, conducted in the field of stylistics, complements this current scholarly landscape, proposing a focus on the aesthetic terrain, in which I trace the core of the radical transformation performed by translingual migrant poetics.

Corpus

As the brief excursus in the section above suggests, the realm of Italophone translingual migrant poetics is an extremely complex one. In this research I have decided to focus on three poets who, despite important differences, share points of contact in their migratory and literary experience, which can be summarized in four main aspects. First of all, Hajdari, Pumhösel, and Al Nassar all migrated to Italy within the substantial immigration wave that took place during the last three decades of the twentieth century. This allows me to analyse their poetics in light of a particular phase of Italian history, which saw a radical socio-cultural transformation and which also, I contend, generated a comprehensive mobilization within the trajectory of the Italophone literary tradition. Second, as mentioned above, these three authors learned Italian as a result of their migration into the country during their adult lives. This enables me to closely observe the effect of linguistic distance in their works, and as such to single out the transformative power of versifying beyond the mother tongue. In this sense, the authors present a radical level of distance, which is then configured in different ways in their verse. Third, and in counterpoint to this, the three poets have also used, and in some cases continue to use, their mother tongue in their writing of poetry. While Hajdari, after his exile, predominantly published bilingual works involving parallel texts, the other two authors kept the two practices more separate, and developed distinct paths in each of their poetic languages. This double practice enhances the opportunity to observe the innermost dynamics of the passage of rhythm between the two languages, as well as the continuous rhythmical iterations generated by the prosodic memory of the mother tongue within the novel expressive potential of the second language. Finally, my desire to develop a gaze upon the diachronic evolution of translingual migrant poetics determined my orientation towards three works (one for each author) that I define as self-anthologies: *Poesie scelte (1990–2007)* for Gëzim Hajdari, *prugni* for Barbara Pumhösel, and *Roghi sull'acqua babilonese* for Hasan Atiya Al Nassar.[126] The three self-anthologies all possess vast chronological depth, containing materials already published by the authors not only in miscellaneous works, but also, in the case of Al Nassar and most importantly Hajdari, in sole-authored volumes. This decision allows me to sketch philological considerations as to what enters the realm of self-anthology and what is retrospectively abandoned by the authors, a process that has not been investigated before and that is central to an assessment of Hajdari's poetics in particular. On the whole, the choice to orient my reading towards style and forms, upon which I will expand in the following section, determines a methodological reorientation towards texts. The restriction of the corpus to three authors and works was regulated by my desire to read texts closely and comprehensively. This choice is obviously conducive to an open structure, which I hope future works will complement in their exploration of other voices.

Methodology

In this section, I delineate the methodological coordinates that guide the analysis of the three self-anthologies, analysis that permeates my critical discussion in the three monographic chapters dedicated to each author. My analysis is conducted on four main levels. The first approach to the texts is of a philological nature.[127] I first of all establish the textual tradition of each poem in the self-anthologies through a comprehensive examination of variants. Although this study does not offer a full critical edition of the self-anthologies, each chapter presents a summary of textual histories, while also referring to variants or sets of variants where relevant.

The second level of analysis pertains to form and metre. As I shall explain, all three authors employ free verse, only occasionally engaging with more formalized or hybrid patterns. The complete metrical scansion of the three works has been conducted on a syllabic basis according to the parameters of Italian metrical conventions, but with the flexibility that analysing free verse always requires.[128] The metrical analysis allows me to conduct a comprehensive evaluation of poetic forms (that is, the number of stanzas and lines per composition, and so on), as well as to observe occurrences of metres and stress patterns, tracing both their conventional and unconventional inflections, and to assess them in light of dynamics of continuity with and rupture from the Italophone tradition. As I shall explain, the analysis of rhythm in particular brings to light significant zones of prosodic transformation, such as for example the centrality of accentual dynamics in the shaping of verse for the three poets. In fact, the metrical-linguistic systems of provenance of Al Nassar and of Pumhösel are accentual, while the Albanian metrical-linguistic system of Hajdari is a hybrid of accentual and syllabic. The analysis brings to the surface an accentual prosodic sensitivity that is found to filter spontaneously into their verse in Italian, thus allowing me to complicate the scholarly discussion on the possibility and the potential of an accentual verse within the Italophone tradition.[129]

My analysis then extends to a third level, the lexical one. In order to collect a comprehensive range of data, I have conducted a full lemmatization of the three self-anthologies. This lemmatization has been realized using digital instruments, employing two natural language processing algorithms, both associated with the Italian language.[130] Automatic lemmatization and tagging is still an emerging field, but one that carries significant potential for textual analysis. The model used for the lemmatization is probabilistic and necessitated a series of manual controls. Nonetheless it demonstrated an overall reliable rate of correctness in the identification of parts of speech and in the quantification of frequencies. The frequency lists obtained were particularly useful in supporting and integrating the qualitative analysis of the words employed by the three poets. This level of analysis was also critical in order to observe on a large scale a series of elements peculiar to translingual verse, such as the use of multilingual inserts, the occurrence of neologisms, calques, linguistic 'forcings' and deformations, morphological processes of suffixation, prefixation and juxtaposition, and so on. In each chapter, I have discussed, where relevant, different inflections of these translingual textual strategies alongside Contini's phenomenology of metaphorical expressionism, so as to delineate the intersections and points of rupture that they embody. Finally, the lexical analysis serves to facilitate the examination of the semantic presence of movement in these texts, an examination conducted through a comprehensive evaluation of two sets of textual referents: spatial deixis and verbs of movement.[131] These many layers of analysis have been used to shape the three monographic chapters. Overall, the multiple orientations of the textual analysis combine to provide a first stylistic evaluation of translingual migrant poetics in contemporary Italy, an evaluation that I hope will provide critical tools for subsequent explorations of this intersection.

Notes to Chapter 1

1. Loredana Polezzi, 'Questioni di lingua: fra traduzione e autotraduzione', in *Leggere il testo e il mondo: vent'anni di scritture della migrazione in Italia*, ed. by Fulvio Pezzarossa and Ilaria Rossini (Bologna: Clueb, 2011), pp. 15–33; Jennifer Burns, *Migrant Imaginaries: Figures in Italian Migration Literature* (Bern: Peter Lang, 2013).
2. Polezzi, 'Questioni di lingua', p. 15.
3. Polezzi, 'Questioni di lingua', pp. 16–17.
4. Burns, p. 3.
5. Burns, p. 8.
6. Burns, p. 8.
7. For this context see Graziella Parati, 'Introduction', in *Mediterranean Crossroads: Migration Literature in Italy*, ed. by Graziella Parati (Madison, NJ: Fairleigh Dickinson University Press, 1999), pp. 13–42.
8. For insights on these migratory dynamics see Asher Colombo and Giuseppe Sciortino, 'Italian Immigration: The Origins, Nature and Evolution of Italy's Migratory Systems', *Journal of Modern Italian Studies*, 9.1 (2004), 49–70; Macioti and Pugliese, *L'esperienza migratoria*.
9. For a critical exploration of these intersections see Bouchard, 'Reading the Discourse of Multicultural Italy'.
10. See Brioni, pp. 46–47.
11. My use of the qualifier *distant* here does not allude to the famous conceptualization elaborated by Franco Moretti (see for example Franco Moretti, *Graphs, Maps, Trees* (London: Verso, 2005)). Rather than indicating a quantitative data-based large-scale approach to studying texts, it points here to approaches that remain substantially outside of insightful text-based explorations of the literary qualities and aesthetic profiles of texts.
12. Chiara Mengozzi, *Narrazioni contese: vent'anni di scritture italiane della migrazione* (Rome: Carocci, 2013), pp. 33–108.
13. See in particular Graziella Parati, 'Introduction', *Mediterranean Crossroads* and *Migration Italy*.
14. See for instance Jennifer Burns and Catherine Keen, 'Italian Mobilities', *Italian Studies*, 75 (2020), 1–15.
15. See Parati, *Migration Italy*, pp. 23–52.
16. See Parati, *Migration Italy*, pp. 70–73.
17. Burns, p. 7.
18. Gnisci's most influential essays are collected in his volume *Creolizzare l'Europa: letteratura e migrazione* (Rome: Meltemi, 2003).
19. Gnisci writes, 'La letteratura italiana non esiste più. È defunta negli ultimi tempi, anche se continua a comportarsi come un corpo oscenamente vivo e a praticare i suoi riti abitudinari' [Italian literature does not exist anymore. It died in recent times, although it continues to behave like an obscenely alive body and to practise its daily rituals]. Gnisci, *Creolizzare l'Europa*, p. 63.
20. See in particular Armando Gnisci, *Via della decolonizzazione europea* (Isernia: Cosmo Iannone, 2004).
21. Carlo Dionisotti, *Geografia e storia della letteratura italiana* (Turin: Einaudi, 1971).
22. See Ugo Fracassa, 'Critica e/o retorica: il discorso sulla letteratura migrante in Italia', in *Leggere il testo e il mondo: vent'anni di scritture della migrazione in Italia*, ed. by Fulvio Pezzarossa and Ilaria Rossini (Bologna: Clueb, 2011), pp. 169–82.
23. Polezzi, 'Questioni di lingua', p. 19.
24. Burns, p. 10.
25. Burns, p. 4.
26. Brioni; Christiane Kiemle, *Ways out of Babel: Linguistic and Cultural Diversity in Contemporary Literature in Italy. Exploring Multilingualism in the Works of Immigrated Writers* (Trier: Wissenschaftlicher Verlag Trier, 2011).
27. Barthes. See also the introductory sections of my article Alice Loda, ' "Dolce era la notte": Iraqi and Iranian Poets in Italy: Metrical-Stylistic Implications of Translingual Versification', *Italian Culture*, 33.2 (2015), 105–25.

28. See for instance Parati, *Mediterranean Crossroads*, p. 18.
29. Guido Mazzoni, *Forma e solitudine: un'idea della poesia contemporanea* (Milan: Marcos y Marcos, 2002), p. 8.
30. Deleuze and Guattari.
31. See Parati, *Mediterranean Crossroads*, p. 14.
32. Mario Fortunato and Salah Methnani, *Immigrato* (Rome: Teoria, 1990); Pap Khouma, *Io, venditore di elefanti*, ed. by Oreste Pivetta (Milan: Garzanti, 1990); Mohamed Bouchane, *Chiamatemi Alì*, ed. by Carla De Girolamo and Daniele Miccione (Milan: Leonardo, 1991).
33. Caterina Romeo, 'Meccanismi di censura e rapporti di potere nelle autobiografie collaborative', *Between*, 5.9 (2015), 1–28.
34. See Parati, *Migration Italy*, pp. 54–55.
35. Lucia Quaquarelli, 'Definizioni, problemi, mappature', in *Leggere il testo e il mondo: vent'anni di scritture della migrazione in Italia*, ed. by Fulvio Pezzarossa and Ilaria Rossini (Bologna: Clueb, 2011), pp. 53–64.
36. This subordinate quality attached to the use of *Francophone* as retraced by Quaquarelli has been decidedly mobilized in the present debate. See for instance Edwards, pp. 1–27.
37. See Graziella Parati and Marie Orton, *Multicultural Literature in Contemporary Italy* (Madison, NJ: Fairleigh Dickinson University Press, 2007), pp. 54–55.
38. For a theoretical discussion of these notions see respectively: Said, *Reflections on Exile*; Deleuze and Guattari; Bhabha.
39. Fracassa, p. 180.
40. Brioni, p. 5.
41. Burns, p. 20.
42. See Kellman.
43. Kellman, p. ix.
44. Leonard Forster, *The Poet's Tongues: Multilingualism in Literature* (London: Cambridge University Press, 1970).
45. Kellman, p. 15.
46. See Stefano Colangelo, 'Fonomanzie: appunti preliminari sul plurilinguismo poetico', *Quaderna*, 2 (2014), 1–17.
47. See Kellman, pp. 1–35.
48. Kellman, p. 12.
49. Kellman, p. 14.
50. Yildiz, pp. 1–29.
51. See Edwards, pp. 15–18.
52. This is the case, for instance, for some of the works of James Joyce, an author who escapes the taxonomy but who is elsewhere redirected by Kellman into the translingual realm. See Kellman, p. 16.
53. For Gadda's plurilinguism see Cesare Segre, 'La tradizione macaronica da Folengo a Gadda (e oltre)', in *Cultura letteraria e tradizione popolare in Teofilo Folengo. Atti del Convegno di studi promosso dall'Accademia virgiliana e dal Comitato Mantova-Padania 77. Mantova 15–16–17 ottobre 1977*, ed. by Mario Chiesa and Ettore Bonora (Milan: Feltrinelli, 1979), pp. 62–74.
54. Kellman, p. 28.
55. Loredana Polezzi, 'Translation and Migration', *Translation Studies*, 5.3 (2012), 345–56 (p. 348).
56. See Polezzi, 'Translation and Migration'.
57. See Brioni, in particular pp. 1–59.
58. Polezzi, 'Translation and Migration', p. 348.
59. See for instance the self-reflective essay by Gerda Lerner, 'Living in Translation', in *Switching Languages: Translingual Writers Reflect on Their Craft*, ed. by Steven G. Kellman (London: University of Nebraska Press, 2003), pp. 267–88.
60. For a theoretical exploration of the notion of translanguaging see in particular Catherine Mazak and Kevin Carroll, *Translanguaging in Higher Education: Beyond Monolingual Ideologies* (Bristol: Multilingual Matters, 2016); Suresh Canagarajah, 'Codemeshing in Academic Writing: Identifying Teachable Strategies of Translanguaging', *The Modern Language Journal*, 95.3 (2011),

401–17 (both quoted by Edwards); Emi Otsuji and Alastair Pennycook, 'Metrolingualism: Fixity, Fluidity and Language in Flux', *International Journal of Multilingualism*, 7.3 (2010), 240–54.
61. Edwards.
62. Edwards, pp. 15–16.
63. Edwards, p. 17.
64. Mike Baynham and Tong King Lee, *Translation and Translanguaging* (New York: Routledge, 2019), pp. 22, 24.
65. See Baynham and Lee, pp. 33–54.
66. Edwards, p. 15.
67. Polezzi, 'Translation and Migration', p. 348.
68. Yildiz.
69. Yildiz, p. 2.
70. Yildiz, p. 2.
71. See Yildiz, in particular pp. 1–29.
72. Dowling, pp. 14–19.
73. See Brioni, in particular pp. 18–59.
74. Yildiz, p. 4.
75. Yildiz, pp. 3–4.
76. Tullio De Mauro, *Storia linguistica dell'Italia unita* (Rome-Bari: Laterza, 1991).
77. See De Mauro, in particular pp. 15–50.
78. For the *questione della lingua*, I refer to the many volumes by linguist Claudio Marazzini, among which is the recent *Breve storia della questione della lingua* (Rome: Carocci, 2018).
79. De Mauro, pp. 235–64.
80. See Pier Paolo Pasolini, 'Nuove questioni linguistiche', in *Empirismo eretico* (Milan: Garzanti, 1995), pp. 5–24.
81. Kiemle, pp. 49–64.
82. Kiemle, p. 49.
83. See Cesare Segre, 'Edonismo linguistico nel Cinquecento', in *Lingua, stile e società: studi sulla storia della prosa italiana* (Milan: Feltrinelli, 1991), pp. 369–96.
84. See Segre, 'Edonismo linguistico', esp. pp. 381–84.
85. Gianfranco Contini, 'Espressionismo letterario', in *Ultimi esercizi ed elzeviri: 1968–1987* (Turin: Einaudi, 1988), pp. 41–105.
86. Contini, p. 41.
87. See Contini, pp. 89–104.
88. Contini, p. 64. The essay by Leo Spitzer cited by Contini is 'Der Unanimismus Jules Romains im Spiegel seiner Sprache (Eine Vorstudie zur Sprache des französischen Expressionismus)', in *Stilstudien, II: Stilsprachen* (Munich: Hueber, 1928), pp. 208–300.
89. Kellman, p. 28.
90. *Exophonie: Anders-Sprachigkeit (in) der Literatur*, ed. by Susan Arndt, Dirk Naguschewski, and Robert Stockhammer (Berlin: Kadmos, 2007).
91. For the notion of exophony see for instance Marjorie Perloff, *Unoriginal Genius: Poetry by Other Means in the New Century* (Chicago, IL: University of Chicago Press, 2010), esp. pp. 123–45; Chantal Wright, 'Writing in the "Grey Zone": Exophonic Literature in Contemporary Germany', *German as a Foreign Language*, 3 (2008), 26–46.
92. See Dowling, pp. 8–10.
93. See also Chantal Wright, 'Yoko Tawada's Exophonic Texts', in *Yoko Tawada's Portrait of a Tongue: An Experimental Translation*, by Chantal Wright and Yoko Tawada (Ottawa: University of Ottawa Press, 2013), pp. 1–21; Chantal Wright, 'Exophony and Literary Translation: What It Means for the Translator When a Writer Adopts a New Language', *Target*, 22.1 (2010), 22–39.
94. Wright, 'Yoko Tawada's Exophonic Texts', p. 2.
95. Yildiz, p. 2.
96. I allude here primarily to Giambattista Vico's conceptualization of poetry as humanity's return to childhood. See Giambattista Vico, *The New Science of Giambattista Vico* (Ithaca, NY: Cornell University Press, 1984). I am grateful to Professor Sonia Gentili who suggested this critical engagement.

97. Ornela Vorpsi and Antonia Pezzani, 'Un oceano di distanza: un'intervista a Ornela Vorpsi', *Osservatorio balcani e caucaso*, 17 April 2007, <http://www.balcanicaucaso.org/aree/Albania/Un-oceano-di-distanza-36549> [accessed 14 October 2016].
98. Yoko Tawada, 'From Mother Tongue to Linguistic Mother', trans. by Rachel McNichol, *Manoa*, 18.1 (2006), 139–43 <https://doi.org/10.1353/man.2006.0039>.
99. Mikhail Mikhailovich Bakhtin, *Speech Genres and Other Late Essays*, ed. by Michael Holquist and Caryl Emerson, trans. by Vern W. McGee (Austin: University of Texas Press, 1986), p. 7, quoted in Polezzi, 'Translation and Migration', p. 351.
100. See *Ritmologia. Atti del convegno 'Il ritmo del linguaggio. Poesia e traduzione'. Università degli studi di Cassino, Dipartimento di linguistica e letterature comparate. 22–24 marzo 2001*, ed. by Franco Buffoni (Milan: Marcos y Marcos, 2002).
101. See in particular Henri Meschonnic, *Critique du rythme: anthropologie historique du langage* (Lagrasse: Verdier, 1982); Henri Meschonnic, *Pour la poétique II* (Paris: Gallimard, 1963); Henri Meschonnic, *Poétique du traduire* (Paris: Verdier, 1999).
102. Meschonnic, *Poétique du traduire*, p. 99.
103. See in particular Shemtov, 'Metrical Hybridization'; and 'Prosody as Content, Ideology as Form: A New Approach to Prosodic Theory' (unpublished doctoral thesis, University of California–Berkeley, 2000). The latter has been translated and published in Hebrew in Vered Shemtov, *Changing Rhythms: Towards a Theory of Prosody in Cultural Context* (Ramat-Gan: Bar-Ilan University Press, 2012).
104. Shemtov, 'Metrical Hybridization'.
105. Shemtov, 'Metrical Hybridization', p. 70.
106. Shemtov, 'Prosody as Content, Ideology as Form', pp. 64–125.
107. Patrizia Violi, 'La spazialità in moto: per una semiotica dei verbi di movimento', *Versus: Quaderni di studi semiotici*, 73–74 (1996), 83–102 (p. 85).
108. Amelia Rosselli, 'Spazi metrici', in *L'opera poetica*, ed. by Stefano Giovannuzzi (Milan: Mondadori, 2012), pp. 181–87.
109. Rosselli, 'Spazi metrici', p. 185; Amelia Rosselli, 'Metrical Spaces', trans. by Jennifer Scappettone, *Chicago Review*, 56.4 (2012), 37–43 (p. 39).
110. Nicola Gardini, 'Amelia Rosselli e lo spazio della fuga', *Italianistica*, 2–3 (2002), 111–23 (p. 127).
111. This context is thoroughly explored by Parati and Burns. See in particular Parati, *Migration Italy*, pp. 96–102; Burns, pp. 198–204.
112. Armando Gnisci, 'La letteratura italiana della migrazione', in *Creolizzare l'Europa: letteratura e migrazione* (Rome: Meltemi, 2003), pp. 73–130 (pp. 84–92).
113. Some of the dynamics that are still in place are traced in Maria Cristina Mauceri, 'La letteratura italiana della migrazione nei curricula universitari europei e nordamericani', in *Diaspore europee e lettere migranti: primo festival europeo degli scrittori migranti*, ed. by Armando Gnisci and Nora Moll (Rome: Edizioni Interculturali, 2002), pp. 145–60.
114. I refer in particular to the yearly anthologies of the literary prize Eks&tra <http://www.eksetra.net/concorso-eksetra/>, dedicated to migrant writers, that was established in 1995.
115. I allude here to a series of *quaderni* [notebooks] edited by Lecomte and Stella: *Quaderno africano I: Nigeria, Camerun, Eritrea* (Florence: Loggia de' Lanzi, 1998); *Quaderno balcanico I: Albania, Bosnia* (Florence: Loggia de' Lanzi, 1998); *Quaderno balcanico II: Albania, Bosnia, Croazia* (Florence: Loggia de' Lanzi, 2000); *Quaderno mediorientale I: Iraq* (Florence: Loggia de' Lanzi, 1998); *Quaderno mediorientale II: Iran* (Florence: Loggia de' Lanzi, 2000).
116. *Ai confini del verso*, ed. by Mia Lecomte (Florence: Le Lettere, 2006). Lecomte edited a second anthology five years later, with a new selection of authors and works: *Sempre ai confini del verso* (Paris: Chemins de traverse, 2011).
117. *A New Map: The Poetry of Migrant Writers in Italy*, ed. by Mia Lecomte and Luigi Bonaffini (Los Angeles: Green Integer, 2007).
118. Hajdari's works were also published in the prize's anthology: *7 poeti del Premio Montale, Roma 1997: Laura Maria Gabrielleschi, Gezim Hajdari, Gabriella Pace, Biagio Salmeri, Oliver Scharpf, Francesca Traina, Sebastiano Triulzi* (Milan: All'insegna del pesce d'oro, 1998).
119. For an historical overview see Mia Lecomte, *Di un poetico altrove: poesia transnazionale italofona (1960–2016)* (Florence: Cesati, 2018), pp. 65–246.

120. On the performative and poetic activities of *La compagnia delle poete*, which was founded by Lecomte and of which Pumhösel, De Oliveira, Taylor, and Serdakowski are active members, see Francesco Armato, *Premiata Compagnia delle poete* (Isernia: Cosmo Iannone, 2013).
121. *Poesia dell'esilio: saggi su Gëzim Hajdari*, ed. by Andrea Gazzoni (Isernia: Cosmo Iannone, 2010).
122. Davide Bregola, *Il catalogo delle voci: colloqui con poeti migranti* (Isernia: Cosmo Iannone, 2005).
123. See for instance Flaviano Pisanelli, 'La Frontière invisible: la poésie italienne de la migration entre diglossie et "dislocation", identité(s) et dépossession', *Italies*, 13.1 (2009), 487–507; Flaviano Pisanelli, 'Pour une "écriture plurielle": la littérature italienne de la migration', *Textes & Contextes*, 2 (2008) <http://revuesshs.u-bourgogne.fr/textes&contextes/document.php?id=693> [accessed 19 October 2013].
124. Two further monographs that have recently issued have been dedicated to Hajdari: Alessandra Mattei, *La besa violata: eresia e vivificazione nell'opera di Gëzim Hajdari* (Rome: Ensemble, 2014); Sara Di Gianvito, *In balia delle dimore ignote: la poesia di Gëzim Hajdari* (Nardò: Besa, 2015). The work of Barbara Pumhösel has been analysed in an article by Barbara D'Alessandro, 'Scavalcare l'orizzonte: movimento e transitorietà in Barbara Pumhösel', *Studi interculturali*, 3 (2014), 161–80.
125. Lecomte, *Di un poetico altrove*; Flaviano Pisanelli and Laura Toppan, *Confini di-versi: frontiere, orizzonti e prospettive della poesia italofona contemporanea* (Florence: Firenze University Press, 2020).
126. Hajdari, *Poesie scelte*; Pumhösel, *prugni*; Al Nassar, *Roghi sull'acqua babilonese*.
127. For this level of analysis I refer to Alfredo Stussi, *Introduzione agli studi di filologia italiana* (Bologna: Il Mulino, 2007).
128. The handbooks of reference used for the metrical analysis are Gianfranca Lavezzi, *I numeri della poesia: guida alla metrica italiana* (Rome: Carocci, 2006); and Aldo Menichetti, *Metrica italiana: fondamenti metrici, prosodia, rima* (Padua: Antenore, 1993). For the conceptualization and treatment of free verse I rely herein on Paolo Giovannetti, *Modi della poesia italiana contemporanea: forme e tecniche dal 1950 a oggi* (Rome: Carocci, 2013); and Paolo Giovannetti and Gianfranca Lavezzi, *La metrica italiana contemporanea* (Rome: Carocci, 2010).
129. See in particular Bernardo De Luca, 'Per una verifica del verso accentuale', *L'Ulisse*, 16 (2014), 20–31.
130. The first algorithm, from Apache OpenNLP (Italian) <https://opennlp.apache.org/>, associates each word of the texts with the relevant part of speech. The second algorithm, contained in the software TreeTagger (Italian) <http://www.cis.uni-muenchen.de/~schmid/tools/TreeTagger/>, was employed for the complete lemmatization. Regarding the use of TreeTragger, I refer to Helmut Schmid, 'Improvements in Part-of-Speech Tagging with an Application to German', in *Natural Language Processing Using Very Large Corpora*, ed. by Susan Armstrong and others (Dordrecht: Springer, 1999), pp. 13–25; Helmut Schmid, 'Probabilistic Part-of-Speech Tagging Using Decision Trees', in *New Methods In Language Processing*, ed. by Daniel Jones and Harold Somers (London: Routledge, 2013), pp. 154–64.
131. For the function of spatial deixis I refer to Cecilia Andorno, *Linguistica testuale: un'introduzione* (Rome: Carocci, 2003); for its role in poetry writing specifically I refer to Paolo Zublena, 'L'infinito qui: deissi spaziale e antropologia dello spazio nella poesia di Leopardi', in *La prospettiva antropologica nel pensiero e nella poesia di Giacomo Leopardi*, ed. by Chiara Gaiardoni (Florence: Olschki, 2010). The taxonomy of verbs of movement that serves as the parameters of my analysis is contained in Violi, p. 60. In her article, Violi identifies 197 verbs of movement in the Italian language, and distinguishes between those that engage with action and those that engage with change. Both her mapping and her classification are extremely pertinent to this study.

CHAPTER 2

Gëzim Hajdari's Poetics between Italy and Albania

Proximity and Distance: A Transmediterranean Poetics

Gëzim Hajdari, born in the small village of Hajdaraj, Albania, in 1957, is one of the most renowned voices within the poetics that emerged as a result of the massive movement of people to Italy during the last three decades of the past century. Anthologized in a number of works that aimed to capture the emergence of translingual Italophone migrant poetics, he now possesses a consolidated corpus of Italian-Albanian works that have been translated into several languages and have attracted a growing number of dedicated scholarly publications worldwide.[1] Before entering an in-depth analysis of his first self-anthology, *Poesie scelte*,[2] this section will reframe Hajdari's path within a transmediterranean and postcolonial perspective. It will then explore some of the foregrounding features of his literary works, and will introduce his distinctive interpretation of translingualism as the expression of a 'double language',[3] one that developed after his displacement.

First of all, Hajdari's work must be immersed in the complex trajectories of literary, cultural, and socio-political transmediterranean entanglements that historically connect Italy and Albania and that escape any linear centre–periphery classification. Emma Bond and Daniele Comberiati have explored the multifaceted nature of these contacts from a socio-historical and literary perspective in an edited volume published in 2013.[4] In the introduction to this volume, Bond and Comberiati suggest the presence of a *confine liquido* [liquid border] between the two countries, to be intended in both a material and a metaphorical sense.[5] In their work, this liquid border is read as an indicator of a 'prossimità della distanza' [proximity of distance] between Albanian and Italy that exists in light of memories of passage that reverberate from one shore to another in cultural productions, productions which in turn challenge 'lo iato culturale e politico perpetuatosi dal dopoguerra in poi' [the cultural and political hiatus which perpetuated itself from the post-war period onwards].[6]

On the whole, three main trajectories of transmediterranean entanglements are recalled by Bond and Comberiati, all of which are relevant to a redefinition of Albanian and Italian identities in a transmediterranean direction. First is the presence in Italy of Arbëreshë communities, an ethnic and linguistic Albanian alloglot minority who settled in the south of the Italian peninsula from the fifteenth century onwards to escape Ottoman domination, and of whom the author Carmine Abate is one of the main literary voices.[7] In fact, Bond and Comberiati stress that the Arbëreshë is 'una delle diverse sfaccettature dell'identità italiana, che è dunque composta anche dall'elemento albanese' [one of the diverse facets of Italian identity, which is thus also composed of an Albanian element].[8] Second, they emphasize the necessity of studying Albanian–Italian relations from a colonial and postcolonial perspective. In particular, expanding on the notion of colonial influence, they recall the pervasive tensions towards the Italian control of Albanian borders and socio-political balances performed throughout the centuries by Italian institutions, which extended beyond the military occupation initiated in 1939 and formally ended a few years later with the fall of the fascist regime. Through this reasoning, the authors identify a series of 'fatti ed eventi che, nel loro insieme, sono da considerare coloniali e post-coloniali' [facts and events that, on the whole, must be considered to be colonial and postcolonial].[9] Among these facts and events are, for instance, Italy's expansionistic aims towards the east that had been on the rise since before unification; the role of Italy in the Balkans during the Cold War and during the last years of the Albanian communist regime; and the influence of Italian popular culture in Albania since the 1960s, in particular through radio and television broadcasting, which have also proved important means of contact with the Italian language. Finally, Bond and Comberiati build on the distinctiveness of works by Albanian translingual migrant writers in contemporary Italy, works which they identify as multi-layered spaces of cultural hybridization deeply informed by all of the above dynamics.[10] Across the works of Albanian-Italian authors, they recognize two main tropes. On the one hand there is the prominence of sea-related imagery, that is, the occurrence of 'il *filtro marino* come condizione specifica dello sguardo del migrante' [the 'marine-filter' as the specific condition of the migrant's gaze].[11] On the other hand there is the centrality, in the authors' imaginary, of a fundamental Albanian trauma, and in particular of dictatorship (or the memory or reverberations of it for the younger generations), an element that determines their frequent seeking of refuge in anti-historical times of childhood, adolescence, and myth. All these points are highly pertinent, as we shall see, to Hajdari's translingual literary path.

A second trajectory that needs to be explored in this introductory section relates to the development of Hajdari's translingual path, as it configures itself through almost three decades of literary activity. As mentioned previously, Hajdari fled Albania in 1992 in order to escape the violent and repressive atmosphere that characterized the post-communist years, and as a consequence of his life having been threatened due to his political and intellectual activities. The full circumstances of his displacement are explicitly recalled in his renowned long poem *Poema dell'esilio*, in which Hajdari writes: 'La mia unica colpa è stata di non aver accettato | compromessi, denunciando gli abusi e i crimini | del vecchio regime e quelli del nuovo regime di Berisha [My only fault was not having accepted | compromises, denouncing the abuses and crimes | of the old regime and those of the new Berisha regime].[12] The author arrived at the port of Trieste on a windy night in April 1992, and after settling in Frosinone he began to reconstruct his scholarly and poetic apprenticeship in his second language, Italian.[13] His first collection, *Ombra di cane*, published one year after his displacement, was followed by an impressive number of publications: poetry collections (the core of his aesthetic research), but also narratives, dramatic pieces, translations, and critical and scholarly publications.[14] In 1997 Hajdari was awarded the Montale prize for an unpublished sylloge in Italian that later became part of *Corpo presente*, one of the capstones of his explorations of body, matter, and mobility.[15] This contributed to the diffusion of his work to a wider national and international audience, a process that has been further amplified by two recent English translations of his verse.[16]

On the whole, the corpus of Hajdari's works constitutes a solid and quite homogeneous body of theoretical and aesthetic research revolving around displacement and the human condition. As Andrea Gazzoni points out, Hajdari's works embody different translations over time of that 'central Albanian trauma' that has been identified by Bond and Comberiati as prominent in the works of Albanian-Italian authors, and that lies at the heart of Hajdari's displacement.[17] Moreover, Gazzoni argues that these consecutive translations correspond to the practice of three different genres in Hajdari's work, which develop in succession: lyric, epic, and history-chronicle. According to Gazzoni, the critical notion of distance plays an important role in the development of these translations. More specifically, he argues that the progression from metaphorical to literal expression, which marks the passage from lyric to history, is enabled and mediated in Hajdari's work by the diverse embodiments of physical and linguistic distance entailed in the different phases of his displacement. In other words, the greater Hajdari's distance from Albania (a distance that increases progressively as his years in exile continue), the easier it is for him to express the central Albanian trauma in direct and unmediated ways. On the whole, Gazzoni's reflection on and critical use of the notions of translation and distance confirms that Hajdari's body of works constitutes a multifaceted inflection of a major central research, upon which physical and linguistic displacement act as primary forces.

From a semantic and formal point of view, two concerns animate Hajdari's cohesive body of works. Firstly, a civil inspiration that leads his work to converge increasingly on a celebration of the displaced community through the different genres practised, and to single out the ontological and epistemological spaces that are created through the experience of movement. This view, which is nourished both instinctively and theoretically from the beginnings of Hajdari's literary activity, eventually leads the poet to identifiy communality in displacement as the sole possible means of recovering beauty, purity, and a form of salvation. The poet explains:

> I harbor immense esteem for exilic poets, who are symbols of the cultures of the worlds, who inspired and continue to inspire entire generations to a better life — a more pacific, human and tolerant one. They teach everybody how to be exiles and migrants, in order to share future and destiny.[18]

Hajdari's exploration of displacement is constantly intersected by reflections on otherness and on the materiality of the body and its connections with the outside world, both of which, as I shall explain, are mobilized by the progressive acquisition of the second language. A second pillar in Hajdari's work is the constitutive focus on mobility. We can trace this focus within the exploration of diverse literary genres and their frequent intermingling, but also within the intratextual dynamics of stylistic and linguistic hybridization that characterize his work. Alessandra Mattei has linked this feature to Hajdari's composite and transnational intellectual background, which generates, she suggests, an extremely mobile transmediterranean word.[19] As I argue in the following sections, all these aspects emerge strongly from the formal and rhythmical strategies that the poet adopts in his verse, and are reinforced through the progression of his translingual practice.

From a linguistic point of view, the poet maintains a distinctive positioning. In fact, for Hajdari, the acquisition of a second language and the practice of literary translingualism as an effect of his displacement do not entail either an abandonment of the mother tongue, or the development of two parallel literary paths, as in the cases of Pumhösel and Al Nassar. On the contrary, in Hajdari, translingualism generates what the author defines as a double language, which arises spontaneously from his skin: 'Scrivo parallelamente in tutte e due le lingue, quindi in albanese e in italiano e viceversa. Non si tratta di bilinguismo ma di una *lingua doppia* [I write in parallel in both languages, so in Albanian and in Italian and vice versa. This is not bilingualism, but rather a *double language*].[20] Consequently, the majority of Hajdari's translingual poetry collections display parallel texts: the Albanian version on the left-hand page and the Italian version on the right-hand page. This choice, I argue, spontaneously uncovers the transformative and translational dynamics that constitute translingual verse more broadly, even in works where one sole language is represented on the page and multilingual inserts are absent.

Many scholars have pointed out that linguistic choices for translingual migrant authors are critical, especially in postcolonial contexts and in the face of dynamics of linguistic resistance and talking back. For instance Brioni, in his monograph, identifies a number of strategies of linguistic interaction active within Italophone postcolonial literature, including the use of parallel texts, which he analyses in light of the notion of 'thick translation' elaborated by Lawrence Venuti.[21] Several aspects of Brioni's discourse are relevant to Hajdari's works. First of all, Brioni, quoting Polezzi, recalls the distinctiveness of the use of parallel texts in the context of translingual migrant and postcolonial writing, wherein 'the boundaries between target and sources text are blurred since the two texts are inseparable,' and 'therefore writing and translation are conflated'.[22] The concept of inseparability, foregrounded by Polezzi and Brioni's reasoning, resonates with Hajdari's double language, and I argue that it must be retained as a central fixture in investigating his translingual experience.

In his study, Brioni also demonstrates that the use of parallel texts can be associated with very different textual practices and authorial or editorial intentions. Brioni closely compares two postcolonial works which both display parallel texts: the novel *La nomade* by Igiaba Scego, which presents parallel Somali and Italian versions, and the long narrative poem *Aulò* by Ribka Sibhatu, published in Tigrinya and Italian.[23] Brioni argues that in *La nomade* the Italian text prevails, based on at least two factors. First, the Somali version is clearly translated from the Italian, with the collaboration of a Somali native speaker. Scego is in fact an author born in Rome to a Somali family, and her first language is Italian, so her positioning in respect to the two languages diverges greatly from that of Hajdari. Second, the Somali version, following the Italian text, reproduces the explanation of some critical Somali passages, an operation which would appear to be redundant if the Somali text were actually directed to readers who are masters of this language. This brings Brioni to identify the Somali text as almost a decorative appendix of the Italian one, a feature that, he argues, compromises the principles of inseparability and reciprocity that parallel texts may otherwise foreground. In counterpoint to this, Brioni discusses the dialogic function of parallel texts in Sibhatu's *Aulò*. In Sibhatu's work, the Italian version is self-translated by the author following the text written in Tigrinya, which is her first language. The non-exoticized and non-decorative interpretation of parallel texts offered by Sibhatu in *Aulò* is read by Brioni as being capable of opening more decisively dialogic and antihierarchical spaces across the languages and cultures involved, and of foregrounding reciprocity as a constitutive function within the text in a more direct manner.

Brioni's analysis offers an insightful exploration of the use of parallel texts and related translational practices in postcolonial literature. Hajdari's use of parallel texts, however, is distinctive in respect to the cases examined by Brioni. First of all, in Hajdari's work, the use of the double language does not correspond to a textual or editorial strategy, or to a process of self-translation, but rather it foregrounds the innermost compositional mechanisms which operate within the author's double translingual imagination, and which he allows to spontaneously surface. It is also a process deeply grounded in the specificity of poetic writing and in particular in the rhythmical qualities brought about by translingual versification. In fact, if we return for a moment to Meschonnic theories, Hajdari's double verse can be read as a powerful manifestation of the translational rhythmical encounter that occurs when poetry moves across languages. In Hajdari's poetry, the syntonic translingual pulsation precedes the actual accumulation of meaning on the page through semantics and rhythm, and thus determines the double flowing of the verse onto the page. Therefore not only is it impossible to understand in which of the two languages Hajdari conceives of and writes his verses, but it can also be said that his versification is indeed founded on the inseparability of languages and constructed across the rhythmical spaces that both connect and foreground them. The relationship between the two languages in Hajdari's poetics is thus strictly non-hierarchical, and, within a postcolonial perspective, it provides a compelling example of the rhythmical erasure of power imbalances, a strategy of talking back that acknowledges and makes visible an inwardly fluid subjectivity. Moreover, this practice is in itself a sign of the radical transformative power that translingualism possesses in the realm of poetics.

Poesie scelte (1990–2007): The Self-Anthology as Long Form

Overall, *Poesie scelte* can be considered the main synthesis and product of the author's circular work towards his corpus of verses. Gazzoni accurately notes that the book represents 'il disvelarsi definitivo di una forma lunga' [the definitive unveiling of a long form],[24] and as such stresses the central presence of centripetal forces herein. The uniformity of this self-anthology makes the work a privileged point of observation from which to measure the diachronic progressions of Hajdari's work, and to acknowledge the dynamics of both unity and variety that qualify it. Moreover, this self-anthology represents an important synthesis of the different translational strategies that are at play in Hajdari's translingual verse, and in particular of the author's progressive transition from lyric to epic. In the following sections, I will retrace these trajectories across the formal qualities of Hajdari's verse, in light of the different responses to distance and displacement that are progressively articulated by the author.

On the whole, the centripetal forces at play in Hajdari's verse, which emerge with increased clarity in the self-anthology, pertain to the formal-metrical level as well as the semantic-lexical one. The poet himself, for instance, refers to the iteration within his poetic corpus of a set of primal elements, such as stone, water, fire, snow, rain, wind, thorns, and earth.[25] While these elements are recurrent in all his works, it is through the development of the translingual practice and the consolidation of the epic turn in particular that their roots in the long tradition of Albanian popular and epic poetry are made more and more explicit by Hajdari. This confirms that a transhistorical force operates constantly in Hajdari's work, a force that enacts a progressive recuperation of a poetic grammar related to centuries of Albanian poetics, while also allowing the poet to articulate his resistance to the trauma of recent history. At the same time, the repetition of these elements, together with other formal and lexical-semantic legacies of Albanian popular and epic poetry, enables the poet to perform a series of translations of the Albanian tradition into a second language-history: the Italian one. This process is made possible by the translingual practice and by the use of the double language in particular, and it becomes central in the mature poetic phase, when languages begin to merge vigorously from a lexical and morphological point of view as well. These aspects allow me to confirm that Hajdari's desire to position his work within a specific tradition is related to a trajectory of resistance, as he himself explains: 'I come from a long epic tradition in the North of Albania. My ancestors were singers of rhapsody and produced a vast cultural patrimony. One of the missions or battles is to give back life to the words, recovering the epic and the music that modern poetry has lost [...]'.[26] At the same time, the infusion of this specific traditional Albanian grammar into the double verse consolidates Hajdari's role as transmediterranean interpreter and translator, a role that the self-anthology allows to emerge with particular strength, and one that must be constantly kept in mind when evaluating the impact of his verse.[27]

A few introductory words need to be given at this point to the structural, philological, and linguistic profiles of the anthology. First of all, *Poesie scelte* is made up of nine sections which are eponymous with Hajdari's main previously published collections: *Erbamara* [Bitter grass], *Antologia della pioggia* [Anthology of the rain], *Ombra di cane* [The dog's shadow], *Sassi contro vento* [stones upwind], *Corpo presente* [The present body], *Stigmate* [Stigmata], *Spine nere* [Black thorns], *Maldiluna* [Maldiluna], and *Peligòrga* [Peligòrga].[28] The collection, written entirely in free verse, numbers 241 poems in all, which were authored across twenty years of translingual poetic activity. Notably, Hajdari reorders the sylloges chronologically, according to the composition date of the corresponding collections. The self-anthology thus opens with two sections, *Erbamara* and *Antologia della pioggia*, which stem from two works written in Albania, before Hajdari's displacement and before his acquisition of the double language. Hajdari would not translate these collections into Italian and publish them in bilingual editions until almost ten years after the publication of his first fully translingual work. The texts of these two sections therefore reflect an early poetic phase on an imaginative level, but they foreground a mature stage in terms of translingual versification. Moreover, they are the sole example of self-translations in the book, representing a unique bridge between the monolingual and double imagination. While the analysis below follows the new order of the sections as presented by the author in his self-anthology, the peculiar positioning of *Erbamara* and *Antologia della pioggia* in terms of translingual practice is to be kept in mind.

Hajdari's examination of the poems' textual history is indicative of his interpretation of the self-anthological operation. On the whole, the variants in the self-anthology as compared to the original collections are articulated across three main levels. First, Hajdari reduces the number of texts in each section, and introduces a number of unpublished compositions, all within the first part of the book.[29] Second, he performs numerous interventions in the formal profile of texts, through insertions, modifications to line divisions, and alterations to punctuation. Significantly, a comprehensive restoration of punctuation marks is performed across the book, and in particular in the sections which correspond to the early translingual works, which were completely deprived of diacritical marks in their original redactions. According to Meschonnic, punctuation plays an important role in regulating rhythmical-semantic balances within a verse, constituting the inner breath of a composition.[30] As I shall explain, the absence of punctuation in the early translingual phase correlates with both a radical sense of loss and woundedness, and the erosion of Hajdari's poetic grammar, an erosion that dominated the first stages of his physical and linguistic displacement. This aspect is domesticated in the self-anthology, which revisits the corpus of poems from an acquired distance, and heightens their uniformity, allowing the book to qualify as a long form. Third, in *Poesie scelte* Hajdari increases the overall indexicality of texts. For instance, places are mentioned more explicitly, corroborating the notion that a more transitive relation to history and to the Albanian past emerges in the mature poetic phase. On the whole, these interventions have the double effect of amplifying the formal and semantic correspondences across the sections on the one hand, and carefully preserving the inner values and individual meanings of each sylloge on the other.

Finally, from a linguistic point of view, the self-anthology is characterized by a particular foregrounding element: the book is presented as a monolingual Italian edition, which displays only the Italian versions of the poems. Significantly, however, the Albanian versions are collected and published in a homologous volume issued concurrently by the same publisher, titled *Poezi të zgjedhura (1990–2007)*.[31] Separating Italian and Albanian verse is an extremely uncommon practice for Hajdari, and in this case may be related to editorial requirements. The production of the two homologous volumes, however, assembled and published in parallel, makes it clear that the self-anthological operation was once again conducted through a double imaginative and compositional process, and hence confirms the principle of inseparability which presides over Hajdari's translingual verse and his syntonic use of Albanian and Italian.

In the following sections, keeping in mind these qualities, I will enter comprehensively into Hajdari's translingual poetic laboratory, providing insights into the evolution of his poetry as it emerges from the articulated and fluid realm of the self-anthology. The analysis is directed to three main levels. In the first section, I investigate poetic forms in light of both the diachronic progression of Hajdari's translingual practice and the different embodiments of distance that characterize almost twenty years of displacement. In the second section, I analyse the occurrences of different metres and in particular the emergence of accentual dynamics in Hajdari's translingual verse, at the intersection with prosodic hybridization, and with a focus on the aesthetic potential that translanguaging holds in the metrical-rhythmical realm. In the third and final section I provide an evaluation of the lexical profiles of the texts, focusing on dynamics of lexical and morphological hybridization, and paying particular attention to the treatment of embodiments of movement and to spatial indexicality.

Poetic Forms: Circularity and Transformation

In this section, I engage with Hajdari's use of poetic forms in the self-anthology; that is, with the general architecture of the poems, including their lengths, number of stanzas, number of lines per stanza, and occurrences of patterns and forms. By so doing, I will foreground two central aspects of Hajdari's poetry practice: a formal circularity, highlighted by the self-anthological dimension, and a constitutive mobility, made visible through the transition from lyrics to epics. Moreover, in my analysis I emphasize the ways in which linguistic distance, which was radical during the early stages of Hajdari's displacement, impacted both on the configuration of poetic forms, and on the ways in which the double language generated novel rhythmical and formal ecologies within the poet's translingual verse. While my considerations below are articulated with reference to a selection of texts that provide examples of the most obvious marked dynamics, they are based on the comprehensive data provided in the tables and in the figures in the Appendix, which are intended as a necessary complement to this discourse.[32]

On the whole, I have identified four different semantic-formal phases within the self-anthology relative to the configuration of poetic forms. The first comprises

Erbamara and *Antologia della pioggia*, which, as I have mentioned, derive from the self-translations of two early works originally written in Albanian. The two sections present many common points. First of all, both depict a solitary subject immersed in the natural spaces of Darsìa, the region where the poet grew up, a place which mostly operates as an innocent counterpoint to a violent and corrupted Albania. In portraying a subject located substantially outside of history, alienated from a closed society, the poet highlights the salvific function performed by nature, and in particular by dialogues with non-human interlocutors, such as plants and animals. Having been written before Hajdari's exile, and in an atmosphere dominated by tension and censorship, both the original collections from which *Erbamara* and *Antologia della pioggia* stem are articulated towards a subtle balance between said and unsaid, and display a metaphorical nature that is revisited through the variants of the self-anthology with the aim of increasing its assertiveness, as will be illustrated. On the whole, the catalogue of Hajdari's poetic grammar and symbols is already present in its substantial components in these early works: for the first time, fruits, birds, snow, and stones make incursions into his verse, and, with few exceptions, do not abandon it thereafter.

Despite an underlying formal and imaginative cohesion, the two sections present a series of differences. More specifically, while *Erbamara* is grounded in Hajdari's juvenile imagery, *Antologia della pioggia* is written in a period that* immediately precedes the poet's exile, and is visited by a more pervasive and explicit tension. As a consequence, the perception of alterity that permeates both sections is configured differently in each of them. In *Erbamara*, for instance, forms tend to be more regular on the whole. Isostanzaic compositions, and in particular those shaped around a succession of quatrains, are highly recurrent:

> Appoggiati al muro della casetta,
> nell'ultimo giorno d'autunno,
> prendiamo il sole che picchia,
> io e una lucertola senza coda.
>
> Nulla accade in questa provincia,
> gli stessi uomini, gli stessi volti.
> Tutto si trascina con fatica
> nel fango incanutito da secoli.
>
> D'ora in poi, nell'arena del gelo,
> ci sentiremo soli nella collina cupa.
> Io e il falco combatteremo
> con i denti e gli artigli.
>
> Sdraiato sulla terra umida
> assaporo l'erbamara dei prati.
> Negli abissi dei cieli impazziti
> si perde il mio sguardo.
>
> Non lontano dalla mia dimora,
> dove fecondano i fulmini,
> il vento del mare porta come misericordia
> le voci degli internati nei Campi. (*PS EM* 7)

> [Leaning against a small house
> on the last day of autumn
> I and a lizard without a tail
> soak in the beating sun
>
> Nothing happens round these parts —
> same people, same faces.
> Everything drags itself through mud
> whitened by centuries.
>
> From now on, in this chilly arena
> we'll be alone on the dark hill.
> The hawk and I will fight with tooth and claw.
>
> Lying on the damp earth
> I savour the fields' bitter grass.
> My gaze is lost in the emptiness
> of crazy skies.
>
> Not far from where I live,
> fertile for storm and lightning,
> the sea wind carries like a call for mercy
> the moans of those interned in the Camps.][33]

The poem above reveals a series of important qualities of Hajdari's verse in this pre-exilic phase. First of all, the sense of alienation from history that permeates the verse confirms that Hajdari's critical reflection on exile in fact precedes his actual displacement, and is configured in his early works as an initial reaction to the central Albanian trauma. This trauma, present from the opening of the poem in the form of a premonition, erupts explicitly at the close, wherein the voices of Lushnjë's political prisoners emerge, carried on the wind. The quatrain is the lyric-narrative form that enables both this scenario and dialogue to take place. As the text shows, its articulation in the first section is quite plain, and marked by a syntactic simplification that also foregrounds the original Albanian version. In fact, an examination of the bilingual collections shows that Hajdari is an extremely conservative self-translator, particularly careful to respect the formal balances of the texts, including length of lines, punctuation, and organization of stanzas. Metre and syntax substantially converge in this phase, a quality transcribed from the Albanian into the Italian diction. Rhythmically, verses present quite a cohesive profile, emphasized by the assonances at the ends of lines and consonances in the openings. In counterpoint to this, each stanza develops a specific focus on a different set of sounds, a process visible for instance in the two diverse inflections of whispered tones in the last two quatrains. Finally, the neologism *erbamara* [bitter grass], which is used as the title of the section and homologous collection, is a translation of the Albanian *barihidhur*. The neologism is significant from a rhythmical-semantic point of view, as it enhances the play on sounds and epitomizes the centrality of more-than-human encounters in the fourth stanza. On the whole, *Erbamara* is a section where the perception of alterity is domesticated into a regular versification, which returns the central Albanian trauma to an overarching and controlled formal order.

This trajectory is complicated in the later *Antologia della pioggia*, where the perception of alterity increases in intensity, beginning to impact on the regularity of forms. This tension also impacts on the productivity of more-than-human encounters, which begin to be compromised. Antonio Crecchia, for instance, explains that, in this collection, rain has an unprecedented anti-redemptive value, which contributes to the subject's constraint.[34] The native region of Darsìa, still the protagonist in this section, is now regarded with a premature sense of loss and melancholy. Contextually, forms begin to break. The relationship between said and unsaid evolves in favour of the latter, and white spaces acquire a novel expressive weight on the page:

> Infanzia solitaria e lontana,
> peligòrga, mio caro uccello,
> caratello d'acqua piovana
> che raccoglieva mia madre
> per lavare i panni,
> campi di brina dove andavo da solo all'alba
> e parole mai dette nascoste tra le labbra,
> solitudini, amarezze, sogni perduti
>   sulle strade di Darsìa,
> come ombre sparite
> e vi affacciate sempre. (*PS AP* 33)

> [Lost and lonely childhood,
> peligòrga, my beloved bird,
> pail of rainwater
> my mother collected
> to wash clothes,
> frosted fields where I walked alone at sunrise
> and words kept hidden behind my lips,
> loneliness, sorrow, dreams lost
>   on the streets of Darsìa,
> like shadows you vanish
> but always return.]

On the whole, the poem above conveys a memory of childhood, which is metonymically recalled through a triple set of references: to the mythical Albanian bird the *peligòrga*, to the daily maternal gesture of collecting water, and to the Darsian fields covered in frost that the subject crosses. Formally, the poem is made up of one sole undivided stanza. While rhythmical cohesion still emerges, the organization of lines and the dialogue with white spaces is more fluid here. Significantly, as part of the variants introduced in the self-anthology, the poet includes a step line containing the reference to Darsìa, completely absent in the first redaction. This variant is relevant to my discourse for two reasons. First, the step line has the effect of increasing the verse's fragmentation, enhancing the expressive function of white spaces, and amplifying as such one of the inner qualities of the section. Second, the insertion introduces a spatial referent, marking an increase in indexicality in the text. If examined within the more general context of the system of variants introduced in *Poesie scelte*, this referential inclusion confirms a path towards assertiveness which Gazzoni relates to a later phase of Hajdari's work, the phase that is most transitively projected towards history, and that corresponds roughly to the years in which Hajdari compiles his self-anthology.[35] On the other hand, the poetic construction of the historical and mythical Darsìa, to which this insertion responds, is also a prominent part of the grammar of recurrent elements progressively developed by Hajdari, a grammar which constitutes the basis of his increasingly openly declared epic inspiration. In this first phase, then, the poet reflects on a perception of alterity which manifests at different intensities within the two sections, and is embodied by two interrelated yet distinctive formal profiles in the texts: one more disciplined, the other more fragmented. While Hajdari works conservatively as a self-translator, attempting to establish *a posteriori* the syntonic rhythmical balances that qualify his double verse, the variants that he introduces in the self-anthology appear at once to increase the distinctive formal qualities of sections and to emphasize internal correspondences across the self-anthology, while also reinforcing the system of iterations that would constitute the core of the epic turn.

A second phase in the configuration of poetic forms corresponds to the three following sections: *Ombra di cane*, *Sassi contro vento*, and *Corpo presente*. These sections derive from three early translingual collections, all authored by Hajdari in the years that immediately followed his displacement. In this second phase, the poet faces physical and linguistic exile for the first time. The perception of alterity now becomes a radical and overarching force, which impacts all levels of versification. Encounters with the human-*other* are impossible, and dialogues with the non-human are largely prevented. As a consequence, the sensual imagery and the more-than-human encounters that permeated the first phase are dramatically interrupted, and poems abruptly lose their ability to name. Verses are broken and traumatized, and the quatrain — still present mostly in the form of a rhythmical memory — is sliced apart and deconstructed. Here, brevity becomes the foregrounding feature, and monostanzaic — sometimes even monolinear — compositions prevail. In these early translingual works, Sara di Gianvito has pointed out the presence of a mark of unbelonging, expropriation, and wounding that impedes the verse from fully flowing.[36] Developing her argument, I maintain that this is the phase in which Hajdari is forced to abandon his monolingual poetic grammar, and begins to build a new one, relying on the distinctive expressive potential of the double language, but also on a different perception of the space that surrounds him, determined by his displacement.

> Fuori della finestra
> la pioggia, come un vetro opaco
> taglia i giorni della mia vita,
> mi bagna la ragione. (*PS OC* 38)
>
> [Outside the window
> the rain, like opaque glass,
> slices the days of my life;
> it soaks my reason.]

> Nessuna donna
> chiama il mio nome
> in questo Paese. (*PS OC* 42)

> [No woman
> calls my name
> in this country.]

> Madre,
> ho perso le metafore. (*PS OC* 44)

> [Mother,
> I have lost my metaphors.]

> Tu stai laggiù
> dietro colonne di pioggia,
> distratta da specchi e abissi.
> Vedo la tua ombra sulle pietre,
> ma non ti trovo.
> È inverno, si chiude il giorno. (*PS SC* 57)

> [You stand there
> behind columns of rain,
> distracted by mirrors and abysses.
> I see your shadow on the rocks,
> but I can't find you.
> It's winter; the day ends.]

> Partiamo di notte,
> dimenticando che siamo ciechi,
> per raggiungere un territorio nudo
> del quale ha bisogno la nostra voce.
> Andiamo al mare per parlare
> e lanciare sassi controvento. (*PS SC* 61)

> [We leave at night,
> forgetting we are blind,
> to reach a bare land
> that our voice needs.
> We walk to the sea to talk
> and throw stones against the wind.]

> Nessun altro gesto è possibile. (*PS SC* 62)

> [No other gesture is possible]

The poems above foreground the laceration embedded in the verses of this phase through the portrayal of a six-dimensional loss: of reason (*PS OC* 38), name (*PS OC* 42), language (*PS OC* 44), love (*PS SC* 57), sight (*PS SC* 61), and gesture (*PS SC* 62). The outer world is now looked at from a radical distance which dissipates the specific connotations of places, elements, and interlocutors. At the same time, words acquire a novel material function. They transitively adhere to the matter that they are called on to embody, and are chosen first and foremost for their sensual and plastic qualities. The development of this novel function is often described by translingual authors as one of the primary effects of the acquisition of a second language, a language in which signifiers can finally be liberated from the multi-layered cage of meaning, to be re-experienced as bodies, in their physical qualities. In the case of Hajdari, this use of words constitutes the core of a novel radical expressive force that arises in this phase. In fact, on the subject of Hajdari's early translingual works, Luigi Manzi significantly states: 'Ho conosciuto Gëzim nel 1995, ad Agnone, durante un reading di poesia [...] Quando fu il suo turno di lettura, i versi caddero sull'uditorio come schegge' [I met Gëzim in 1995, in Agnone, during a poetry reading [...] When it was his turn to read, the verses fell on the audience like splinters].[37] This assertion stresses the novel weight that Hajdari's words acquire through the translingual practice, and their innovative potential within the Italophone scene.

The poems above also allow further central qualities of this phase to emerge. First of all, the verse is now more decidedly open to expressionist marks, such as metalinguistic inserts and, more generally, a forced use of structures, particularly verbal forms. The syntax remains extremely plain, and the sentences appear dry and cut to the bone. Manzi rightly speaks of an overall lack of polysemy in these works,[38] which I maintain is related to the material function allocated to words, and to the loss of Hajdari's poetic grammar as an effect of physical and linguistic displacement. Moreover, the absolute absence of punctuation in the original collections corresponds to the loss of coordinates and poetic grammar. The former is fully restored in the self-anthology, where the poet also performs a strategic inclusion of a number of unpublished poems. On the whole, the variants demonstrate once again the double drive towards both unity and variety that presides over the self-anthological operation at large.

The following section, *Corpo presente*, marks a development within the early translingual phase in formal terms, as well as in regard to the progression of the poet's theoretical reflection on displacement. As the title suggests, this section explores both the qualities of the body and its constitutive immanence. More specifically, the body, and its material presence in space, now become a possible horizon of belonging for the poet. As Hajdari explains, this development is related to novel epistemological spaces that are opened as the experience of displacement progresses: 'Oggi non si migra solo da un paese all'altro, ma anche da una lingua all'altra. Il bilinguismo mi ha insegnato che il mio corpo è la mia patria e il mio nome è la mia identità. Anzi, ogni giorno creo una nuova patria, in cui muoio e rinasco' [These days one does not only migrate from one country to another, but also from one language to another. Bilingualism taught me that my body is my homeland and my name is my identity. In fact, every day I create a new homeland, in which I die and am reborn].[39] On the whole, *Corpo presente* represents the most materialistic phase of Hajdari's research. Uprooted and disappointed, the poet eventually finds a complete and self-sufficient form of being and belonging in corporeality. The body — extremely vulnerable, yet also extant, actual, true, impossible to be overlooked — remains a consistently tangible and visible point across space. Its immanence makes it become both an embodiment of resistance and an instrument of empowerment for the displaced subject. The declaration of the body's immanence and the dissolution of the perception of alterity into the material horizon of corporeality, which this section foregrounds, do not prevent the onset of a sensual dialogue with the outer world, but in fact re-enable it. In other words, when a novel possible homeland is discovered and declared, Hajdari's verse begins to unseal itself anew. As a consequence, the verse is populated once again, and for the first time is grounded in the landscape of Ciociaria, where the poet has lived since the early days of his displacement.

Formally, some of the dynamics that we saw at play in *Ombra di cane* and *Sassi contro vento*, such as the constitutive brevity and the material relief of words, are still active in *Corpo presente*. In this section, however, the new faith in the body determines an overall relaxation of forms, which begin to be extended and are slightly rhetoricized. Monostanzaic patterns rarely occur, and the division of stanzas foregrounds the poet's desire to inflect his double verse in more articulated textual geographies:

> Stringiamo i nostri nomi
> strappati come l'erba
>
> e non sappiamo da dove ci viene
> questa solitudine.
>
> Forse dovevamo stare
> più vicino agli alberi
> o ai marmi riversi.
>
> Da anni camminiamo
> nei campi brulli
> senza infanzia.
>
> Scende una neve lenta
> sui nostri corpi. (*PS CP* 69)
>
> [We hold on to our names
> torn like grass
>
> and we do not know where
> this loneliness comes from.
>
> Maybe we should have stayed
> closer to the trees
> or the fallen marble.
>
> For years we have walked
> in dry fields
> without childhood.
>
> A light snow falls
> on our bodies.]

In this section, as the agile verse above shows, forms are still sharp and are impacted by the poet's search for essentiality and precision. Nonetheless, they begin to recuperate a lyrical-narrative function. The progression of translingual versification is reflected in the beginnings of a rhetoricization of the diction, visible here in the anaphoric occurrences of verbal forms, for instance. Forms, as identified by the division of stanzas, are more fragmented, and the pact between metre and syntax is sporadically interrupted. On the whole, the verses in *Corpo presente* adhere to the body and its complexities, simultaneously foregrounding its novel function: to provide a shelter through which to survive storms, passages, and the loss of one's name, and to embody a terrain of resistance, identification, and communion.

This section closes the early and more confessional phase of Hajdari's translingual work, a phase that is entirely directed towards the displaced and post-migratory condition, and that translates the central Albanian trauma, through the greatest linguistic distance, into a verse structured towards brevity and across a novel transitive relation between word and world. In later works, Hajdari's verse undergoes a process of progressive extension, rhetoricization, and epicization, which relies primarily on a mounting recovery of the tropes of Albanian popular and oral epics. In parallel, a more mediated relationship between signifier and signified will be established. This process begins to become central in a third phase, through three intermediate steps that are represented by the three following sections of *Poesie scelte*: *Stigmate*, *Spine nere*, and *Maldiluna*. The works that emerge across this phase reflect on in-betweenness as a permanent condition of the poet's existence, and of humanity at large. As such, they establish a direct dialogue with both Albania and Italy, which are often personified and assume the roles of major interlocutors. At the same time, the verse points more explicitly to a celebration of the displaced community, and collectivity is placed at the centre of the scene. The verses undergo a process of pluralization and are informed by an increased relationality. As a result, not only does the number of interlocutors increase, but also the verse opens itself more decidedly to sensual and then openly erotic imagery. Among the catalogue of human interlocutors who populate Hajdari's verse in this phase is the figure of the mother, who emerges as the first epic character. Within her profile, which enters the verse extensively, especially in *Spine nere*, the trauma of displacement crystallizes, while personal and collective histories begin to merge. Moreover, the melancholic and sensual imagery of this phase abundantly converge on the figure of the mother, thus providing a model for the shaping of all the human encounters that begin to increasingly foreground Hajdari's verse. The increased relationality of these poems also concerns the more-than-human encounters, which evolve in the direction of interpenetration and transformation. Consequently in these sections there is a central occurrence of transitional imagery, and in particular of metamorphosis and personification.

On the whole, these sections represent a zone of contact between the semantic nodes of the first translingual phase and later polyphonic and epic developments. Formally, they are characterized by a binary development. On the one hand, they all accommodate brief compositions, still related to the sharp forms of the first translingual phase. In the case of *Maldiluna*, which is the most openly lyrical section, the poet predominantly works with short undivided forms, while more textual mobility is recorded in *Stigmate* and *Spine nere*. On the other hand, in *Spine nere* and *Maldiluna*, long poems begin to appear. These are the poems that most notably start to host references to the tradition of rhapsodies and Albanian oral poetry, and to insert the transfigured narration of the poet's personal history into a collective one; as such, they prepare the poetic ground for the epic turn. A few examples of the first and more laconic trajectory active in this phase are found below.

> Anche tu, pino, che ti affacci alla mia finestra, sei in esilio
> lontano dal mare sogni le onde blu salate, lo iodio, la sabbia,
> i rumori dei pescatori al crepuscolo, i fichi d'India
> e i gridi dei gabbiani agli orizzonti sottili.
> Solo tu sei testimone delle donne nude nel mio letto
> e dei miei amori clandestini. (*PS SN* 155)

> [Even you, pine tree, appearing through my window, live in exile
> far from the sea you dream the salty blue waves, the iodine, the sand,
> the sounds of fishermen at sunset, the prickly pears
> and the call of seagulls against fragile horizons.
> You are the sole witness of the naked women in my bed,
> of my secret loves.]

> Quella mela rossa
> dimenticata sui rami denudati dall'autunno,
> è il mio cuore appeso. (*PS SN* 156)

> [That red apple,
> forgotten on branches bared by autumn,
> is my hanging heart.]

> Ieri sera,
> insieme ad un bicchiere di vino,
> ho bevuto la tua immagine color viola,
> i tuoi occhi castani, i tuoi inni.
> Ho bevuto le tue labbra gonfie di passione,
> le tue notti e le tue albe,
> tutti i tuoi incendi ho bevuto.
> Verranno altre sere
> con nuovi crepuscoli appesi
> ed io altri bicchieri di vino berrò,
> ma sarà tardi,
> la tua immagine e i tuoi occhi,
> le tue labbra e i tuoi inni
> non riusciranno a riportarmi a riva. (*PS MD* 204)

> [Last night,
> along with a glass of red wine,
> I drank your violet image,
> your brown eyes, your hymns.
> I drank your passion-swollen lips,
> your nights and your dawns,
> all your fires I drank.
> There will be other nights
> with other suspended sunsets
> and I will drink other glasses of wine,
> but it will be too late;
> your profile, your eyes,

your lips, your hymns,
will never bring me back to the shore.]

As the examples shows, short texts in *Stigmate* and *Spine nere* foreground the subject's in-betweenness. Moreover, the poems highlight the increased centrality of more-than-human encounters and the identification between body and nature, which is a major trope in this phase. From a formal point of view, lines begin to stretch horizontally. On the whole, the verse in short compositions is still mostly characterized by a scarcity of rhetorical superstructures. Syntax tends not to follow metre, and enjambment acquires a central expressive role.

In counterpoint to these forms, all sections also present more extended structures, which raise the formularity of the diction and work decisively in the direction of the epic turn. This is a phase in which Hajdari deepens his research into long forms, which he had experimented with in parallel to this work in the long poem *Poema dell'esilio*, his sole poetry book not to enter the self-anthology.[40] For his *Poema*, which brings together lyrics, epics, and history-chronicle, Hajdari had engineered a specific long metre, with stanzas composed of a quatrain of long lines plus a one-line refrain, repeated with *variatio* throughout the whole length of the composition. Inspired by the narrative power and potentially infinite length of Dante's *terzina*, this metrical hapax provided Hajdari with a fertile ground in which to experiment with the rhythmical balances and expressive potential of the long form. This specific research informs the emergence of two main types of long poem in this phase. On the one hand, Hajdari inflects the long poem in isostanzaic forms wherein the pact between syntax and metre is re-established, and stanzas are permeated by an extreme metrical and rhythmical regularity, based first and foremost on a calibrated system of repetitions. On the other, the poet infuses long compositions with dialogic and polyphonic developments, wherein the alternation of different voices becomes a central feature. These compositions tend to be more irregular in terms of the organization of the stanzas, and to be shaped on a succession of rhythmically distinctive utterances. Both types of long form, however, begin to host a complex catalogue of conventional motifs of the Albanian popular poetry tradition, and overall they present a high degree of polysemy and intertextuality.

> C'era una volta un ragazzo magro dall'animo fragile
> con occhi castani e sguardo penetrante come un corvo nero,
> nato in un inverno magico di lampi e tuoni marini
> e cresciuto sulla collina brulla vicino alle stelle ardenti.
>
> Quando vide i primi raggi del sole pallido:
> 'Il suo nome vivrà in eterno — dissero i laghi e le nebbie cieche —
> di pietra in pietra verrà scolpito il suo verbo,
> nei secoli la sua storia d'uomo verrà narrata. (*PS SN* 172, 1–8)
>
> [Once upon a time there lived a boy with a fragile soul,
> with brown eyes and a piercing gaze, like a black crow.
> He was born in a magic winter of storms and tempests,
> and raised on a barren hill close to the burning stars
>
> When the first rays of the pale sun touched him:
> 'His name will live forever,' the lakes and blind fogs said,

'from stone to stone his word will be sculpted;
through the centuries his tale will be told.']

Perché questi uomini vestiti di nero
bussano alla mia vecchia porta?
Vengono per gioia o per lutto?
Perché si ferma il vento in montagna
e l'usignolo resta in ascolto?
Ditemi, al mio Gëzim cos'è accaduto?
Sono sua madre e devo sapere.
È insieme a voi la mia peligòrga?
Ditemi se è spirato per strada,
o nella stanza sgombra?
Misera me! che grande *gjam*!
[...]
Occidente, dov'è la tua *besa*
che mi avrebbe restituito Gëzim salvo? (*PS SN* 173, 1–11; 27–28)

[Why do these men dressed in black
knock at my old door?
Do they come carrying joy or grief?
Why does the wind rest on the mountain
while the nightingale stops to listen?
Tell me, what happened to my Gëzim?
I am his mother; I need to know.
Is he with you, my peligòrga?
Tell me if he died in the street,
or in the empty room?
Alas! What a great *gjam*!
[...]
West, where is your *besa*
that would have safely brought my Gëzim home?]

Here, the diction is extended in all directions in comparison to the preceding phase. Lines are opened up to a catalogue of traditional Albanian motifs, which multilingual inserts may highlight. We see this in the allusion to the *gjam*, which is a celebration of the merits of a dead person, and the *besa*, a binding promise which, according to the poet's explanation, 'è principio d'onore, regola di vita, è qualcosa di assoluto e complesso, nello stesso tempo è un patto di fedeltà che si stringe con un uomo, vivo o morto, con un'istituzione (l'ospitalità), con la propria terra' [is a principle of honour, a rule of life, something absolute and complex, and at the same time it is a pact of loyalty that is established with a person, dead or alive, with an institution (hospitality), and with one's own land].[41] The opening up of the verses to the intertextual and multilingual, upon which I will expand in the final section, also informs the reconstruction of the poet's own life and work in an epic key, including the celebration of his mythical origins and name through the verse. This is a radical turn, considering that only ten years previously Hajdari had denounced in his verse the loss of his name as an effect of displacement. Here, with the long poems openly declaring his belonging to the tradition of Albanian oral epic and popular poetry, and confirming his mission to celebrate, from exile, the displaced community and the significance of the experience of movement, Hajdari thus begins to close an important circle. Simultaneously, he reinforces, through the increased relationality of texts, and through a more explicit inclusion of the Albanian tradition within the double verse, his role as transmediterranean interpreter and translator.

A few more words need to be given to the textual histories of the texts that flow into these sections, in particular in *Stigmate* and *Spine nere*. In these two sylloges Hajdari introduces the highest number of variants in the entire book. The variants include not only the meticulous restoration of the punctuation marks that were substantially missing from the first redactions, but also, and extensively, the paratextual materials. In fact, as the Italian and Albanian poetic grammar also tends to merge from a lexical-morphological point of view in this phase, Hajdari increasingly provides the readers with coordinates they can use to navigate the references to the Albanian tradition and the multilingual inserts, and introduces a substantial apparatus of explanatory notes. This practice is reinforced and made uniform in the self-anthology. This is an interesting aspect, especially if we read it in relation with Brioni's analysis of paratextual explanations and glosses in postcolonial Italophone literature.[42] In the works analysed by Brioni, notes and glosses seem to be related to a chronologically early or central phase of the authors' work, while in later phases Somali-Italian authors tended more frequently to domesticate other languages internally within the Italophone text, without recourse to an explanatory apparatus. In this sense, Hajdari's process is once again distinctive. Indeed, in the self-anthological process, which occurs in a mature phase, while separating languages, the poet increases the explanations of his translingual poetic grammar in a space which is located beyond the verse itself. This attitude reinforces the positioning of the author as a transmediterranean translator, and also foregrounds the transition from lyric to epic and history, and the related path towards assertiveness already identified by Gazzoni.[43]

The shift towards a full polyphony, a collective and universal dimension, and a symbolic eroticism is performed in the following and concluding phase, which includes the final section *Peligòrga*. The poems of this particular section derive from a collection that could be framed as the rewriting of the Albanian past within a translingual present. This crucial juncture is announced from the very title, which alludes to the mythical Darsian bird *peligòrga*, one of the symbols of Hajdari's poetry, which visits the self-anthology extensively and circularly, as I shall explain in the next section. In the introduction to the original collection, the poet clarifies that the book contains

> versi scritti ieri per oggi e oggi per ieri. Essi *giacevano* in me da decenni, erano *seppelliti* nella mia pelle [...] Più passavano gli anni, più i loro gemiti non si placavano; così ho deciso di dare volto e voce a questi versi, che hanno sconvolto profondamente il mio io centrale, lasciandomi segni strazianti e indelebili.
>
> [verses written yesterday for today and today for yesterday. These were *lying* in me for decades, they were *buried* beneath my skin [...] The more the years passed by, the more their moans did not subside; so I decided to give a face and a voice to those verses, which has profoundly shocked my deepest self, leaving excruciating and permanent signs].[44]

This assertion allows me to reinforce the idea that, for Hajdari, the emergence of the double verse is rooted in a physical-rhythmical process grounded in the body itself. Moreover, Hajdari's words reveal that the poet's tradition of origin is mediated through the progression of his physical distance from Albania, and the concurrent shortening of linguistic distance from Italian, which occurs after almost twenty years of translingual practice. Once the double language reacquires its polysemantic qualities, the verses can thus open up anew to the past.

Finally, the transhistorical dimension brought about by the polysemantic nature of the diction in *Peligòrga* allows for a rereading of Hajdari's entire corpus of works in a new figurative and symbolic key. It is therefore crucial to uncover the catalogue of allusions that the poet has covertly disseminated in the preceding phases. This section is thus significant per se, as the pinnacle of the epicization that is Hajdari's objective, and as a tool to unveil the profundity of memories and transmediterranean interconnections. Within a now-mythologized and eternalized Darsìa, Hajdari completes the rewriting of his story in light of the ensuing experience of displacement and sheds light on the ultimate function of his contrapuntal word. Personal and collective history are merged, and the central Albanian trauma is translated into narrative and rhetoricized forms. Located at the crossroads between the juvenile quatrains and the more mature narrative metre, the epic forms of *Peligòrga* complete the memorialization of the poet's mission, a poet who is now explicitly depicted as the witness and cantor of Albanian glories and tragedies, a heroic figure. The mythic narration of his origins and of his first approaches to poetry stresses this celebratory intention, while also defining Hajdari's mature mission: to redeem Albania's unfortunate past, to denounce and defeat oppression and censorship, and to celebrate an oppressed transnational community through a reconnection with its mythical past. Here, the quatrain returns to formally dominate the diction, yet it has profoundly mutated as a result of the translingual journey that divides its present inflection from that which we find in the early juvenile works. In parallel, the appearance of more irregular and highly polyphonic forms (similar to the long poems that emerged in the preceding phase) foregrounds the translation of these dialogic forms into an intertextual and polysemantic grammar. The excerpts below account for both of these dynamics:

> Nel villaggio corse la voce
> e si diffuse di casa in casa:
> 'Il figlio della povera Nur
> è uscito fuori di senno, è impazzito!'
>
> I parenti e i vicini
> mi guardavano storto.
> I contadini, appena mi vedevano,
> cambiavano strada.
>
> Piangeva la mia Nur,
> mentre raccoglieva le olive.
> Ogni giorno supplicava il Signore
> per una benedizione.

Nella casetta di pietra nera
la sera veniva tanta gente.
'Devi andare da un hoxha per una preghiera! —
le dicevano le amiche —

l'hanno legato i xhin
all'una di notte;
qualcuno che non vi vuole bene
gli ha fatto la fattura!' (*PS PG* 215, 1–20)

[Through the village the word spread
from house to house:
'The son of poor Nur
has lost his mind!'

Family and neighbours
looked askance.
As soon as the farmers saw me,
they turned the other way.

My Nur was crying
while she harvested olives.
Every day she prayed to God
for a blessing.

Every night people came
to the black stone house.
'You have to go to an *hoxha* for a prayer!'
her friends said,

'The *xhin* have trapped him
at one at night;
someone who wishes you evil
has cast a spell!']

Fanciulla della Ciociaria,
mia dolcezza, fiore selvatico delle colline di Saturno,
sei una puledra focosa che corre per i campi trebbiati
tirando calci al vento,
piena di odori e fiumi femminili,
profuma la tua pelle mora e inebria gli erranti.
[...]
sono ardente, attraversami con i tuoi xhin,
  con le tue Zanat
   con i tuoi oracoli,
    con le tue pietre
seminami, fecondami,
mordimi come mordevi le more,
toccami come toccavi le visciole,
succhiami come succhiavi la melagrana spaccata della tua collina,
inondami della schiuma bianca del tuo fiume in piena,
inonda la mia valle di papaveri rossi
e fa che il tuo dio fertile si perda nella mia luna oscura!
      (*PS PG* 241, 1–6; 218–28)

[Maiden of Ciociaria,
my sweetness, wild flower of Saturn's hills,
you are a lively horse who runs through winnowed fields
kicking against the wind,
full of feminine odours;
your dark skin's scent makes travellers drunk.
[...].

I am burning! Transport me with your xhin
    with your Zanat
        with your oracles
            with your stones
sow me, fertilize me,
bite me as you bit the blackberries,
touch me as you touched the wild cherries,
sip from me as you sip from the broken pomegranate on your hill,
flood me with the white foam of your full river,
inundate my valley with red poppies,
and may your fertile God become lost in my dark moon!]

The vigorous recourse to a catalogue of symbols and intertextual references generates the more explicit emergence of Albanian grafts onto the Italian diction. As the first example shows, the quatrain of *Peligòrga* is more extended, dialogic, and formulaic with respect to that of *Erbamara*. Moreover, it embodies a series of more-than-human entanglements that are mediated by filters of memory and displacement. The second excerpt, drawn from the final long poem of the collection, *Contadino della tua vigna*, demonstrates that the eros of *Peligòrga* is a different eros: it is mediated, polyphonic, hybrid, and intertextual. Here, the lover gains a voice, which is configured as a counterpoint to that of the subject. The two utterances are characterized by diverse rhythmical profiles, with internal cohesion created through repetitions and correspondences such as the insistence on proparoxytones in the lover's discourse. Linguistically, the diction is hybridized, and accommodates a wide range of transliterations and calques, again accompanied by paratextual explanations. We see this for example with *xhin*, alluding to mythological domestic predatory spirits, and *Zanat*, demigoddesses of the mountains; but the process is far more extensive. As I shall explain, these inserts are not simply signs of formal hybridization, but instead serve to mark the transition to the epic. Within the interweaving of tropes and iconic love figures in this composition, which are undoubtedly indebted to the biblical Song of Songs, Laura Toppan rightly observes extensive references to transnational erotic and love poetry far beyond the Albanian-Italian horizon: from Konstantinos Petrou Kavafis to Adonis, from Nâzım Hikmet to Amaruka, from Jacques Prévert to Pablo Neruda.[45] In light of the present discourse, it is important to underline that *Peligòrga* also marks the passage to a full germination of Hajdari's erotic imagery, and closes on a deeply intertextual figuration of universal fertility. As Toppan observes, 'tutto converge nella parola Amore' [everything converges in the word Love].[46] This concluding image confirms the emergence of a Hajdarian word that, in this late phase, arrives deeply transformed, and announces its novel collective, plural, relational, and epic qualities.

Hajdari's Metres: Between Syllabic and Accentual Verse

The qualities of Hajdari's double verse may also be observed on a fine-grained rhythmical level; that is, in light of the interaction between the Italian syllabic prosodic system and the Albanian one, which is mostly accentual, but can better be considered to be a hybrid accentual-syllabic.[47] This translingual prosodic interaction tends to covertly move Hajdari's double verse towards an accentual isochronism, which emerges in several compositions within *Poesie scelte*. Stemming from the prosody of the mother tongue, the accentual inclination configures in Hajdari as a hidden metre that is profoundly inscribed in his diction.[48] This translingual rhythmical sensitivity is particularly visible in the self-translations, as well as in the formulaic diction of the final epic phase. The ensuing metrical-rhythmical analysis conducted on the entire body of *Poesie scelte* follows, out of a descriptive necessity, the syllabic Italophone conventions. Yet the centrality of the accentual dynamics that emerge in the Italophone diction as an effect of translanguaging must be considered crucial to Hajdari's versification practice, and as such are referred to in the analysis when relevant.

As with the majority of Hajdari's collections, the self-anthology is entirely constructed in free verse. Nonetheless, the occurrence of lines of different lengths, and the analysis of internal metrical-rhythmical balances, is highly relevant to this discourse, as it allows me to elaborate on the stylistic implications of translingual versification, an area which is still significantly under-investigated, especially within the Italophone realm. Table 2.1 provides a comprehensive mapping of the types of lines in *Poesie scelte*, which is useful in pinpointing the predominant balances.

Type	*Count*	*Percentage*
BS	21	0.53%
TS	53	1.35%
QS	115	2.92%
QN	197	5.00%
SN	331	8.41%
ST	430	10.92%
OT	431	10.95%
NO	463	11.76%
DS	413	10.49%
ED	361	9.17%
VL	1122	28.49%
Total	3937	100%

TABLE 2.1 Types of lines in *PS*

Overall, the poet seems to prefer lines of medium length, which constitute the basis of one of his favourite forms, the quatrain, and of the long poem too. However, short and long lines also carry a significant weight in his diction. In fact, their occurrence is related to the different functions that the translingual verse performs over time, and hence to the transition from lyric to epic. These lines also reveal some of the foregrounding stylistic marks of Hajdari's verse, such as its iterative nature and its increasingly dialogic articulation.

In the following paragraphs, I will examine the occurrence of different metres in the self-anthology at the intersection with the rhythmical profile of lines and the progression of the translingual verse. This analysis allows me not only to discuss central forms in Hajdari's Italophone verse, but also to discuss the constitutive diversity of his lines and their progressive transformation from a metrical-rhythmical point of view, as well as the significance of this process in the context of translingual versification. With the aim of providing a comprehensive picture of the balances that preside over Hajdari's use of metres and rhythms in his Italophone verse, the analysis develops vertically, and visits in succession short, medium, and long measures.

Short metres up to the *senario* recur overall quite frequently in the book (18.21% in total). Of the very short measures, from the *bisillabo* to the *quinario*, we witness limited but crucial occurrences. On the whole, these are used to fragment the diction, to introduce pauses, and to emphasize the dialogue between words and white spaces. Their occurrence is central in the early translingual phase, where the radical dryness of the diction determines an unprecedented cluster of short lines. Often employed in combination with allocutions, figures typical of Hajdari's verse, short lines are frequently called on to foreground a dialogic development, to perform a coordinative or iterative role, or to rhythmically qualify the central subject. More rarely, particularly from the central phase onwards, they may spring up as a result of a collision between metre and syntax.

PS CP 83, 1–3
Albania,	QS	3					
che amarezza	QS	3					
il nostro destino,	SN	2		5			
[Albania | what bitterness | our fate,]							

PS CP 93, 7–8
Padre,	BS 1						
salvami dal mio impietoso destino.	ED 1				7		10
[Father, | save me from my pitiless fate.]							

PS MD 208, 93
Ridi tu, valle,	QN 1	3	4				
[Laugh, valley,]							

★ ★ ★ ★ ★

PS EM 14, 1–2
Non piangere,	TS	2					
è il pettirosso che corre	OT		4		7		
[Do not cry | that's the robin running]							

7–8
Non piangere,	TS	2					
ho percorso la tua ferita	NO	3			8		
[Do not cry | I have travelled your wound]							

PS SN 160, 6
Chiamami,	BS 1						
ti risponderà la mia voce sparsa sull'erba	VL		5		8	10	13
[Call me, | my voice scattered on the grass will answer you]							

PS MD 207, 121–22
 Chiamami,   BS 1
 dall'immenso dell'esilio ritornerò   VL   3   7   12
 [Call me, | from the immensity of exile I will return]

       ★ ★ ★ ★ ★

PS CP 65, 10–11
 Ed io,   TS   2
 scavato da ombre e pietre,   OT   2   5   7
 [And me, | drawn by shadows and stones]
PS CP 81, 7–8
 Accanto a me   QN   2   4
 sei come una collina,   ST 1   2   6
 [Beside me | you are like a hill,]

       ★ ★ ★ ★ ★

PS CP 71, 4–6
 e vogliono uccidere la mia carne   ED   2   5   10
 affidata all'acqua e alla memoria   DS   3   5   9
 degli alberi.   TS   2
 [and they want to kill my flesh | given to the waters and to the memory | of trees.]
PS MD 207, 91–93
 La mia voce orfana   SN   3   5
 sotto l'ombra   QS 1   3
 del flauto.   TS   2
 [My orphan voice | beneath the shadow | of the flute.]

These excerpts demonstrate the employment of short metres in coordination with allocutions (*PS CP* 83; *PS CP* 93; *PS MD* 208). The latter may occur at the ends of lines, tending in this case to be graphically relieved by punctuation. Short metres may also perform a coordinative function, connecting segments in the texts (*PS EM* 14) and creating prominent metrical resonances across the book, which amplify its epic breath (*PS MD* 207). Moreover, they are frequently used in coordination with pronominal deixis and expressions that point to the subject. In this case, the short line tends to isolate the subject from interlocutors and the surrounding space, foregrounding its distinctive positioning. This use is particularly pervasive in *Corpo presente*, where the focus on matter corresponds to a more physical relief of the subject and its embodiments on the page. Finally, as the last set of examples shows, when short metres are the result of an enjambment (quite rare in *Erbamara*, *Antologia della pioggia*, and *Peligòrga*; more frequent in other works), they tend to isolate qualifiers.

From a rhythmical point of view, pentasyllabic and hexasyllabic lines begin to perform a solid unifying role within the composition into which they are inserted, contributing to the construction and propagation of accentual dynamics. First of all, both Hajdari's *quinario* (5.00%) and *senario* (8.41%) usually present a binary and fast-paced structure. Generally, lines tend towards the polarization of stresses at the borders of the line. Both regular and irregular rhythmical profiles are recurrent:

PS EM 1, 12				
rose e coltelli.	*QN*	1		4
[roses and knives.]				
PS EM 6, 6				
piume e richiami.	*QN*	1		4
[feathers and calls.]				
PS EM 6, 8				
nidi e rumori.	*QN*	1		4
[nests and noises.]				
PS OC 40, 2				
queste città	*QN*	1		4
[these cities]				
PS SC 58, 3				
Sotto le pietre	*QN*	1		4
[Beneath the stones]				
PS CP 90, 4				
delirio e polvere;	*QN*		2	4
[delirium and dust;]				
PS PG 227, 30				
polvere e cenere —	*QN*	1		4
[dust and ash —]				
PS CP 80, 1				
Resterò io	*QN*		3	4
[I will stay]				
PS PG 239, 8				
Porti erba verde	*QN*	1	2	4
[You bring green grass]				

★ ★ ★ ★ ★

PS EM 6, 3–4				
A stormi le rondini	*SN*	2		5
nei cieli volarono.	*SN*	2		5
[In flocks the swallows | in the skies they flew.]				
PS CP 68, 1–4				
Siamo qui tra i sassi	*SN*	1	3	5
[We are here between the rocks]				
PS AP 34, 10				
e dimenticati.	*SN*			5
[and forgotten.]				
PS PG 224, 16				
che ti terrà in vita!	*SN*		4	5
[which will keep you alive!]				
PS PG 241, 219				
con le tue Zanat	*SN*			5
con i tuoi oracoli,	*SN*			5
[with your Zanat | with your oracles]				

The first set of examples shows the three main embodiments of the *quinario*, all presenting a rhythmical insistence at the edges of the line. The *quinario* is also frequently used in combination with proparoxytone forms, another stylistic marker of Hajdari's Italophone verse, and may occur, in its most irregular embodiments, in coordination with *accenti ribattuti* [double stresses], which both increase the verse pace and infuse it with an element of dissonance and dynamic tension. Similar dynamics are involved in the rhythmical profile of the *senario*. A regular double-stressed dactylic development of the *senario* is common in both the self-translations and the later mature translingual phase, while elsewhere, triple-stressed trochaic and irregular patterns are recurrent instead (*PS CP* 68; *PS PG* 224). The search for accentual isochronism appears to be interrupted in the early translingual phase, which is rhythmically heterodox. This is an important feature, as it demonstrates that the accentual sensitivity takes a certain amount of time to rhythmically rearticulate itself across the translingual vibration of the double verse.

The discourse on rhythm in Hajdari's translingual verse, analysed here in its Italophone embodiments, can be complicated further if we analyse the configurations of lines of medium length (from the *settenario* to the *endecasillabo*, 53.29% in total). These metres more profoundly characterize the rhythm of Hajdari's verse; but they also contribute more crucially to the enactment of the process of epicization therein. Furthermore, the use of medium-length lines, and in particular heptasyllabic and octosyllabic ones, reinforces the entanglements between Hajdari's poetry and the Albanian popular poetry and epic tradition, where both metres are central.[49] The metrical translation of medium-length lines into the double verse resonates with the concept of a hidden metre; but due to their centrality within the Italophone poetry tradition as well, it also works as an important point of transmediterranean contact.

The employment of the *settenario* (10.92%), one of the most central metres in the Italophone tradition, and of the *ottonario* (10.95%), both of which perform similar functions in the self-anthology, is quantitatively and qualitatively significant. Both measures, and the first in particular, reveal themselves to be strategic vehicles for the rhythmic qualities of compositions, and undergo a significant process of metamorphosis throughout the book, acting increasingly as a metrical bridge between the Italophone realm and the Albanian popular and epic poetry tradition. Highly attested to in *Erbamara*, the *settenario* reappears in a transformed form in *Peligòrga*, where it performs a central role in the epicization of the diction. On the whole, the *settenario* of *Erbamara* displays primarily a binary rhythmic pattern and often embodies slow-paced pulsations of anapaestic memory. Rarer, though still attested to, are the triple-stressed patterns. In the early translingual phase, irregular patterns are more frequent, while regularity is attained once more in *Peligòrga*. The *ottonario* in *Poesie scelte* is instead inflected mostly with triple-stressed and fast-paced patterns, and occurs in both canonical and irregular rhythmical configurations, the latter being particularly frequent from *Stigmate* to *Maldiluna*. As was the case for the *quinario* and the *settenario*, the two measures tend to support accentual isochronism in the self-translations and the final epic phase. Their role is particularly effective in compositions that hold three dominant beats.

PS EM 6, 17–20
    Le primavere fuggirono,   OT   4   7
    per gli abissi gocciolarono.   OT   3   7
    Come i cieli grigi   SN 1 3 5
    anche noi invecchiamo.   ST   3   6
    [Springs fled, | they leaked across the abysses. | Even we get old | like grey skies.]
PS EM 15, 9–10
    I tronchi degli alberi spezzati,   DS 2   5   9
    tu li conti in silenzio.   ST   3   6
    [The trunks of the broken trees, | you count them silently.]
13–14
    Intristiti dagli echi e dalle voci di allora, VL   3   6   10
    rimaniamo in silenzio.   ST   3   6
    [Disheartened by echoes and voices from the past, | we remain in silence.]
PS EM 16, 7–8
    I miei versi m'inseguono   ST   3   6
    come vecchi assassini.   ST   3   6
    [My verses chase me | like ancient assassins.]
PS OC 38, 1–4
    Fuori della finestra   ST 1 3   6
    la pioggia, come un vetro opaco   NO 2   6   8
    taglia i giorni della mia vita,   NO 1 3   8
    mi bagna la ragione.   ST 2   6
    [Outside the window | the rain, like opaque glass | slices the days of my life, | it soaks my reason.]
PS CP 69, 1–2
    Stringiamo i nostri nomi   ST 2 4 6
    strappati come l'erba   ST 2 4 6
    [We hold on to our names | broken like grass]
PS STG 120, 3–4
    lucciole nelle valli,   ST 1   6
    [fireflies in the valleys,]
PS MD 199, 4
    Ora sei una dea antica   ST 1 3   5 6
    [now you are an ancient goddess]
PS MD 207, 100
    pungono la mia carne   ST 1   6
    [they bite my flesh]
PS SN 173, 16
    — Vattene, strega morte!   ST 1   4 6
    [Get out, death witch!]
62
    non voglio pianti in casa,   ST 2 4 6
    [I do not want tears in the house,]
67
    è stato lungo il viaggio,   ST 2 4 6
    [the journey has been so long,]
PS PG 233, 13–34
    Qui non avrai fortuna,   ST 1   6
    vivrai nella pazzia;   ST 2   6
    [here you will not find luck, | you will live in madness]

PS PG 241, 91
   Voglio toccarti il fondo,   ST 1   4
   [I want to touch your core]

                  ★ ★ ★ ★ ★

PS EM 3, 5–7
   la melagrana spaccata   OT   4   7
   [the broken pomegranate]
PS SC 57, 6
   È inverno, si chiude il giorno.   OT 2   5 7
   [It is winter, the day ends]
PS CP 65, 1
   Sono campana di mare   OT 1   4   7
   [I am diving bell]
PS CP 79, 4–6
   Alberi stretti tra loro   OT 1   4   7
   come negli anni di fame.   OT 1   4   7
   Gridano al cielo parole   OT 1   4   7
   [Trees cling close to one another | like they did during the years of hunger. | They scream words at the sky]
PS MD 197, 1
   I versi mi fanno male.   OT 2   7
   [The verses hurt me.]
PS PG 220, 3
   Fiabe di cerbiatti e boschi   OT 1   5 7
   [Tales of fawns and forests]
PS PG 221, 20
   d'acqua, salici e cicogne.   OT 1 3   7
   [of water, willow, and storks.]
PS PG 223, 21
   'Cosa sei venuto a fare? —   OT 1 3 5 7
   ['What you are here to do?']

The opening excerpt is drawn from a text entirely composed of quatrains of medium-length lines. Here, the *settenario* functions to rhythmically close the composition and to summarize its predominant double-stressed profile. The *settenario* may also be used to establish intratextual homologies and to reinforce anaphoric iterations (see *silenzio* 10: 14 in *PS EM* 15), or to more broadly enhance intrastanzaic sound correspondences as in (*PS EM* 16). In contrast to these unifying functions, the *settenario* of the early translingual phase appears to be rather dissonant and acute, and to reflect the wounding brought about by linguistic displacement in this phase (*PS OC* 38). As the examples show, from *Corpo presente* onwards more fast-paced triple-stressed configurations emerge, and the iambus enters forcefully onto the scene, becoming prominent from *Spine nere*. The iambus, traditionally a metre of invective, is generally connected to the most assertive phase involving the long poems and to the most assertive mature translingual phase. It is also employed to foreground a particular voice in verses shaped around dialogic and polyphonic articulations. Moreover, from *Corpo presente* onwards, irregular patterns and double stresses appear more visibly (*PS STG* 120; *PS MD* 199). Finally, the *settenario* of *Peligòrga*, as it emerges in the examples, is distinctive in respect to earlier embodiments. Even though patterns of double pulsations do later return to prevalence, the first beat is now more often anticipated in the first or second position (*PS PG* 233; 241). More than merely placing a rhythmical pressure on the extremities of the lines, the configuration of the *settenario* seems to ripple outwards in this last section: the metre is frequently hypotactic and is relieved by punctuation; it increasingly plays host to rare, epicizing, symbolic, and multilingual inserts; and it is significantly employed to emphasize anaphoric identities, thus playing a strategic role in increasing the iterative qualities of the diction. Its natural and instinctive seat is still the quatrain, which, with respect to the early Albanian phase, has again been rhythmically transformed within a more openly epic, iterative, and formulaic trajectory.

In contrast to the constitutive rhythmical diversity that presides over the use of heptasyllabic forms, the *ottonario* tends to be most commonly inflected with triple-stressed patterns. Dactylic developments, as well as irregular configurations, are highly recurrent in the early translingual phase, and particularly in *Sassi contro vento*. Here, Hajdari infuses the metre with novel rhythmic possibilities, creating fast-paced sequences that underline the material relief accorded to his words (*PS SC* 57). Overall, the initial stress again appears to be slightly retrograded in *Peligòrga*, resulting in a frequent rhythmic focus on the first position (*PS PG* 220, 221, 223). This further foregrounds *Peligòrga* as a rhythmically peculiar section, and confirms the extensive attention directed towards the borders of the lines. Furthermore, octosyllabic lines in *Peligòrga* may lead to a multiplication of stresses (*PS PG* 223), another process which is related to the increase in the dialogic and polyphonic qualities of the diction, which is as such inscribed in the rhythmical texture of poems.

Both the *novenario* (11.76%) and the *decasillabo* (10.49%) are also well attested. The *novenario* appears frequently in the self-translations and in the later mature phase. It may occur as a rhythmic complement to the *settenario* and the *ottonario*, whose triple-stressed patterns it frequently reproduces, presenting both the dactylic and irregular configurations that prevail overall. The *decasillabo* marks the transition towards more highly structured and extended forms. As such, it is not homogeneously distributed. It occurs more often in the self-translations, where it may represent a distended insert in laconic texts, having the function of relaxing the diction and supporting the regularity of *Erbamara* in particular. The metre significantly loses centrality within the early translingual phase. Overall, the *decasillabo* of *Poesie scelte* is generally a slow one, with three prevailing stresses, and it may rely on anapaestic rhythmic memories, especially in the first phase. Fast-paced and irregular structures may occur in combination with proparoxytones, from the central phase onwards. While quantitatively less attested, these inflections are rhythmically foregrounding:

PS EM 15, 5–8

In mezzo ai fitti rami dei platani,	DS	2		4	6	9
per prima tu trovi il sentiero.	NO	2			5	8
Nella tua fronte e nelle tue mani	DS			4		9
si fermano tortore e merli.	NO	2			5	8

[Across the dense branches of the sycamores, | you, before everyone else, find the path. | On your forehead and in your hands | turtledoves and merlons rest.]

PS AP 23, 1–2
 In questa dimora di pioggia   NO 2 5 8
 un filo sottile ci separa.   NO 2 5 8
 [In this house of rain | a subtle thread separates us.]

PS SC 55, 5–7
 respirando il nostro silenzio   NO 3 5 8
 (...)
 per fuggire oltre i confini   NO 3 5 8
 [breathing our silence [...] to flee beyond the borders]

PS CP 82, 1
 Tu esisti di fronte all'inverno   NO 2 5 8
 [you exist before winter]

PS STG 125, 1
 In quale stagione ti cerco,   NO 2 5 8
 [In which season will I look for you,]

PS MD 201, 1–2
 Ritornare dal tempo al tempo, NO 3 6 8
 [To return from one time to another,]

PS PG 216, 7–8
 quando nell'umida casetta   NO 1 4   8
 mi circoncisero in fretta.   OT 4   7
 [when in the humid hut | they circumcised me with haste.]

★ ★ ★ ★ ★

PS EM 16, 9
 Ogni notte si rompe qualcosa   DS 3 6 9
 [Every night something breaks]

PS AP 37, 3
 E il mio corpo leggero non regge DS 3 6 9
 [my light body does not hold]

PS CP 65, 17
 che non tornano (e mai torneranno!) DS 3 6 9
 [which do not return (and never will!)]

PS STG 109, 7
 unica gioia nelle *domeniche*   DS 1 4   9
 [the sole joy of Sundays]

PS SN 163, 5
 tieni a bada i *demoni* che *mordono*, DS 3 5 9
 [come hold the demons who bite,]

PS MD 208, 8
 sono *maschera* della mia *maschera*, DS 1 3   9
 [I am a mask of my mask,]

PS MD 208, 134
 in questa notte di stelle *gelide*,   DS 2 4 7 9
 [In this night of frozen stars,]

PS PG 211, 11
 salivano vestite da sposa   DS 2 6 9
 [they climbed in their bridal dress]

PS PG 225, 8
   pun*go*no la tua debole carne.   DS 1   6   9
   [they bite your weak flesh.]
PS PG 227, 6–7
   mi *dissero* le sue notti oscure —   DS 2   7   9
   una luna *gelida* invernale   DS 3   5   9
   [they said his obscure nights — | an icy winter moon]
PS PG 233, 11
   '*Vattene* — mi ha detto una veggente —   DS 1   5   9
   ['Leave,' a seer told me,]

The first block of examples shows dactylic developments of the *novenario* (with a prevailing initial stress in the second and third positions and the second stress in the fifth position). The first example (*PS EM* 15), for instance, displays a use of the metre in a light and agile quatrain, forming a pattern in *Erbamara* that is often related to descriptions of nature and the subject's engagement with it. Further examples display the use of the *novenario* in the openings, occurring especially in *Corpo presente*. In *Peligòrga* the configurations of the *novenario* confirm the usual rhythmic attention towards the openings of the lines. Overall, the metre complies with the function of a rhythmically unifying centre that has already been identified in other medium-length measures, but it reveals itself to be quantitatively less incisive, particularly in the central phase of *Poesie scelte*. The second block of examples highlights the constitutive dynamics of iteration that interest Hajdari's *decasillabo*, and that may extend to the individuation of internal rhymes (see for example *PS MD* 208). Starting with *Corpo presente*, and particularly in *Maldiluna*, the occurrence of this metre appears to be strongly related to the employment of proparoxytone words, which lend a fluid rhythmic articulation to Hajdari's Italophone diction. On the whole, the *decasillabo* is thus a transitional metre into which Hajdari introduces rhythmic geometries on the basis of the position of stresses, the choice of words, and the quality of iterations that it is called on to foreground.

   The rhythmical inflection and mode of employment of the *endecasillabo*, the most conventional and canonized metre of the Italophone tradition, may reveal interesting dynamics in the context of translingual versification. Considering Hajdari's tendency to inflect his voice in shorter lines, the employment of the *endecasillabo* is quantitatively significant (9.17%), especially from *Stigmate* onwards, and thus in the epic phase. Moreover, the metre usually appears in topical positions, such as at the edges of a composition and within refrain-like inserts.

PS EM 15, 1–2
   Il mattino imbiancato di rugiada,   ED   3   6   10
   camminiamo nel bosco senza un'anima. ED   3   6   10
   [the dawn whitened by dew, | we walk soul-less in the wood.]
PS AP 25, 16
   come il soldato la propria ferita.   ED 1   4   7   10
   [like the soldier his own wound.]
PS STG 127, 1
   Per voi belle ragazze d'Albania,   ED 2 3   6   10

7								
	Per voi belle ragazze d'Albania,	ED	2	3		6		10
11								
	Per voi belle ragazze d'Albania,	ED	2	3		6		10
	[for you beautiful girls from Albania,]							
PS MD 185, 8								
	Dalle tue labbra fioriscono uccelli,	ED		4		7		10
	[From you lips birds bloom,]							
PS MD 186, 2								
	con la tua lingua mi conduci all'Eden,	ED		4			8	10
	[with your tongue you transport me to Eden,]							
PS MD 202, 13								
	In una città di mandorli amari,	ED			5	7		10
	[in a city of bitter almond trees,]							
PS PG 241, 223–24								
	mordimi come mordevi le more,	ED	1			7		10
	toccami come toccavi le visciole,	ED	1			7		10
	[bite me as you bit the blackberries, | touch me as you touched the wild cherries,]							

*The *endecasillabo*, in its regular and irregular embodiments, always carries a strong rhythmic characterization in *Poesie scelte*. On the whole, Hajdari favours forms with three and four stresses and shows both a qualitative and quantitative sensitivity to dactylic (*PS EM* 15) and anapaestic patterns (*PS AP* 25). In the long poems, which entail polyphonic dynamics, the distinctive rhythmical inflections of hendecasyllabic lines serve to contrastively characterize the diverse utterances. More generally, the *endecasillabo* is used by the poet to raise the tone of the diction, and to enhance both elegiac and epic functions, especially if it occurs within conventional rhythmical configurations (*PS STG* 127). From *Maldiluna* onwards, its presence also foregrounds the peak of more-than-human encounters and transformations, as well as of erotic tensions (*PS MD* 185; *PS PG* 241).

Finally, the long line (28% of the total) presents an interesting rhythmical diversity. First of all, even in its most extended forms, Hajdari's verse never indulges in prosaic modes. On the contrary, the poet tends to expand the lines while at the same time retaining them within solid rhetorical and rhythmic boundaries. Long lines are especially attested in the central sections (from *Spine nere* to *Maldiluna*) and are related to the first occurrence of the long dialogic and more irregular poems, as well as to the most horizontally extended short compositions that emerge therein. On the whole, long lines are less frequent in self-translations and in the final epic phase, and are rarely brought into the quatrain:

PS SN 157, 4–6	seppellitemi sulla collina, all'ombra del pioppo,						
	con la luna piena.						
	Mettetemi nudo sulla terra fresca,						
	VL		3			9	11	14
	SN		3	5				
	VL	2		5		9	11	

[Bury me on the hill, in the shade of the poplar | under a full moon. | Place me naked on the fresh soil,]

PS STG 139, 7–10 Tu amavi l'Europa senza muri in cui regnasse la poesia,
addio all'Europa di ipermercati che non fa più Storia.
Tu amavi i tuoi amici, i tuoi lettori, i tuoi editori,
addio ai tuoi amici, ai tuoi lettori, ai tuoi editori.

VL	2	5	9	13	17
VL	2	4	9	13	15
VL	2	5	9	13	
VL	2	5	9	13	

[You used to love a Europe without walls, governed by poetry. | Goodbye to the Europe of supermarkets, which no longer makes History. | You used to love your friends, your readers, your publisher; | goodbye to your friends, your readers, your publishers.]

PS SN 154, 1–2 Di quel pomeriggio ricordo le sue parole:
'Non nominare il mio nome nei tuoi versi!'

VL	2	5	8	13
VL	4	7	11	

[I recall her words from that afternoon: | 'Do not spell my name in your verses!']

PS PG 241, 186–87 per queste mani cresciute sotto la nudità della pioggia,
per queste labbra che tremano sotto il cielo oscuro

VL	4	7	9	14	17
VL	4	7	12	14	

[For these hands grown beneath the nudity of the rain, | for these lips which tremble beneath a dark sky]

PS PG 241, 202–04 e all'alba rinasciamo di nuovo in questo mondo di terrore,
baciamo i nostri corpi innocenti condannati al confine
come se fosse l'ultimo bacio dell'ultimo giorno,

VL	2	6	9	13	17
VL	2	6	9	13	16
VL	4	6	9	12	15

[And at dawn we are born anew in this world of terror, | we kiss our innocent bodies | condemned to the border | as if it were the final kiss of the final day,]

The examples above show that the employment of the long line does not entail a transition towards prose, but works instead on establishing and reinforcing rhythmical balances. Its employment becomes crucial in the central section, where the diction opens up to plural and more relational developments and the poet's research opens more vigorously to the collective. As the excerpts reveal, patterns with four stresses are highly recurrent (*PS SN* 157; *PS STG* 139). The long line is frequently employed in rhythmic homogeneous couplets and stanzas (*PS PG* 241), and may accompany the characterization of the diverse voices at play in the mature phase (*PS SN* 154).

On the whole, accentual sensitivity emerges in the metrical-rhythmical configuration of Hajdari's Italophone verse, and is intersected by the impact of different embodiments of linguistic distance. The self-translation compositions are mostly tuned towards two prevailing beats, while in the early translingual phase, when linguistic distance reaches a peak and Hajdari loses his poetic grammar, the search for accentual isochronism is temporarily compromised. Within the ensuing phases, in parallel with the progressive horizontal stretching of the lines, Hajdari begins to orient his compositions towards three and, in rare cases, four prevailing beats. This trajectory demonstrates that the prosodic encounters with the Albanian language augment over time, rather than decreasing with the progression of translingual practice. On the other hand, the foregrounded use of the *endecasillabo*, a central and strategic configuration in Hajdari's Italophone diction, announces that the rhythmical exchange is mutual, and that the double verse performs a synthesis of translingual balances that preside over a double and increasingly inseparable rhythmical sensitivity.

Double Language: Translingualism, Space, and Movement

From a linguistic viewpoint, Hajdari's poetry embraces the same increasingly epicizing movement that we have seen informing the evolution of forms and metres. The overall values, as they emerge from a full lexical concordance of *Poesie scelte*, bring into focus two main aspects. First of all, they signal a high incidence of pronominal and adjectival deixis referring to the central subject and its interlocutors. Words such as *mio* [mine], *tuo* [yours], *ti* [to you], *io* [I], and *tu* [you], for instance, are among the first twenty most frequent forms. This aspect foregrounds a dialogic vocation that exists in essence from the very first sections, but that acquires centrality towards the end of *Poesie scelte*. Moreover, these occurrences pinpoint that the central subject, despite opening up to polyphonic structures and increasing its relationality in the mature phases, remains prominently present through the whole articulation of the self-anthology. As we shall see, this aspect differs significantly from Pumhösel's experience, wherein translingualism and migration generate instead a progressive erasure of the central subject and a simultaneous search for a constitutively relational, transindividual, and even transhuman voice.

On the other hand, the concordance illuminates Hajdari's overall preference for plain diction, which is highlighted by the notable recurrence of words such as *notte* [night] (95 occurrences), *giorno* [day] (90), *corpo* [body] (66), *collina* [hill] (64), *pietra* [stone] (56), *tempo* [time] (61), *anno* [year] (58), and *pioggia* [rain] (57).[50] Significantly, these terms point most of all to a non-human temporal and spatial dimension. On the whole, they highlight the dialectic past–present that permeates Hajdari's poetics, the progression of his gnoseological research, and the materialistic turn inscribed in his investigation of the body. Finally, they make explicit the poet's preference for a set of fixed primordial elements that he translates and inflects differently in the various phases of his translingual journey, as illustrated above.

If we now leave the frequency lists and turn instead to the evolution of Hajdari's use of the Italian language over time, as it emerges from the data collected through the concordance, further interesting data emerge. Within the translingual verse, as previously mentioned, a tension towards an expressive forcing of words and expressions emerges. At large, this tension can be related to some of the qualities that Contini ascribed to the realm of metaphorical expressionism, such as violations of linguistic norms, a predominance of action in the diction, a focus on the sensuality and corporeality of language, and a taste for plastic deformation.[51] This forced use of language may also respond to the need for mimetic allusions to loss, tension, and may stem from a high rate of metaphorization within the diction. In all these cases, language enacts a pressure on the norm, a process which is chiefly visible in the treatment of verbal forms.

> la pioggia [...] | taglia i giorni della mia vita [the rain [...] | slices the days of my life] (*PS OC* 38, 3); respirando il nostro silenzio [breathing our silence] (*PS SC* 55, 5); passa sotto la pelle di neve [it passes under the snow-made skin] (*PS SC* 56, 4); che aggravano il linguaggio [which aggravate the language] (*PS CP* 79, 7); per assetarmi di cielo [to make me sky-thirsty] (*PS AP* 28, 6); arano la mia carne oscura [they plough my dark skin] (*PS MD* 197, 3); i mari dove navigo arrugginiscono [I sail on rusting seas] (*PS MD* 199, 10); ho bevuto la tua immagine color viola [I drank your violet image] (*PS MD* 204, 3); ingannerà il tuo cammino [will deceive your route] (*PS PG* 227, 8).

As the comprehensive lexical analysis reveals, this expressive tension is greatest in the early translingual phase, and it returns, albeit in a rather more mediated and metaphorical inflection, in later phases. In its more powerful embodiments, the deformative charge attributed to language is thus intrinsically related to the first phases of linguistic displacement, and is then progressively attenuated as the translingual practice progresses.

Another important element emerges from an investigation of the progressive positioning of Hajdari's Italophone verse with respect to rare and literary language. In the early translingual phase, as I have explained, Hajdari develops a novel and transitive relationship with language, which quickly reaches a maximum level of reification: words in this phase adhere to the matter, and are selected by the poet first and foremost for their plastic and sensual qualities. It is only in ensuing phases, when the linguistic distance and the exophonic effect have decreased, that this transitivity between signifier and signified begins to become complicated. In fact, as a result of the progression of the translingual practice, novel metaphorical and mediated connections blur the linear bounds between word and world. In Hajdari's double verse, this juncture corresponds to a rise in intertextuality and, more specifically, to an incursion of tradition motifs of Albanian epic and popular poetry, as previously noted, which reaches a peak in the last epic phase. This progression has a manifold effect on the Italophone side of Hajdari's double verse, which not only begins to play host to many multilingual inserts, but also starts to open up vigorously to literary terms, accommodating intertextual references from the Italophone poetic tradition, and from authors such as Dino Campana, Camillo Sbarbaro, and Eugenio Montale in particular. This novel taste for the rare and literary word, and its intertextual interpretation through a more direct incursion into the Italophone tradition, is particularly visible from *Corpo presente* onwards, and is confirmed by the occurrence of forms such as *crepuscolo* [crepuscule], *abisso* [abyss], *avo* [ancestor], *dimora* [abode], *eunuco* [eunuch], *fanciullo* [child], and *forestiero* [foreigner], as well as uncommon verbal forms such as *ardere* [to flare], *arrochire* [to indurate], *attendere* [to bide], *condurre* [to conduct], *condottiero* [condottiero], *decedere* [to decease], *gocciare* [to drip], *poggiare* [to lay], *rammentare* [to bethink], and *sorgere* [to arise] in the final sections. Beyond foregrounding the transition to the epic and the shift in focus from the individual to the collective (which intertextuality, as a relational process, highlights), these occurrences also allow Hajdari to infuse historical depth into his translingual discourse, and to introduce a further element of mediation between signifier and signified. It is thus not by chance that this process occurs in a mature phase, in which the poet rewrites the past in light of the present, and when the physical distance from Albania increases and the linguistic one from the Italian language decreases. Finally, through its remodulation of a set of Albanian and Italian voices, this process emphasizes the function of transmediterranean connections upon which Hajdari's double verse increasingly plays.

As I have explored above, the progression of Hajdari's translingual verse is accompanied by a heightened frequency of multilingual inserts, as well as by an increased presence of calques and neologisms. In fact, the ways in which Hajdari's two languages intersect on the page change with time, in parallel with the evolution of his reflection on exile, the progressive epicization of his diction, and the increase in polyphonic dynamics. In the earlier collections, the double verse flows substantially through parallel routes, in a dialogue that is mostly structural, metrical, and rhythmical, but does not involve in-depth lexical or morphological hybridization. In parallel with the maturing of the translingual experience and the progressive epicization of the diction, these exchanges between the two languages become more visible on the lexical level. If we return to Brioni's taxonomy, we could argue that dynamics of thick translation, conveyed by the parallel texts, progressively intersect in Hajdari's work with foreignizing and domesticating translational trajectories. These latter correspond respectively to multilingual inserts and to calques or neologisms primarily coined from Albanian words. This discourse can be broadened through a reflection on the inseparability and reciprocity that qualifies the double verse, and as such through the assertion that the translingual verse progressively becomes a space where Hajdari domesticates Albanian into Italian and vice versa: predominantly through processes of lexical modification, the two languages increasingly intersect each other on a morphological level too. From a lexical perspective then, Hajdari's path, even within its own distinctive unfolding, foregrounds the chronological movement from distance to proximity that is likewise identified by Brioni as marking the diachronic evolution of Somali-Italian literature in linguistic terms.[52]

Multilingual inserts and calques are abundant in the mature phase, while in the earlier sections they are rare occurrences that are mostly related to onomastic or toponomastic indications. Among the multilingual inserts that appear in *PG* we find: *Kanun*, a traditional Albanian oral legal code; *Xhin*, mythological domestic predatory spirits; *Bektashì*, a mystical Albanian confraternity to which the poet's family belongs; *Kulak*, a Russian word that alludes to landowners; *robinje*, a prisoner of war; and the aforementioned *besa*, which arises as a central concept in Hajdari's poetics through its diverse embodiments.

The presence of neologisms is equally extensive, although they are disseminated more uniformly through the self-anthology. Neologisms are generally created through compositional mechanisms, such as combining words in forms like *erbamara* and *maldiluna*, or prefixation and suffixation as in *impiccoliti*, *rimpiccoliti* and *pagliuri*, the latter being a word that Hajdari introduces to translate the Albanian *drizat* [thornbush]. Among the most innovative inserts are certainly the calques, which transform and domesticate Albanian terms, some of which have become iconic of Hajdari's double expression. The most famous is *peligòrga*, which the poet introduces into his Italophone poetic grammar to translate the Albanian *peligorgë*, the name of a solitary bird with green feathers native to the northern region of Darsìa, a creature who has inhabited his verse since the juvenile works, who loses her name in the early translingual phase, and who later becomes one of the focal points of the mythical and epic reconstruction of the poet's origins. The *peligòrga* undergoes a series of important transformations across the self-anthology, working synecdochically to indicate a lost place or land (*Dove sei fuggita città di Lushnje? | città della peligòrga* [where did you flee, city of Lushnje? | city of the peligòrga] *PS SN* 162, 1–2), and even the poet himself (*È insieme a voi la mia peligòrga?* [Is my peligòrga with you?] *PS SN* 173, 8). Her translation into the double verse foregrounds her main function of rewriting the past in light of the present, a function inscribed in the morphological transformation that the term undergoes in order to enter the Italophone diction. Towards the final sections, however, the *peligòrga* becomes an actual interlocutor (*Ah, peligòrga stanca* [Ah, tired peligòrga] *PS MD* 207, 84), and a crucial actor in more-than-human bonding and communion (*le peligòrghe che ci cantano nelle dita* [the peligòrgas who sing within our fingers] *PS PG* 241, 239).

In terms of the diachronic evolution of the translingual verse, one further aspect should be mentioned, which relates to the increased specificity in the use of language, and particularly in the loss and subsequent reacquisition of a referential grammar. As I have mentioned, Hajdari's early translingual verse loses the ability to name the outer world in its specificities, and as such is oriented towards embodying primordial symbols and raw matter. The ability to name is progressively recuperated, a process that is made visible particularly through the reappearance of the many named species of plants and animals that begin to foreground his verse from *Corpo presente* onwards.[53] More specifically, Hajdari's language shows a progressive interest in a botanical and ornithological vocabulary, which is present in the juvenile phase, absent in the early translingual one, and reconstructed again in the central phase through novel references to the landscapes and non-human inhabitants of Ciociaria. The loss and eventual recovery of specificity is confirmed by the values that emerge from the comprehensive lexical analysis. Transcribed below are some central occurrences from the botanical catalogue, to give an idea of the range of inflections:

> Presto fiorirà il mandorlo [soon the almond tree will bloom] (*PS EM* 14, 4); In mezzo ai fitti rami dei platani [Across the dense branches of the sycamores] (*PS EM* 15, 5); un nuovo biancospino [a new hawthorn] (*PS EM* 18, 14); per gli olmi vaga la furba civetta [around the elms the clever owl wanders] (*PS EM* 19, 15); una nuvola bianca si posa sul pioppo [a white cloud rests on the poplar] (*PS EM*

19, 3); nel giardino dei melograni dove partoriva la cagna [in the pomegranate garden where the dog gave birth] (*PS EM* 19, 7); Si è seccato anche il gelso rosso nella siepe [even the red mulberry on the bush has dried out] (*PS EM* 19, 12); assediato dall'edera invadente [besieged by invasive ivy] (*PS CP* 80, 5); come il grano del campo la rosa canina del bosco oscuro [like the wheat in the field the rosehip in the dark wood] (*PS STG* 116, 2); io ti copro con fiori di ginestra e canti di merlo [I cover you with gorse flowers and merlon songs] (*PS STG* 125, 8); cresciuto con l'amore per l'albicocco [raised with love for the apricot] (*PS STG* 131, 12); come i salici del nostro paese [like the willows in our country] (*PS SN* 146, 3); Respiriamo odore di pini bagnati [we breath the scent of wet pine] (*PS STG* 152, 1); La tua bocca fiore di pesco [your mouth, peach blossom] (*PS STG* 164, 5); come questo nespolo alla scarpata [like this medlar on the escarpment] (*PS SN* 152, 10); coltiveremo grano e girasoli [we will grow wheat and sunflowers] (*PS SN* 173, 53); Rosse di sangue | le corniole del bosco di Canterno [Blood red | the cornel berries in Canterno's wood] (*PS MD* 207, 47–48); ricordi, era marzo, fiorivano i siliquastri [do you remember, it was March, the Judas trees were blooming] (*PS MD* 181, 4); e nei cespugli assolati profumavano le viole [and in the sun-kissed bush, the scent of violets] (*PS MD* 194, 14); giuggiole e corniole rosse come un rosario intorno al tuo collo di cerbiatta [jujube and red cornel berries like a rosary around your fawn-like neck] (*PS PG* 241, 45); inonda la mia valle di papaveri rossi [inundate my valley with red poppies] (*PS PG* 241, 227).

Within the privation and progressive repopulation of Hajdari's referential grammar, there is thus an initial dominance of matter and pure sense over referentiality. The latter then emerges precisely from the poet's faith in matter, which then enacts the progressive recovery of the ability to name, and of the great significance of that ability. This lexical trajectory in Hajdari's poetics thus identifies the multiple ways in which translingualism intervenes in the configuration of the complex relationship between signifier and signified, and displacement mediates the development of connections between subject and space.

Similar progressions are traceable in the use of metalinguistic inserts, which occur abundantly and extremely significantly in the works of translingual authors. Explicit allusions to language are numerous in the self-anthology, although they appear in *PS* through differing embodiments that mark an overall mutation. In the early translingual phase, allusions to language are rare, and are overall associated with a frustrated physical desire, an impossibility to say, or a mistrust of the language itself (*La lingua di questo paese | non serve più a niente* [the language of this country | no longer serves any purpose] *PS CP* 66, 1–2). Progressively, the qualities of Hajdari's double language, including the productivity and transformative nature of the act of translanguaging, begin to be placed at the centre of his discourse (*La nostra lingua si riveste | di un'altra lingua che germoglia | corvi* [Our language dresses itself | with another language that sprouts up | crows] *PS CP* 70, 3–5). In a later period, when the reliving and rewriting of the past begins to be enacted, language is often foregrounded by images that convey a retrospective sense of loss or danger (*fuori dai tuoi confini e dalla tua lingua* [outside of your borders and your language] *PS STG* 130, 22). Finally, in the later epic-mythical phase in particular, language not only recuperates its relational qualities and its ability to facilitate human dialogue, thus performing a novel collective function (*ci chiameranno all'alba,* | *con la lingua dei profughi* [they will call us at dawn, | with the language of refugees] PS MD 207, 130), but also operates as a crucial means of connection between human and non-human spheres (*cantando e danzando nella lingua dei fiumi* [singing and dancing in the language of the rivers] PS SN 172, 66).

Another central quality that emerges from metalinguistic inserts, and even more directly from metapoetic ones, is the idea of the autonomy, the independence, and even the animation of language and verses (*I miei versi m'inseguono* | *come vecchi assassini* [my verses chase me | like old assassins] PS EM 16, 7–8). As I shall illustrate, this is a feature that is quite common in translingual authors, and it is also traceable in the works of Pumhösel and Al Nassar. Significantly, an analysis of metapoetic inserts reveals an identification between verse and body (*Un verso cieco* | *senza memoria* | *è il mio corpo* [a blind verse | with no memory | is my body] PS OC 39, 1–3) or between verse and place (*All'improvviso ti affacci alla finestra,* | *ed io ai miei versi* [suddenly you look out the window | and I look at my verses] PS SN 165, 15–16), both of which are particularly strong in the early translingual phase. On the whole, then, both metalinguistic and metapoetic inserts suggest a progression, illuminating the autonomous force of words and the transformative nature of the experience of translanguaging, which is portrayed as a physical and embodied experience.

A few final considerations must be elaborated on Hajdari's use of words at the intersection with embodiments of movement and spatial indexicality. First of all, if we analyse, in light of Violi's taxonomy, the occurrence of verbs of movement, Hajdari seems to more frequently employ forms that allude to crossing and to linear movement, such as *venire* [to come] (56 occurrences), *portare* [to bring] (41), and *andare* [to go] (37), rather than forms referring to plastic transformation or metamorphosis such as *crescere* [to grow] (24). The way in which crossing and linear movement manifests across the diction also undergoes an important diachronic evolution, which makes visible the transition from plain to rare words — such as *procedere* [to proceed], *errare* [to wander], and *giungere* [to reach] — that is active within Hajdari's translingual diction more generally. Among the forms that convey dynamicity, the poet seems to favour those that allude to rupture, and sharpness or velocity of movement. Finally, it is interesting that *migrare* [to migrate], a verb of crucial semantic weight in Hajdari's work, always appears in the transitional form of the present participle, and is related in all its occurrences to poetry or to the act of writing poetry (*Con le mie ceneri fertili* | *nutro i miei versi migranti* [with my fertile ashes | I feed my migrant verses] PS MD 207, 111–12). This feature further stresses the impact of movement on the inner mechanisms of versification, as well as on the transient qualities of the translingual verse.

Unlike that of Pumhösel, Hajdari's diction demonstrates an impressive rate of indexicality. Spatial deixis (and especially demonstratives) can be used to analyse the positioning of the central subject, and to acquire indications of the spatial coordinates that preside over the self-anthology. Below is a list of the inflections of *questo* [this] and *quello* [that] as they emerge from the self-anthology.

in *quest'angolo* di terra arsa [in this corner of scorched land] (*PS EM* 1, 2); Nulla accade in *questa provincia* [nothing happens in this province] (*PS EM* 7, 5); di *queste cose* visibili [of these invisible things] (*PS AP* 22, 17); In *questa dimora* di pioggia [In this house of rain] (*PS AP* 23, 1); È tra *queste conchiglie* che ho perso il Tempo [Within these shells I have lost Time] (*PS AP* 26, 4); in *questa collina* brulla e impazzita [on this barren, insane hill] (*PS AP* 27, 12); *queste città* [these cities] (*PS OC* 40, 2); in *questo Paese* [in this country] (*PS OC* 42, 3); Cosa attendo in *questa stanza* sgombra? [what do I wait for in this empty room?] (*PS OC* 45, 1); in *questo | Paese* [in this | country] (*PS OC* 48, 2–3); *Queste cose* visibili [these visible things] (*PS OC* 49, 6); *questo cielo* di segni [this portentous sky] (*PS OC* 49, 8); su *questo territorio* sterile [on this sterile territory] (*PS SC* 54, 9); di *questo territorio* impazzito [of this territory gone mad] (*PS SC* 55, 8); *Questo cielo* chiuso [this closed sky] (*PS SC* 56, 1); nato da *questo freddo spazio* [born from this cold space] (*PS CP* 63, 2); La lingua di *questo paese* [the language of this country] (*PS CP* 66, 1); Da *questa parte* del mondo [in this part of the world] (*PS CP* 66, 5); sotto *questi cieli* inchiodati [under these fixed skies] (*PS CP* 70, 2); dietro *questo volto* quotidiano [behind this quotidian face] (*PS CP* 72, 5); sono diventato come *questa penisola* di terremoti [I have become like this earthquake peninsula] (*PS CP* 91, 5); su *questa Pietra* di Cervara [on this Cervaran stone] (*PS CP* 94, 13); in *questo verde* [in this green] (*PS CP* 95, 17); in cima a *questa collina* buia [on top of this dark hill] (*PS CP* 98, 3); in *questo Paese* sterile [in this sterile Country] (*PS CP* 99, 10); *questo mondo* maledetto dove fuggo senza sosta [this cursed world where I flee without rest] (*PS STG* 111, 2); Ancora resisto in *questa strana città* [I still resist in this strange city] (*PS STG* 117, 1); come *questo nespolo* alla scarpata [like this medlar on the escarpment] (*PS SN* 152, 10); non me ne andrò da *questo mondo* [I will not leave this world] (*PS SN* 173, 94); che ho lanciato lungo *questa costa* [which I threw along this coast] (*PS MD* 184, 7); Raccolgo *questi fiori* [I gather these flowers] (*PS MD* 207, 80); Dove ti perdi in *questo mondo* perduto? [Where do you lose yourself in this lost world?] (*PS MD* 207, 147); un domani in *queste pianure* [one day on these plains] (*PS PG* 209, 2); Andrò via da *questo mondo* contadino [I will leave this provincial world] (*PS PG* 209, 9); nel lasciare *questo mondo* [in leaving this world] (*PS PG* 230, 10); — Baciami e abbi pietà di *questo corpo* martoriato [— Kiss me and have mercy for this shredded body] (*PS PG* 241, 179); per *queste mani* cresciute sotto la nudità della pioggia [For these hands grown beneath the nudity of the rain] (*PS PG* 241, 186); per *queste labbra* che tremano sotto il cielo oscuro [for these lips which tremble beneath a dark sky] (*PS PG* 241, 187); per *questo Verbo* diventato amore e sacrificio [for this Word, become love and sacrifice] (*PS PG* 241, 189); accogli *questi occhi* sconfitti e insanguinati [embrace these eyes, defeated and blood-shot] (*PS PG* 241, 190); benedici *questo sguardo* sepolto dal Tempo [bless this gaze buried by Time] (*PS PG* 241, 193); togli *queste spine* nere dalla mia pelle [Pull these black thorns from my skin] (*PS PG* 241, 194); e all'alba rinasciamo di nuovo in *questo mondo* di terrore [and at dawn we are born anew in this world of terror] (*PS PG* 241, 202).

e le pietre di *quel paese* [and the rocks of that country] (*PS SC* 56, 10); lontano da *quella terra* che impietosamente [far from that land that pitilessly] (*PS STG* 110, 11); *Quella mela* rossa [that red apple] (*PS SN* 156, 1); Sia orgoglioso *quel grembo* pietroso e fertile, [may that stony and fertile womb be proud] (*PS MD* 174, 4); *quelle ceneri* leggere come la rugiada [those ashes, light as dewdrops] (*PS MD* 179, 8); *quelle ceneri* gonfie di grida [those ashes, swollen with screams] (*PS MD* 179, 9).

Proximity is more frequently expressed than is distance. On the whole, the numerous inflections of *questo* connote the exilic space, as well as enhancing the focus on matter and on the sensing of the body within space. Through spatial deixis, Hajdari clarifies the subject's positioning, with the intention of sketching the context from which his gaze originates. A different scenery, however, is conveyed by deixis when it engages with distance, a process which is overall less frequent. In fact, the demonstrative *quello* may refer to the exilic reality as it is seen before the actual departure, conveying an image of loss, pain, and premonition regarding the future. It may also refer to pictures from Hajdari's childhood or juvenile years, a feature that is quite frequent from *Spine nere* onwards.

As these references have shown, the analysis of Hajdari's use of vocabulary delineates some of the poet's main lines of research. First, the lexical values show a progressive specification, the acquisition of poetic grammar, and the concurrent mobilization of the relationship between signifier and signified, all of which intersects the evolution of Hajdari's translingual practice. Second, through innovative grafts and metalinguistic inserts, Hajdari emphasizes the transformative nature of the process of translanguaging, founding a novel translingual poetic grammar which is based on notions of inseparability and reciprocity. Third, the abundant occurrence of verbs of movement, and the forms they take in the text, suggest a focus on sudden linear movement towards space, and foreground the intermingling of migration and poetic writing. Finally, spatial deixis allows for a dichotomic anchoring of texts to two different landscapes: a pre-exilic and an exilic one. Space is thus polarized more than it is hybridized. Overall, the lexicon is informed by an extreme mobility, one that has been proven herein to evolve diachronically, in parallel with Hajdari's reflection on his double language and transient verse.

Notes to Chapter 2

1. See in particular Gazzoni, *Poesia dell'esilio*; Mattei; Di Gianvito.
2. Gëzim Hajdari, *Poesie scelte*.
3. Hajdari and Inverardi, p. 307.
4. *Il confine liquido: rapporti letterari e interculturali fra Italia e Albania*, ed. by Emma Bond and Daniele Comberiati (Nardò: Besa, 2013).
5. Emma Bond and Daniele Comberiati, 'Narrare il colonialismo e il postcolonialismo italiani: la "questione" albanese', in *Il confine liquido*, pp. 7–30.
6. By *hiatus* the authors allude to the establishment of the Hoxha communist regime on the Albanian side and the joining of Italy to NATO on the other. See Bond and Comberiati, *Il confine liquido*, p. 7.
7. On the work of Carmine Abate see two studies by Rosanna Morace, 'Carmine Abate', in *Letteratura-mondo italiana* (Pisa: Edizioni ETS, 2012), pp. 131–64; 'Carmine Abate: un mosaico identitario ricco per adozione', in Bond and Comberiati, *Il confine liquido*, pp. 98–116.
8. Bond and Comberiati, *Il confine liquido*, p. 11.
9. Bond and Comberiati, *Il confine liquido*, p. 15.
10. The extensive presence of authors of Albanian origin and mother tongue within the Italophone contemporary literary landscape is to be read in relation to the significant movement of people towards the Italian shores that occurred throughout the 1990s, in parallel with the weakening and the subsequent fall of the Albanian communist regime. In the last *Bolletino di sintesi* of BASILI, a database that recorded translingual migrant writers who had published at least one

work in Italian, there are 41 authors of Albanian origin, making them the most numerous group. BASILI, 'Banca Dati sugli Scrittori Immigrati in Lingua Italiana, University of Rome La Sapienza', <http://www.disp.let.uniroma1.it/basili2001/> [accessed 10 August 2013].
11. Bond and Comberiati, *Il confine liquido*, p. 10.
12. Gëzim Hajdari, *Poema dell'esilio* (Santarcangelo di Romagna: Fara, 2005), pp. 12–14. On the circumstances of Hajdari's exile and the situation of poets and writers from Albania throughout the troubled decades of its recent history, see also the essay by Gëzim Hajdari, 'Breve panorama della poesia albanese dagli anni Trenta ad oggi', *Kúmá*, 3.1 (2002), now fully available online <http://www.arbitalia.it/letteratura/hajdari_poesia_albanese.htm>.
13. The poet attended university in Rome, graduating with a degree in literature, and as a student had already begun collaborating with several Italian journals and publishers (see Andrea Gazzoni, 'Introduzione: cantare nel sisma dell'esilio', in *Poesia dell'esilio: saggi su Gëzim Hajdari*, ed. by Andrea Gazzoni (Isernia: Cosmo Iannone, 2010), pp. 9–61. Today Hajdari is the director of the Erranze series for the publisher Ensemble.
14. Gëzim Hajdari, *Ombra di cane* (Frosinone: Dismisura, 1993).
15. The sylloge was originally published in *7 poeti del Premio Montale, Roma 1997: Laura Maria Gabrielleschi, Gëzim Hajdari, Gabriella Pace, Biagio Salmeri, Oliver Scharpf, Francesca Traina, Sebastiano Triulzi* (Milan: All'insegna del pesce d'oro, 1998) and later became part of Gëzim Hajdari, *Corpo presente* (Tirana: Botimet Dritëro, 1999).
16. Gëzim Hajdari, *Stigmata*, trans. by Cristina Viti (Bristol: Shearsman Books, 2016); Gëzim Hajdari, *Bitter Grass*, trans. by Ian Seed (Bristol: Shearsman Books, 2020).
17. Andrea Gazzoni, 'Una terra scritta nell'esilio: rappresentazioni e traduzioni dell'Albania nell'opera di Gëzim Hajdari', in *Il confine liquido: rapporti letterari e interculturali fra Italia e Albania*, ed. by Emma Bond and Daniele Comberiati (Nardò: Besa, 2013), pp. 137–48.
18. Gëzim Hajdari and Anita Pinzi, 'An Ode to Exile: Anita Pinzi in Conversation with Gëzim Hajdari', *Warscapes*, 2013 <http://warscapes.com/conversations/ode-exile> [accessed 23 April 2019].
19. Mattei, in particular pp. 56, 60–61, 71.
20. Hajdari and Inverardi, p. 302. Emphasis mine.
21. Brioni, in particular pp. 18–59. See also *The Translation Studies Reader*, ed. by Lawrence Venuti (London: Routledge, 2000).
22. Brioni, p. 21. See also Loredana Polezzi, 'La mobilità come modello: ripensando i margini della scrittura italiana', in *Studi europei e mediterranei*, ed. by Armando Gnisci and Nora Moll (Rome: Università degli Studi di Roma, La Sapienza, 2008), pp. 115–28 cited by Brioni.
23. Igiaba Scego, *La nomade che amava Alfred Hitchcock = Ari raacato jecleeyd Alfred Hitchcock*, Somali trans. by Zahara Omar Mohamed (Rome: Sinnos, 2003); Ribka Sibhatu, *Aulò: canto-poesia dall'Eritrea* (Rome: Sinnos, 2004).
24. Andrea Gazzoni, 'Nel tempo, in relazione, per frammenti: leggere due decenni attraverso Gezim Hajdari', in *Leggere il testo e il mondo: vent'anni di scritture della migrazione in Italia*, ed. by Fulvio Pezzarossa and Ilaria Rossini (Bologna: Clueb, 2011), pp. 119–218 (p. 217).
25. See the interview included in Davide Bregola, *Il catalogo delle voci: colloqui con poeti migranti* (Isernia: Cosmo Iannone, 2005), p. 55.
26. Hajdari and Pinzi.
27. Hajdari has played an important role as translator and editor of Albanian works within the Italophone literary scene. See for instance his translations of popular and epic poetry in Gëzim Hajdari, *I canti del Nizam* (Nardò: Besa, 2012).
28. These are the details of the original collections: Gëzim Hajdari, *Erbamara* (Santarcangelo di Romagna: Fara, 2001); *Antologia della Pioggia* (Santarcangelo di Romagna: Fara, 2000); *Ombra di cane*; *Sassi contro vento* (Milan: Laboratorio delle Arti, 1995); *Corpo presente*; *Stigmate* (Nardò: Besa, 2002); *Spine nere* (Nardò: Besa, 2004); *Malديluna* (Nardò: Besa, 2005); *Peligòrga* (Nardò: Besa, 2007). Henceforth with these titles I will be alluding to the sections of *Poesie scelte*, unless otherwise specified. In the excerpts I use the following abbreviations to allude to the self-anthology and the sections: *Poesie scelte (1990–2007)* PS, *Erbamara* EM, *Antologia della pioggia* AP, *Ombra di cane* OC, *Sassi contro vento* SC, *Corpo presente* CP, *Stigmate* STG, *Spine nere* SN, *Maldiluna* MD, *Peligòrga* PG.

29. The poet introduces seven unpublished texts in the self-anthology (two in the section *Erbamara* and five in the section *Ombra di cane*).
30. See Henri Meschonnic, *Poétique du traduire* (Paris: Verdier, 1999).
31. Gëzim Hajdari, *Poezi të zgjedhura (1990–2007)* (Nardò: Besa, 2007).
32. For a comprehensive mapping of the structure of poems in *Poesie scelte* see Figures A.1 and A.2 in the Appendix.
33. Translation by Ian Seed in Hajdari, *Bitter Grass*, p. 29.
34. Antonio Crecchia, 'Prefazione', in *Antologia della pioggia*, by Gëzim Hajdari (Santarcangelo di Romagna: Fara, 2000), pp. 7–18.
35. See Gazzoni, 'Una terra scritta dall'esilio'.
36. See Di Gianvito, p. 18.
37. Luigi Manzi, 'La notte straniera di Gëzim Hajdari: la luna e la melagrana', in *Poesia dell'esilio: saggi su Gëzim Hajdari*, ed. by Andrea Gazzoni (Isernia: Cosmo Iannone, 2010), pp. 317–21 (p. 317).
38. Manzi, 'La notte straniera di Gëzim Hajdari', p. 320.
39. Gëzim Hajdari and Francesco Zurlo, 'Intervista in Workout', n.d. quoted in Di Gianvito, p. 38.
40. Hajdari, *Poema dell'esilio*.
41. Hajdari, *Poesie scelte*, p. 203.
42. See Brioni, in particular pp. 21–28.
43. See Gazzoni, 'Una terra scritta dall'esilio'.
44. Hajdari, from the introductory note to *Peligòrga*, p. 15.
45. Laura Toppan, 'La *Peligòrga* di Gëzim Hajdari: "regina degli esuli in fuga"', *Italies: littérature, civilisation, société*, 13 (2009), 243–60.
46. Toppan.
47. For an introduction to Albanian prosody and metre see Arshi Pipa, 'Albanian Metrics', *Südost Forschungen*, 34 (1975), 211–33; Arshi Pipa, *Albanian Folk Verse: Structure and Genre* (Munich: Trofenik, 1978).
48. Rhythm in the second language has been proven to be influenced by the typology of the mother tongue. For the impact of stress-timing patterns for L1 Albanian speakers of L2 Italian and related rhythmic implications in the natural language, see Luciano Romito and Andrea Tarasi, 'A Rhythmic-Prosodic Analysis of Italian L1 and L2', in *Prosodic and Rhythmic Aspects of L2 Acquisition: The Case of Italian*, ed. by Anna De Meo and Massimo Pettorino (Newcastle upon Tyne: Cambridge Scholars Publishing, 2012), pp. 137–52.
49. Pipa, *Albanian Folk Verse*; Adam Goldwyn, '"Go Back to Homer's Verse": Iliads of Revolution and *Odysseys* of Exile in Albanian Poetry', *Classical Receptions Journal*, 8.4 (2016), 506–28.
50. See the frequency list in Table A.1 in the Appendix.
51. See Contini.
52. Brioni, pp. 18–59.
53. On this process see Silvia Vajna De Pava, 'La peligorga canta in italiano: la poesia di Gëzim Hajdari e i suoi apporti interculturali', in *Poesia dell'esilio: saggi su Gëzim Hajdari*, ed. by Andrea Gazzoni (Isernia: Cosmo Iannone, 2010), pp. 189–210.

CHAPTER 3

Dissolving Boundaries: Mobilization and Transformation in Barbara Pumhösel's Poetry

Translingualism, Ecopoetics, Ecofeminism

Barbara Pumhösel, 'mancina poi "corretta", indecisa e da sempre immersa nelle parole e nelle figure retoriche' [born left-handed and later 'corrected', indecisive and forever immersed in words and figures of speech],[1] was born in 1959 in Neustift bei Scheibbs, Austria, and migrated to Italy in a very different set of circumstances from those of Hajdari. In fact, Pumhösel arrived in Italy after several experiences of living elsewhere in Europe (including the United Kingdom and France) and after graduating from the University of Vienna with a thesis on Italian children's literature.[2] She eventually settled in Bagno a Ripoli, a small town near Florence, in 1988, where she still lives today. She currently works in intercultural education projects in public schools and libraries, and pursues her creative writing career in parallel to this work. Regarding her move to Italy, she points out:

> Mi sono sempre sentita in colpa quando qualcuno usava la parola 'emigrazione' in riferimento a me. Certo, ho cambiato paese e lingua [...]. Ma rimane il fatto che semplicemente, un giorno, ho preso un treno. Mi sono mossa all'interno dell'Europa [...] non sono stata criminalizzata perché volevo decidere dove vivere.
>
> [I have always felt guilty when someone has used the word 'emigration' to refer to me. Yes, I did change country and language [...]. But the fact remains that one day I simply got on a train. I travelled within Europe [...] I wasn't criminalized because I wanted to decide where to live].[3]

As in the case of Hajdari, Pumhösel's literary commitment is articulated within various genres. First of all, she is a very well-known, prize-winning author of children's literature.[4] She has concurrently authored both short stories and scholarly works in German and Italian,[5] and has developed an increasingly solid poetic production in the two languages.[6] Pumhösel is also particularly active within the network of publishers and cultural associations that has been working extensively on themes of migration and transculturation in contemporary Italy over the past four decades.[7] Moreover, she is a member of *La compagnia delle poete*, a project that has allowed her to cultivate the collective and relational side of her poetry, and which represents an important part of her trajectory. As I shall explain, the reflection on the positioning of translingual migrant women configures itself as an essential part of Pumhösel's research as it unfolds in its various emanations.

On the whole, three main aspects foreground Pumhösel's work, and her poetry more specifically, all of which deserve a brief exploration in this introductory section. First of all, Pumhösel's verse, like her writings more generally, definitively escapes any national affiliation, on the level of its imaginary as well as its linguistic profile. The author herself speaks to this feature:

> Sono state create tante scacchiere di tante letterature nazionali con confini lineari e netti, ma mai le grandi storie, i grandi narratori, hanno osservato il loro diktat. Si potrebbe dire che le grandi storie sono come certi animali [...] che non rispettano confini politici, sto pensando ai lupi, alle volpi, agli orsi, agli uccelli migratori [...].
>
> [So many chessboards have been created out of so many national literatures with linear and clear-cut borders, but the great stories, the great narrators, have never observed their rules. One could say that great stories are like particular animals [...] that do not respect political borders; I am thinking about wolves, foxes, bears, migratory birds [...].][8]

Rather than a national affiliation, Pumhösel's work foregrounds instead a translocal dimension, where *translocal* refers to the demonstration of emotional attachments to places and the simultaneous acknowledgment of their constitutive multiplicity and relational nature, following Scott Slovic's definition.[9] Moreover, in her writings, Pumhösel aims to reveal the artificiality of borders and the constitutive interconnectedness that extends not only across geopolitical barriers but also, and even more significantly, across the human and the non-human realms.

In her article dedicated to Pumhösel's work, Barbara D'Alessandro has identified one of the central semantic fields in the author's entire literary production, which is the notion of crossing.[10] Building on D'Alessandro's argument and developing a specific focus on Pumhösel's poetry, I maintain that the constitutive mobility of her verse, combined with her focus on crossing and on the absence of boundaries between species, matters, and elements, can be inscribed in an ecopoetic trajectory. In previous studies, I have argued for the presence of a consistent yet under-investigated ecopoetic stream in contemporary Italophone poetics.[11] This stream develops primarily at the crossroads between the past and the present century, and represents both a point of rupture with postmodern studies and a development of them, insofar as it engages more closely with environmental awareness and demonstrates a more radical and explicit anti-anthropocentric positioning. The emergence of this ecopoetic trajectory is related, among other things, to the worsening of conditions of life on the planet, and to the visibility of the environmental crisis that is now constantly in front of authors' eyes.[12] These dynamics determine a more pervasive engagement on the part of authors with a series of powerful ecocentric nodes, nodes that emerge decisively in Pumhösel's poetics and in her understanding of language as well.

In theoretical terms, the concept of ecopoetics is still a mobile one, and largely remains to be explored at the intersection with the Italophone realm. In previous studies, I have relied on two famous ecocritical studies by Lawrence Buell and Scott

Bryson in order to conceptualize it, and as such I have inscribed within ecopoetic frameworks experiences that engage with a series of specific features that the two scholars have identified in their works.[13] These features include: the treatment of the non-human as more than a background; a focus on interconnectedness and interdependence between species; a fluid understanding of the environment as a process and a cycle of feedback; the firm anti-anthropocentric positioning of the author; and finally a pervasive perception of the environmental crisis and of the need for human accountability in the face of it. It is within these ecopoetic trajectories that I confidently inscribe both the work that Pumhösel has carried out through the years of her translingual production, and *prugni* in particular, as the main synthesis of the foundational values of her verse.[14] As I shall explain, translingualism, in its transformative nature, has impacted on the affirmation of this ecopoetic force within Pumhösel's work.

A second aspect that is crucial in Pumhösel's verse, and that stems directly from its ecopoetic qualities, is the pervasiveness of what I call *transitional imagery*; that is, of figures and structures that embody transitions between species, objects, and elements. Grazia Negro has pointed out the centrality of the trope of transformation in Pumhösel's work, arguing for the presence therein of an 'interscambiabilità degli oggetti e dei vari aspetti del reale' [interchangeability of objects and of various aspects of reality].[15] This interchangeability is particularly powerful when it develops across the human and non-human. As I shall illustrate, transitional imagery is mostly present in Pumhösel's poems through diverse inflections of animation, personification, and metamorphosis. In *prugni*, these features are so central that they represent the main terrain of research and formal-semantic experimentation for the author, and are configured as sites of linguistic innovation. On the whole, in *prugni*, transitional imagery embodies the main effect of crossing, epitomizing the transformative nature of the experience of physical and linguistic movement.

The central occurrence and specific inflection of transitional imagery in Pumhösel's writings can be placed in relation with another ecocritical trajectory, that of ecofeminism. In 2013, Serenella Iovino authored a study that joined ecofeminist theories, and specifically works by Val Plumwood and Donna Haraway, with the writings of the contemporary Italophone author Anna Maria Ortese, and the novel *L'iguana* in particular.[16] In her work, Iovino foregrounds ecofeminism as a field that advocates 'for the dismantling of the "intersectional oppressions" which encapsulate women, nonhuman animals, "non-normative humans," and whatever subject has been marked as "alien" by dominant systems of power, including the earth'.[17] Ecofeminist thought thus works to deconstruct both hierarchies and the systems of oppression that generate them. Moreover, within an ecofeminist perspective, difference is conceived as a generative force and not a sign of vulnerability. Iovino demonstrates that, as in the cases of Ortese and Pumhösel, the exploration of difference may occur through aesthetic strategies that foreground a process of mutual transformation across species and beings. In fact, in *L'iguana*, Ortese uses what Iovino terms 'transition forms or hybrids'[18] — that is, fluid and transformative forms that make visible the constitutive interconnectedness and mutual embeddedness of the human and non-human — and it is in these forms that Iovino sees the core of the literary embodiments of the ecofeminist perspective.

Iovino's work on ecofeminism and Italophone literature is ground-breaking on many levels. First of all, she confirms that transitional figures, such as metamorphosis and personification, possess an ecocentric and radical power that can generate social change. This power has otherwise been extensively questioned within ecocritical scholarship, and specifically within interpretations that conceive of transitional figures involving the human as constitutively anthropocentric.[19] In Iovino's analysis, on the contrary, figures of transformation such as metamorphosis and personification are instead conceptualized as the core of a novel form of more-than-human binding. As such, transitional imagery in literary works creates a moral, bodily, and affective bridge between the human and non-human, foregrounding reciprocity and interdependency, and favouring exploration of the ways in which 'the human is hidden in the non-human itself'.[20] Its presence in *prugni*, which will be textually mapped in the final section of this chapter, responds to these trajectories and to the interrelated building of an interspecies 'ethic of proximity',[21] which Pumhösel explores through the specific positioning of a migrant translingual woman voice. In this system, as it emerges from *prugni*, the non-human *other* is acknowledged not only as kin, but also, in Iovino's words, as a 'fundamental element of our own becoming'.[22]

As I have briefly mentioned above, the development of both ecopoetics and ecofeminist perspectives in Pumhösel's works is highly interconnected with the experience of physical and linguistic movement. A few preliminary considerations of Pumhösel's interpretation of translingualism may be useful before this juncture can be explored in more detail. First of all, unlike Hajdari, Pumhösel does not publish her works in bilingual German and Italian editions. On the contrary, over time she establishes a parallel production in the two languages, which she regularly alternates in her writings. She describes the process of creating poetry as a 'non-scelta' [non-choice], the spontaneous emergence of words in one language or in the other. She explains: 'Io, però, non ho scelta quando mi affiora il primo verso in italiano, un verso qualsiasi, gli altri li devo costruire in relazione a quello' [I, however, have no choice when the first line surfaces in Italian, any line — I have to build the other lines in relation to that first one].[23] As I shall discuss below, despite the fact that Pumhösel maintains substantially separate paths in the two languages, her poems still demonstrate an important level of internal linguistic hybridization, which arises from the frequent prosodic and morphological encounter between German and Italian. The author also opens her verse to other languages, such as English, and she demonstrates a crucial engagement with her native Austrian dialect, the presence of which is recorded through metalinguistic inserts and reflections. Regarding her dialect, Pumhösel explains:

> i dialetti austriaci hanno residui di latino, di gotico, di longobardo, di molto yiddish e di molto slavo, perché c'è tutto un sostrato della monarchia. Mentre la lingua tedesca è stata 'purificata' durante il Nazismo, nei dialetti è sopravvissuto tutto.

> [Austrian dialects have residues of Latin, Gothic, Lombard, and very much of Yiddish and of Slavish, because there is the presence of a whole substratum of the monarchy. While the German language was 'purified' during Nazism, in the dialects everything survived.][24]

Although occupying opposite ends of the linguistic experience, for Pumhösel the Austrian dialect (in its plural nature) and the Italian language (as a novel and untouched territory) are two equally pure and fluid means of expression, and both are therefore capable of foregrounding a focus on transformation. The recovery of an instinctual and material element in the use of language, which the author states is possible for her within her dialect but not within German, is one of Pumhösel's main aims, and one that she also carries out through her use of the second language. Consequently, in her employment of the Italian language, as Negro explains, the poet consistently attempts to recreate 'un gesto di meraviglia, il gesto filosofico per eccellenza' [a gesture of wonder, the philosophical gesture *par excellence*].[25]

As I shall explain, linguistic complexity and the occurrence of multilingual inserts in Pumhösel's verse are often related to intertextuality, which is used by the author to enhance the relational quality of her poetry, and hence to amplify its ecocentric force.[26] In previous studies, I have recalled Julia Kristeva's concept of intertextuality, which the scholar distinguishes from that of intersubjectivity, with the former pointing to the interweaving of textual and socio-historical aspects and the latter pointing instead to ideological-emotional consonances between authors.[27] Similarly to other contemporary Italophone ecopoetic voices, Pumhösel employs intertextuality primarily in the first textual inflection, in order to multiply and then erase the central subject's voice, which in turn facilitates the disposition of her verse to embrace the other and co-become with it. This use points to what Lidström and Garrard would define as a *trans-individual* force in her verse;[28] that is, an erasure of individual instances in favour of plural, relational, and ecological ones.

The ecologizing effect of translingualism is not only connected to the use of multilingual inserts and intertextuality, but must also be placed in relation to the transformative power of translanguaging as a practice more broadly. Clive Scott has explored this force in the realm of poetry translation, which he reads as a process that is able to cultivate a crucial 'ecological consciousness'.[29] More specifically, Scott conceptualizes language itself as an environmental medium, and as a full constituent of the environment. In his view, translation, as an act of translanguaging, allows for a 'multiplication of linguistic and sensory contact' that, in turn, enhances the perception of outside space and the 'participational consciousness' of the subject in the process of environing.[30] If we uphold the critical bridge between translingualism and translation discussed in the opening chapter, it is clear that Scott's study becomes highly relevant to Pumhösel's case, because it relates the emergence of an ecologizing force to the embodied experience of languaging, and simultaneously acknowledges the ecocentric potential of the experience of moving across different languages.

Significantly, Pumhösel herself has described the change of language as a generative and game-changing event, and one that significantly impacted her way of viewing, approaching, and then writing the surrounding world. This process of epistemological opening up, enacted by translingualism, is grounded first and foremost in a novel and physical experience of language, and particularly in the disengagement between signifier and signified that is possible only in a non-maternal language, according to the trajectory already encountered as a driving force in Hajdari's early works. On these novel material qualities of language and on the path that foregrounds her approximation to words in the second language, Pumhösel notably explains:

> Io sento una parola e dal suo suono la collego ad un'immagine e prima di imparare cosa davvero vuol dire, posso anche toccare quella parola come un oggetto da guardare che mi suggerisce delle cose che poi non sono.
>
> [I hear a word, and from its sound I connect it to an image, and before learning what it actually means, I can even touch that word, as an object to look at, that suggests things to me that in the end are not there.][31]

As such, the approximation to the second language occurs firstly through hearing, glancing, and touching; that is, through a sensual-affective path that now presides over the experience of languaging.

On this point, Pumhösel's words resonate with those of Yoko Tawada, another translingual author who shares a focus on the more-than-human and the accelerated contact of beings and objects within a hyperconnected environment. In fact, in a famous narrative, Tawada describes her first encounter with her second language, German, as a physical interaction with a typewriter. In her eyes, this typewriter becomes a materialization and animation of language itself:

> There was a female object on the table too: a typewriter, *die Schreibmaschine*. She had a large, broad body tattooed with all the letters of the alphabet. When I sat down in front of her, I felt as if she were offering me a language.[32]

In the same narrative piece, regarding the epistemological possibilities offered by the use of a second language, Tawada writes:

> In your mother tongue, thoughts cling so closely to words that neither can take flight independently. In a foreign language, however, you have something like a staple remover: it removes what makes things cling to one another.[33]

From the excerpts above, we can see that, for these authors, translingualism entails not only a radical disengagement of the signifier from the signified, but also the establishment of a novel connection with the outer world through a language that becomes language-object and language-body. All of these aspects constitute the backbone of the translingual ecopoetic operation that Pumhösel carries out with her first self-anthology, *prugni*, the analysis of which will be the object of the following sections.

A More-Than-Human Book: *prugni*

Pumhösel published *prugni* in 2008, when her voice was already quite well established within the Italophone literary scene. Surprisingly though, *prugni* is her very first book of poetry, and it collects verses and sylloges previously published in journals and periodicals, on paper and online, as well as many unpublished poems, which form the majority.[34] As such, the volume has a composite and unique nature: encompassing roughly two decades of Pumhösel's translingual poetic production, it represents at once a debut and a retrospective. On the whole, the self-anthology performs a synthesis of Pumhösel's research on the interconnectedness and mutual embeddedness of human and non-human.

In the foreword to the book, Grazia Negro illuminates three central aspects that qualify the poetic experience of *prugni*. First of all, she explains that nature is configured therein as a 'polo di attrazione forte a cui l'umano si adegua' [strong pole of attraction to which the human adapts],[35] foregrounding as such the profound anti-anthropocentric nature of the book. This trajectory entails an immersion of the human in the non-human realm, which gives shape to the act of thinking and to intellectual processes themselves: 'i pensieri allora possono avere corpi sferici o essere urticanti come una medusa' [thoughts can then have spherical bodies or sting, like a jellyfish].[36] In the context of the acceleration of more-than-human encounters that the self-anthology prominently reflects, synaesthesia, a figure that identifies a sensorial shift, is configured as a further ecocentric instrument. In fact, the convergence of different senses across synaesthetic movements supports Pumhösel in corroborating the trope of transformation.

Secondly, Negro rightly explains that *prugni* depicts the act of poetry-making as a process that is first and foremost 'concreto, corporeo, artigianale: rimozione di sassi e costruzione di recinti' [concrete, corporeal, artisanal: the removal of rocks and the construction of fences],[37] consequently deconstructing and reinterpreting the role of the poet. This feature is connected to the author's extensive playing with language and words-objects, a game that translingualism, as I have explained, is able to amplify through enacting a radical liberation of signifiers. Notably, in regard to moving across two languages, Pumhösel explains 'non ho visto un confine, piuttosto un fiume grande, con fondali, vite sconosciute sotto la superfice, banchi di sabbia e sterpaglie. Pesci e serpenti d'acqua. E due rive' [I didn't see a border, but rather a large river, one with multiple riverbeds, unknown lives under the surface, sandbanks, and brushwood. Fish and water snakes. And two banks].[38] The natural metaphor filters in and, as such, permeates the literary realm.

Finally, Negro recalls how the poetry of *prugni* is substantially configured in tension with dominant structures of power, which are extensively and persistently challenged, not only through Pumhösel's important reflection on women's positioning, but also through her environmental discourse.[39] Grounded in the specific positioning of a migrant translingual woman, the self-anthology establishes a bridge of solidarity between oppressed creatures, while configuring itself as a space where that which is conventionally considered peripheral is allowed to speak, often using the subtle weapons of irony and surrealism. All of these critical aspects deeply nourish the verses of *prugni*, and, as I shall illustrate, they are profoundly inscribed in its formal, rhythmical, and linguistic profile.

From a structural point of view, the self-anthology contains 172 texts organized in eight sections: *bioluminescenze* [bioluminescence], *lezioni di poesia* [poetry lesson], *prugni* [plum trees], *guadare* [fording], *simmetrie mancine* [left-handed symmetries], *la maniglia di ghiaccio* [the ice handle], *poesie sparse* [scattered poems], *haiku* [haiku]. The eight sections are unequal in terms of the number of poems included. On the whole, they share a substantial programmatic affinity, yet they inflect Pumhösel's ecopoetic inspiration in different ways. Notwithstanding important areas of transition and overlapping, and the iteration of a series of key nodes, the eight sylloges foreground respectively: the entrance of humans into non-human realms (*bioluminescenze*); the understanding of poetry as a natural, scientific, technical, or mechanical process (*lezioni di poesia*); the breaking of affective and material barriers between beings and elements (*prugni*); the reflection on alterity, hybridity, and the overturning of power dynamics by means of crossing (*guadare*); the mobilization performed by changes of positioning and perspective (*simmetrie mancine*); the power of languaging as a material experience (*la maniglia di ghiaccio*); the transformative nature of movement (*poesie sparse*); and the material and sculptural qualities of language and its embeddedness in nature (*haiku*).[40]

The semantic affinity across the sections is mirrored by a radical homogeneity on the formal level. Brevity is the norm in *prugni*, with extremely rare exceptions, and, as I shall explain, the short poem is the protagonist of the book. Unlike the case of Hajdari, the different embodiments of linguistic distance that foreground the various sections of *prugni* do not imply noticeable mutations or transformations of the diction, nor do they generate transitions across different genres. Rather, in *prugni*, distance operates towards another, and sometime opposite, trajectory. In fact, once linguistic distance is confronted and traversed by the author for the first time, 'quasi senza accorgermi, piano piano' [almost without me realizing it, very slowly], it is thereafter cultivated as a tool with which to access a novel vision of the world. Pumhösel explains:

> cercavo di muovermi nel paesaggio linguistico in cui mi trovavo, ma scoprivo con il tempo che quello spazio tra le lingue [...] mi permetteva [...] una visione privilegiata, obliqua, dal di fuori e dall'interno, una visione sullo stesso concetto da posizioni opposte.
>
> [I was trying to move in the linguistic landscape in which I found myself, but over time I discovered that the space between languages [...] was providing me with [...] a privileged vision, an indirect one, from the outside and from the inside, a vision of the same concept from opposite positions.][41]

Distance is thus programmatically preserved, explored, and even radicalized in some of her most recent texts.

From a philological point of view, Pumhösel appears to operate across a far more conservative trajectory than Hajdari. The two self-anthologies are differently conceived and configured, especially given that in *prugni* the number of unpublished texts (122 in total) is significantly higher than in Hajdari's *Poesie scelte*. This happens despite the fact that the texts of *prugni*, similarly to those included in Hajdari's self-anthology, have been composed across quite an extended period of time. In this regard, Pumhösel explains that in her case, the disclosing and then publishing of her translingual verse was an extremely slow process: 'ho scritto per anni senza confrontarmi con nessuno' [I wrote for years without discussing it with anyone].[42] As such, the self-anthology is configured as a collection of writings that correspond to different stages of Pumhösel's translingual trajectory, writings which are also reworked and remediated for a significant amount of time by the author.

On the whole, only five previously published sylloges have become sections or parts of sections of the book: *prugni*, *guadare*, *simmetrie mancine*, *la maniglia di ghiaccio*, and *haiku*.[43] Interestingly, Pumhösel does not follow chronological order in arranging the poems and sylloges in her book. The first two sections of *prugni*, for instance, both include unpublished compositions that are among the most recent in the whole self-anthology, while *guadare* and *simmetrie mancine*, which collect verses published by the author quite early on, in 2004 and 2005 respectively, are placed at the centre of the book. However, when a previously published sylloge filters into the self-anthology, the poet meticulously maintains the same order in the succession of texts as in their first redaction. Finally, most of the previously published texts do not present significant variants in their self-anthology versions, with the majority of interventions involving only graphical uniformity and minor adjustments to punctuation. For instance, in the book, all titles tend not to be capitalized, and diacritic marks, which are scarce overall, are sometimes restored. In a very few cases, Pumhösel reworks the metrical and structural balances of poems (e.g. of *PN MG* 86; *PN GD* 69; *PN PS* 100; *PN SM* 84) with the aim of increasing the compactness of the texts. In other cases, variants may involve slight differences in lineation; for instance, an increase in enjambments (*PN PN* 39; *PN PN* 42; *PN MG* 92), and the insertion of hybrid pausing devices such as slashes and dashes (*PN PN* 40; *PN MG* 88), indentations (*PN MG* 90, 91), and step lines (*PN PS* 96). These variants seem to work towards increasing the plastic qualities of the poetic forms, qualities which, as I shall explain, are one of the central drivers in the shaping of *prugni*'s textual ecologies.

In the following sections, I propose an exploration of the main formal qualities of Pumhösel's translingual verse as it is configured in the self-anthology. As in the study of Hajdari, the analysis revolves around three main levels. In a first section, I explore the use of poetic forms in *prugni*, expanding on their constitutive brevity as well as their distinctive material and visual unfolding. I argue that, through a concrete sensing of forms on the page, Pumhösel creates a series of poem-bodies, poem-objects, and poem-worlds which support her in articulating her discourse on contact, mobility, and transformation. Furthermore, in this section, I explore in detail the morphological qualities of the two most frequent inflections of the short poem in *prugni*: the undivided and the heterostrophic short poem. In the second section my analysis then extends to the use of metres, and identifies the presence of a transient rhythm in Pumhösel's verse, which arises as an effect of its translingual qualities. Finally, in the concluding section, I expand on the linguistic profile of the texts, paying particular attention to the emergence of transitional imagery, as well as multilingual inserts, neologisms, and spatial indexicality. On the whole, the analysis demonstrates that the focus on interconnectedness and transformation that animates Pumhösel's ecocentric verse is thoroughly inscribed in the formal qualities of her translingual verse, which becomes in and of itself a fluid, relational, and translational body.

Poetic Forms: A Semantics of Brevity and Contact

Due to the formal and semantic homogeneity that characterizes *prugni*'s profile, my discourse on poetic forms will be conducted on the whole body of the self-anthology, rather than on individual sections, as was the case in the study of Hajdari. As briefly mentioned above, the poems of *prugni* are first of all foregrounded on a formal level by a constitutive brevity.[44] In fact, brevity allows Pumhösel to enhance the phonosemantic value of words, while also foregrounding a material interpretation of language that she has maintained at the centre of her work across three decades of translingual practice. On the centrality of individual words in her writings, Pumhösel explains: 'potrei chiamare i miei testi insiemi di parole, mosaici o composizioni, ma forse prima di tutto sono tentativi di scambio' [I could call my texts sets of words, mosaics, or compositions, but maybe they are first and foremost attempts at swapping places].[45] In fact, the following examination of textual histories reveals that a process wherein words are isolated and linear elements are graphically dislocated is increasingly brought into focus along the way, thus configuring itself as one of the effects of the progression of the translingual experience. This is an interesting aspect, as, in Pumhösel, the decrease in linguistic distance which comes with the progression of the translingual practice does not entail a distension of the verse, as was the case in Hajdari, but on the contrary determines an increase in the semantic concentration of words and fragments.

On a broader imaginative level, the brevity that formally foregrounds the poems of *prugni* is to be placed in relation to the need for subtraction, which is one of the forces that the author describes as being dominant in her writings, and which, again, grows with time. Regarding this need, Pumhösel significantly states: 'ammiro chi scrive un diario, senza esserci mai riuscita. Quando ho provato, talvolta, ho sentito la necessità di tagliare, subito dopo, e di tagliare ancora, fino a che non rimaneva che un attimo, un'immagine' [I admire those who write diaries, I never succeeded at it. When I tried, sometimes, I immediately felt the need to cut, and to cut again, until all that was left was an instant, an image].[46] Notably, subtraction is a process that also occurs in Pumhösel's Germanophone writings (though less predominantly), but it only grows therein after the development of her translingual practice. This aspect is significant, as it shows that the experience of translingualism can create a series of important reverberations that also impact on the mother tongue, as returning waves. As such, this feature stresses another component of the transformational potential of the translingual practice.

A second aspect that markedly characterizes the verse of *prugni* is its ability to transitively embody human and non-human characters, encounters, and environments. Pumhösel employs words and lines to plastically recreate bodies and figures on the page, as well as to mimetically reproduce movement and action.[47] Consequently, in *prugni* poetic forms have an accelerated expressive visual and material function. The examples of this are numerous.

sotto la pergola un ramo	[beneath the pergola a branch
ha puntato una sua foglia	drove its leaf
rossa sangue a cinque punte	— blood red, with five points —
contro la mia gola	to my throat
mentre	while
alzandomi stavo per pensare	standing up I was about to think
le solite cose	the usual things
sulle foglie che muoiono (*PN GD* 69)	about leaves that die][48]

The short untitled poem above embodies one of the many more-than-human encounters of *prugni*. It belongs to *guadare* [fording], a crucial sylloge in *prugni*. In fact, the idea of *guadare* is central to the development of Pumhösel's translingual works, and its importance and generative power is stressed by the author herself: 'Il guado — come realtà, come parola e metafora — mi era sempre piaciuto, anche quando ancora non conoscevo il termine nella nuova lingua. Quando l'ho trovato per la prima volta in italiano, ho voluto prolungare l'incontro, girandogli intorno' [I had always liked fording — as a reality, as a word and as a metaphor — even when I did not yet know the term in the new language. When I found it for the first time in Italian, I wanted to extend the encounter, circling around it].[49] As such, it is not surprising that it is from the metaphorical act of fording that Pumhösel's early verse springs. The poem above portrays the sudden assault performed by a tree, using one of its red leaves, on a human subject which is eventually disarmed. The textual geography follows the unfolding of this assault, highlighting the sudden change in power balance between the human and non-human. The isolation of the conjunction *mentre* [while] separates the tree's attack from the subject's initial thoughts, while also foregrounding a synchronous more-than-human movement across the two bodies. Versification is thus employed to materially establish novel anti-hierarchical and anti-anthropocentric movements and balances.

Similar dynamics govern the shaping of one of Pumhösel's most famous poems, *Eva*, which represents another notable example of the concrete use of the poetic form:

Eva	[*Eve*
Sono stufa	I am tired
di vedere Eva	of seeing Eve
che morde	who bites
la mela	the apple
sotto lo sguardo	under the gaze
del serpente.	of the snake.
Eva che quadro	Eve who, painting
dopo quadro	after painting,
viene ricacciata	is expelled
dal paradiso.	from paradise.
Vorrei vederla	I would like to see her
seduta sul ramo	sitting on the highest branch
più alto del melo	of the apple tree
con le gambe	with her legs
penzoloni.	dangling.
Vorrei vederla	I would like to see her
sorridere	smiling
mentre prepara	while she prepares
una torta di mele	an apple pie
o ancora mentre	or even when —
cantando pianta	while singing — she plants
i semi. (*PN PS* 100)	the seeds.]

Eva is located in the section *poesie sparse*, which contains previously published as well as novel texts, and which builds extensively on the trope of transformation. On the whole, the poem engages with the overturning of the conventional figuration of Eve in the earthly paradise by depicting her progressive empowerment and departure from the established narrative.[50] By verticalizing the diction, and constructing an agile poem articulated in four syntactical phrases visited by a chain of enjambments, Pumhösel embodies Eve's progressive climbing of the apple tree and her parallel liberation. As such, the poem foregrounds a double ascension carried out by Eve: that of the actual tree, from which she now surveys the world with different eyes, and that of the poem-tree itself, of which she herself plants the seed in the last line of the composition.

A final example of this concrete use of the poetic form is provided by another famous text, that of the poem-river (*rovesciare l'ossimoro*) [reverse the oxymoron]. The river is a central presence in Pumhösel's writing, and one to which she has dedicated two of her poetry collections in German. She herself explains how this presence is intimately connected to her past: 'Vivevo in una fattoria nella zona delle prealpi, tra il Danubio e le prime montagne veramente alte. C'è un fiume freddissimo e pulito (ancora oggi) che viene dalle montagne, e ricordo una zattera e il tentativo di navigare conclusosi con un naufragio quasi immediato' [I used to live on a farm in the pre-Alps zone, between the Danube and the first really high mountains. There is an extremely cold and clean river (still there today) that comes from the mountains, and I remember a raft and an attempt to sail that ended with an almost immediate shipwreck].[51] The author alludes here to the Erlauf river, which is a recurrent presence in her writings. Eva Taylor has analysed the embodiments of the Erlauf in one of Pumhösel's collections in German, individuating therein the triple-layered nature of the river, which she identifies as historical-geographical, autobiographical, and metaphorical.[52] The manifestations of the river in *prugni* assume the same three-fold value.

anche riposarsi	[even to repose
è diventata una corsa	has become a race
un'azione veloce	a quick action
ho cercato di	I tried to
adeguarmi ho perso	adjust I lose
il sonno e ora	sleep and now
provo a tornare	I try to return
a quel corso	to that slow water-
d'acqua lento	course
con le pietre variegate	with marbled stones
foderate di muschio	lined in prostrate
prostrato torno	moss I return
per guardare quel	to stare at that
fluire piano	quiet flow
e immaginare	and imagine
su quei cuscini	on those pillows
in quel letto a poco	in that bed slowly
a poco e lieve	slowly a light
un riposo (*PN LP* 27)	repose]

The poem-river above belongs to the section *lezioni di poesia* [poetry lessons], in which acts of thinking and writing are reinterpreted from a more-than-human perspective. In this verse, sleep is metaphorically depicted as a coursing of water, the textual morphology of which follows its sinuous unfolding. The synaesthetic tension, and in particular the commingling of visual and aural perceptions within the poem, suggests once again the interconnectedness and mutual embeddedness of the human and non-human, and the concrete quality of the poetic form accompanies and foregrounds this trajectory. On the whole, the material nature of poetic forms, as it emerges from the three poems above, permeates to differing degrees of intensity the entire collection, and must be regarded as central to the unfolding of Pumhösel's translingual ecopoetics.

Turning now to a fine-grained structural discourse, the first thing to mention is that the comprehensive textual analysis confirms an essential uniformity in textual morphologies. Free verse dominates the diction. Aside from the final section, which contains sixty-eight haikus constructed on a rigorous 5+7+5 syllabic model, the anthology does not engage with formal or regular metres. Across the book, two main textual typologies emerge. On the one hand, there are undivided poems, which represent the vast majority (141 occurrences). On the other, there are compositions made of two (17), three (11), and, in rare cases, four (3) stanzas. Both typologies are articulated around a foregrounding brevity.

On the whole, undivided compositions are usually short and plain, and rarely include punctuation, with the author preferring hybrid suspensive devices such as steps, indentations, dislocations, dashes, and slashes. Here, enjambment is a central figure and often occurs in a series. I transcribe two examples below:

Hommage à Charles A. Brown

I figli dei figli di quell'usignolo
oggi sono antenati e i loro nipoti
in sogno talora cantano odi
davanti alla stessa casa ancora oggi
sta un prugno — ma non è quello con il nido
poiché i prugni non sono eterni
ma certo le sue radici non sono state tolte
e forse quelle nuove le sfiorano crescendo
oggi quella casa si chiama Casa di Keats
e ogni autunno cadono prugne
proprio in quel luogo nell'ombra
della chioma in cui un anno prima di morire
sedette il poeta e scrisse:
Thou wast not born for death, immortal Bird! (PN PN 42)

[*Hommage à Charles A. Brown*

The children of the children of that nightingale
are ancestors themselves today and their descendants
sometimes in a dream sing odes
in front of the same house still
a plum tree rests — but it is not that one with the nest
because plum trees are not eternal

> yet surely its roots have not been removed
> and maybe the new ones touch them lightly while growing
> today that house is called *Keats House*
> and every autumn the plums fall
> right in that place in the shade
> of the tree's crown where one year before dying
> the poet sat and wrote:
> *Thou wast not born for death, immortal Bird!*]

In this poem, Pumhösel performs a revisited heterometric, multilingual, unrhymed, and undivided version of the sonnet, wherein a single syntactical sentence develops across fourteen lines. Significantly, the poem is dedicated to Charles Armitage Brown, friend and biographer of John Keats. Intertextuality is present in a multi-layered form in this text. It is first of all infused in the poem through the inclusion of a whole line from Keats's *Ode to a Nightingale*. Secondly, it is inscribed in the presence of the *prugno* [plum tree], as it is in fact Brown who reported that Keats composed the ode in his garden, and precisely under the plum tree.[53] Intertextuality contributes here to the complication of referential coordinates, stressing the mutual embeddedness of past and present, which is also epitomized by the encounter of the roots of the old plum tree with those of the new one. As such, the plum tree is configured as an important instrument of more-than-human knowledge, and a creature that foregrounds at once the vulnerability and the permanence of life.

The poem *a/simmetrie* [a/symmetries] displays the typical use of dislocations in *prugni*:

> *a/simmetrie*
> sbuccio verdure mentre da qualche parte
> nel nord lunghe colonne di caribù
> continuano a migrare lenti nella neve
> mangiamo in silenzio
>   nella radura
> non lontano dal loro sentiero
> si mimetizza una pernice bianca
> lavo i piatti e come me una volpe
> è sulle tracce di una possibile
>   preda (PN MG 90)

> [a/symmetries
> I peel the vegetables while somewhere
> in the north long columns of caribous
> continue to migrate slowly across snow
> mutely we eat
>   in the glade
> not far from their trail
> a white partridge hides
> I wash the dishes and like me a fox
> is chasing its potential
>   prey]

The poem belongs to *la maniglia di ghiaccio* [the ice handle], a section that revolves around the material experience of languaging and the dissolution of the body. The poem itself exemplifies the interdependency and syntonic movement of the human and non-human across physical distances, establishing an affective and visual more-than-human binding. In this case, dislocation serves to isolate the spatial aspect and to highlight a sudden change of tone, with the final word, *preda* [prey], alluding to the hunting role of both the human subject and the fox, which eventually mingle. The form foregrounds the alternation between stillness and dynamicity, and the entanglement of human and non-human perspectives.

Finally, to close the discourse on *prugni*'s monostrophic compositions, a few paragraphs must be dedicated to Pumhösel's interpretation of the haiku, which entirely occupies the final section (65 texts in total). Stefano Colangelo has poignantly defined the original Japanese form as 'un armistizio tra soggetto, oggetto e evento' [an armistice between subject, object, and event],[54] which is realized through a distinctive balance between words and white spaces. It is this suspensive function that most attracts Pumhösel to the form, which she inflects in Italian by constructing a rigorous metrical cage. In fact, the classical monostrophic Japanese configuration of the haiku envisages three lines containing a total of seventeen units of sound (*morae*), organized in the fixed scheme 5+7+5.[55] The conventional form is syntactically plain, necessarily contains a caesura, and includes a fixed seasonal reference (*kigo*), which is often evoked metonymically (for example, the rain to signify autumn, the snow to signify winter and so on). As is well known, the haiku is classified as a world poetry form, and has been inflected in several languages, including Italian and German.[56] As such, Pumhösel is able to refer to a series of previous interpretations in both her first and second language in approaching the form herself, although she develops a distinctive path.

Prosodically speaking, the Italophone interpretation of the haiku is a complex task. In reality, the haiku's sound units (*morae*) do not completely overlap with syllables, and, for this reason, the form has been most frequently interpreted outside of preoccupations with regularity. Pumhösel, on the contrary, demonstrates a desire to infuse her translation of the form with metrical regularity, and attempts to reconstruct therein a set of fixed rhythmical balances. More specifically, all her haikus are made up of seventeen syllables, except for three cases of hypermeter (*PN HK* 110, 2; 138, 2; 165, 1). Syllables are counted according to a purely syllabic criterion, and as such follow a 5+7+5 pattern regardless of where the final stress falls. For this reason, in terms of Italian metres, the five-syllable line oscillates between the *ternario* and the *quinario*, while the seven-syllable line oscillates between the *quinario* and the *settenario*. Moreover, Pumhösel's haiku tends to maintain the traditional caesura, as well as the engagement with the natural sphere and the seasonal reference (either metonymic or direct):

> i germogli nel
> campo memorizzano
> la prima pioggia (*PN HK* 129)

> [the sprouts in the
> meadow memorize
> the first rain]

> brina e orme sui
> ciottoli. a qualcuno fa
> freddo alle zampe (*PN HK* 144)
>
> [frost and footprints on
> the pebbles. someone got
> cold paws.]
>
> fine estate
> parto con un soffio di
> libeccio in borsa (*PN HK* 154)
>
> [end of summer
> I leave with a puff of
> *libeccio* in my bag]

As these three examples show, Pumhösel's haiku is a place in which more-than-human entanglements crystallize and are amplified. With respect to other types of compositions, haikus are particularly concerned with figures of sound, and chiefly with onomatopoeia. The latter, the receptive figure par excellence, has been identified as a further important carrier of ecocentric force.[57] Pumhösel employs it in all three of the above poems: to embody the fall of rain in the field (*prima pioggia* [first rain] *PN HK* 129), to accompany the muffled movement of paws (*fa freddo alle zampe* [got cold paws] in *PN HK* 144), and to give voice to the end-of-summer wind (*fine estate |... soffio* [end of summer | puff] in *PN HK* 154). From a formal viewpoint, the haiku closes the circle of Pumhösel's semantics of brevity, epitomizing her phonosemantic vocation and material-synaesthetic understanding of the experience of languaging. Furthermore, the translingual work that she performs on the haiku as a form of world poetry, and her commitment to translating it within a regular metrical pattern, underline her desire to continuously move across languages and traditions while experimenting with the spaces that both connect and foreground them.

The second typology attested to in *prugni* is that of compositions which, while still brief, are articulated in more than one stanza. In morphological terms, stanza divisions in this kind of composition may produce either substantially equivalent sections or, in a majority of cases, highly unequal segments. The second articulation in particular suits Pumhösel's attraction for very short and sharp closures, which often create unexpected turns. In both cases, the use of stanzas responds to dynamic and figurative exigencies, and as such reflects the material function of the poetic form, which I have foregrounded as foundational in the self-anthology. I transcribe below an example of the morphologies of balanced stanzas.

> *(ferri di un mestiere)*
>
> Mi abbaglia l'elenco degli strumenti
> tenuti nella sua capanna da un cavatore
> di marmo del quattrocento: una mazza,
> di ferro, un piccone, un martelletto,
> una squadra, dieci cunei, una zappa,
> quattordici libbre di mollette,
> un palo, una seghetta.

> Con questi strumenti mi chiedo che cosa
> si potrebbe fare oggi: una poesia scolpita
> un falso in versi, incidere segni, cercare
> altri già incisi o inseguire invece la vita
> di una scultura a ritroso fino alla nascita
> sua o perfino a quella della pietra. (PN LP 26)
>
> *(work tools)*
>
> [It dazzles me, the list of instruments kept
> in his hut by a marble quarryman
> from the fifteenth century: an iron
> mallet, a pickaxe, a little hammer,
> a set square, ten wedges, a hoe,
> fourteen pounds of small pegs,
> a pole, a hacksaw.
>
> I wonder what one could do
> with these instruments today: a sculpted poem
> a counterfeit in verse, engraving signs seeking
> others already carved or chasing instead the life
> of a sculpture in reverse all the way to its birth
> even back to the birth of the stone.]

The poem *(ferri di un mestiere)* compares the act of poetry-writing to the work of a quarryman, foregrounding as such Pumhösel's ethics of subtraction. Here, stanzas are end-stopped and syntactically autonomous, and they constitute two segments of almost the same length. Nonetheless, a certain cohesion is achieved through the iteration of the keyword *strumenti* [tools] at the opening of each stanza. This type of correspondence allows the poet to reinforce the strong parallelism between the first and last part of the text, and to build a comparison between the quarryman and the poet, and thus between poetry and stone. Another significant type of cohesion is also gained through the sequence of asyndetic coordinations, as well as through the rapid triadic syntactic composition of lines.[58] Rhythmically speaking, the first stanza is the fastest, containing alternations between quick pauses and extremely fast-paced sounds that mimetically reproduce the rhythm of work in the quarry. The second stanza rhythmically recalls the first, although here the tones are more nuanced; nonetheless, the chains of enjambed lines occurring in both segments still act as a strong intrastanzaic cohesive factor. Pumhösel thus breaks her poem into two segments, and then makes the segments substantially self-sufficient in order to clearly identify the two terms of comparison. However, she also makes the two verses interact through iterations and parallelisms. The poem also exemplifies another fundamental feature of Pumhösel's poetry at the level of sounds: the centrality of alliteration. This is an important feature from a translingual point of view. Alliteration is in fact a key figure in Germanophone poetry, where it may occur as a rhythmic memory of the *Stabreim*, the ancient Germanic rhyme-like consonant iteration that was in use before the introduction of Romance assonance.[59] This memory drives Pumhösel's Italophone diction towards a marked and uncommon sensitivity towards consonants, which is particularly evident here.

The poem *il tempo* [the time], on the other hand, is made up of strongly uneven segments:

il tempo	*the time*
riavvolgerlo	[roll it back
prima veloce	fast at first
poi sempre più	then more and more
lentamente fino al	slowly until
krampus di cioccolata	the chocolate Krampus
nell'involucro rossonero	in the red and black wrapping
in basso a sinistra	bottom left
zoom in direzione centro	zoom to the centre
dell'immagine quel pugno	of the image that handful
di neve sulla tua	of snow on your
nuca dal ramo nudo	nape from the naked branch
del prugno sopra di te	of the plum tree above you
la mia pelle d'oca	my goosebumps
le tue labbra e	your lips and
stop (*PN PN* 38)	stop]

The text is entirely shaped around fragments portrayed in backwards succession. Its articulation is made very rapid by the chain of enjambments that necessitates the progression of very short lines, given in their extreme essence and deprived of punctuation. The stanza division stresses the isolation of the final *stop*, which marks an extremely strong closure not only of the flashback, which is suddenly interrupted, but also of the captured image, quickly suspended and crystallized.

On the whole, the comprehensive analysis of poetic forms confirms at once the emergence of a semantics of brevity, Pumhösel's work on synthesis and subtraction, and most centrally the pervasiveness of a material and concrete function of textual geographies within Pumhösel's verse. All these aspects infuse Pumhösel's texts with an element of transition and mobility, which is accompanied and enhanced, as I shall explain in the following section, by metrical and rhythmical articulations.

A Transient Rhythm: Pumhösel's Metres

On the whole, *prugni* is a collection that demonstrates quite a variegated metrical profile. In rhythmical terms, the book demonstrates a permeability to accentual dynamics, which filter into the Italian verse as a legacy of the mother tongue, similarly to the case of Hajdari. This rhythmical action of the first language within the second one acts as a hidden metre, and leads the author to develop a particular sensitivity for accentual isochrony in her verse and to organize texts around two or three linear pulsations. The analysis of the linear development of lines confirms the central nature of brevity in the book. In fact, the metres employed most often in *prugni* are short and medium-short (see Table 3.1).

Type	Count	Percentage
BS	6	0.42%
TS	32	2.23%
QS	57	3.97%
QN	198	13.78%
SN	147	10.23%
ST	170	11.83%
OT	189	13.15%
NO	184	12.80%
DS	143	9.95%
ED	126	8.77%
VL	185	12.88%
Total	1437	100%

TABLE 3.1 Types of lines in *PN*

The very short metres, up to the *senario*, still hold a significant weight with respect to the overall occurrences (30.63% in total). They are widely employed to enhance the verticality of texts, as well as to isolate and foreground individual words. While some compositions are structurally built entirely around short lines, the cases in which short lines are employed as isolated inserts are more numerous. In these instances, they tend to occur in liminal positions, chiefly at the close of a poem, or they may instead appear as discrete segments of stepped lines. Their insertion in texts that otherwise demonstrate a more extended linear profile serves, again, to enhance the phonosemantic charge of individual words. Below is a map of significant uses of very short lines.

PN GD 66, 12–13
    lo rimango in terra.   SN   3   5
    I cocci brillano.   QN   2
    [I remain on the floor. | the shards shine.]
PN SM 85, 14–15
    per tornare verso l'infanzia   NO   3   5   8
    contropelo   QS   3
    [to go back to childhood | against the grain]
PN SM 85, 1–3
    È la sinistra che scrive   OT 1   4   7
    parte ancora dal lato destro   NO 1   3   8
    del foglio   TS   2
    [it is the left that writes | it still starts from the right edge | of the paper]
PN PS 94, 1–3
    migrando   TS   2
    la luna cambia   QN   2   4
    lingua genere paese   OT 1   3   7
    [migrating | the moon changes | language gender country]

                ★ ★ ★ ★

PN LP 30, 10
    sedimentato   QN   4
    [sedimented]

PN PN 38, 14
    le tue labbra e   QN   3 4
    [your lips and]
PN PN 53, 7
    pronuncia *prugne*.   QN   2 4
    [pronounces *plums*]
PN LP 33, 3
    che parla di pietre   SN   2   5
    [who speaks about stones]
PN PN 35, 21
    di aria notturna e   SN 1   4 5
    [of nocturnal air and]
PN PN 52, 10
    sputo un altro nocciolo   SN 1   3   5
    [I spit out another pit]

Overall, the first set of excerpts identifies short lines occurring at the end (*PN GD* 66, *PN SM* 85), within the body (*PN SM* 85) and, in one case, in the opening line (*PN PS* 94) of a poem. In these cases, short metres tend to identify a key word consisting of a segment rejected by enjambment and dislocation; more rarely, short metres are autonomous and syntactically self-contained.

The second set of excerpts foregrounds some significant embodiments of the *quinario* and *senario*, two metres that are quantitatively well attested (13.78% and 10.23% respectively). In terms of rhythm, both metres see a prevailing binary development, which may be mirrored by a two-fold syntactic articulation (*PN PN* 53). In the case of the *quinario*, the iambic configuration is generally preferred. Less often, the metre is characterized by a dissonant rhythmicization (*PN PN* 38), which occurs especially when the line is composed of a single word (*PN LP* 30, 10). Similarly, the *senario* occurs with a prevailing double pulsation and a consequent binary accentual vocation. The preferred configuration is dactylic (*PN LP* 33), although in certain cases the first accent may rise to the first position. The trochaic form, fast-paced and agile, also occurs quite frequently (see *PN PN* 52), even though the first position may be unstressed in order to comply with the binary rhythmicization of poems, which is overall prevalent in *prugni*. As in the case of the *quinario*, stresses can sequentially multiply and reduplicate, foregrounding more dissonant developments (*PN PN* 35).

The high frequency of short measures is, once again, significant in the broader context of Pumhösel's translingual practice. In fact, short metres frequently occur in combination with a phenomenological, paratactic, and transparent use of syntax. More specifically, short metres support the author in articulating lists which phenomenologically deconstruct objects, bodies, and matter in general. This is another feature that holds ecopoetic implications. Andrea Afribo, in analysing the verse of Fabio Pusterla, another Italophone ecopoet, introduced the concept of 'sintassi presentativa' [presentative syntax], which refers to syntactic articulations favouring listings and enumerations.[60] In a previous study, I inscribed this presentative syntax within an ecocentric trajectory, as in Pusterla's case it represents an attempt to get closer to the matter, to receptively observe it, and at the same time to silence the dominating presence of the central subject through a verse that can achieve a maximum level of adhesion to the observed reality.[61] In a similar manner, the use of this kind of transparent and phenomenological metrical-syntactical articulation enhances the transindividual and ecocentric qualities of Pumhösel's verse, as it facilitates the adhesion of her words to the matter that they come to embody. The distinctive use of short metres in *prugni* amplifies this trajectory.

Medium-short measures, from the *settenario* to the *novenario*, are also consistently employed by Pumhösel (24.98% in total). Among them, the *settenario* (11.83%) plays a central role in metrical-rhythmical terms. It may occur with both regular and irregular rhythmicization; it often accompanies enjambed structures; and it is frequently found in couplets or tercets:

```
PN SM 83
     Ho aspettato la sera           ST     3     6
     per toccare il colore          ST     3     6
     delle loro parole              ST     3     6
     [I waited till sunset | to touch the colour | of their words]
PN PS 96, 1–2
     Scacciato ovunque e nero       ST     2     4     6
     svolazza il corvo              QN     2     4
     [cast out from everywhere and black | the crow flutters]
PN PS 99, 1
     alcune frasi in Jiddish        ST     2     4     6
     [some phrases in Yiddish]
PN PS 96, 13–16
     Sorride poi e scaccia i pensieri — NO  2     5     8
          è suo                     TS  1  2
             il nero                TS     2
                e gli dona.         QS           3
     [he laughs then and casts the thoughts away | it's his | the black | and it suits him]
```

The first excerpt (*PN SM* 83) shows the anapaestic use of the *settenario*, which prevails in *prugni*. Fast-paced and iambic-like articulations are rare, but they may occupy strategic positions such as openings and closes (*PN PS* 96; 99). Interesting rhythmical results are then produced by Pumhösel through her use of irrelative and dissonant stress patterns, especially when combined with hybrid suspensive devices. For instance, noteworthy interpretations of the metre are obtained through its deconstruction in different steps. In the last excerpt transcribed here (*PN PS* 96), the deconstructed *settenario* embodies the movement of a crow, and recreates its steps.

A similar rhythmical mobility foregrounds the *ottonario* (13.15%) and *novenario* (12.80%), both recurrent in the book. On the whole, the *ottonario* and parisyllabic lines are generally employed to establish rhythmical balance and homogeneity in the poems. On the contrary, the *novenario* occurs more often in irregular and dissonant inflections, and to create a tension in the diction:

```
PN BL 8
     Ferma su una roccia sempre     OT     1     5     7
```

in ombra vivo una vita	OT	2	4		7	
da felce e non posso fare	OT	2		5	7	
a meno: devo — osservo	OT	2	4		7	

[Fixed on a rock forever | in shadow I live the life | of a fern and I cannot | help it: I must — I observe]

PN BL 8, 7

cacciare, leccare ferite,	NO	2		5	8

[hunting, licking wounds,]

PN BL 8, 10

diventare preda, finire.	NO	3		5	8

[becoming prey, falling.]

PN PN 42, 6

poiché i prugni non sono eterni	NO	2	3	6	8

[because plum trees are not eternal]

PN MG 88, 8

lei lo sa e brilla umilmente	NO	3	4		8

[she knows and modestly shines]

The first excerpt displays a series of *ottonari* with a dactylic-like rhythm (*PN BL* 8), a particularly frequent feature in texts that are accentually organized through the search for a triadic pulsation. This distinctive rhythmicization foregrounds the appearance of both human and non-human actors, highlighting their convergence. Usually, the employment of the *ottonario* with regular and canonical rhythmicization does not correspond to a rise in the literariness of the diction. On the contrary, Pumhösel tends to allow regular inflections to embrace a plain language, creating an expressive collision in her verse.

Similarly to the *ottonario*, the *novenario* may be employed in dactylic-like embodiments (*PN BL* 7). Nonetheless, this metre is more often translated into heterodox configurations, frequently carrying double stresses and performing a rhythmically destabilizing function within the unfolding of the verses (*PN PN* 42; *PN MG* 88). In both cases, the rhythmicization of this metre tends to interact with and foreground sound iterations, and in particular alliterative dynamics.

A similar generative dialogue between regular and irregular configurations, as well as a similar tendency to amplify the play on sounds, emerges from Pumhösel's use of medium-long metres such as the *decasillabo* (9.95%) and the *endecasillabo* (8.77%). The former occurs more often, yet as we shall see, the latter performs an accelerated strategic rhythmical function:

PN GD 66, 1

La poesia mi salta addosso quando	DS		3	5	7	9

[Poetry jumps on me when]

PN PN 53, 3

le mie braccia diventano rami,	DS		3		6	9

[my arms become branches,]

PN PN 41, 1

Un raggio di sole si inginocchia	DS	2		5		9

[a ray of sunshine kneels]

PN PN 56, 8

Qualche mese più tardi vengo a	DS 1	3		6	8	9

[a few months later I come to]

PN MG 88, 4
    buio paura veleno e giallo   DS 1   4   7   9
    [darkness fear venom and yellow]

          ★ ★ ★ ★ ★

PN PS 97, 1
    dal niente spunta un filo di parole   ED   2   4   6   10
    [from nothing a thread of words appears]
PN PN 47, 1
    Vento forte stanotte e la mattina   ED   3   6   10
    [strong wind tonight and the morning]
PN PS 102, 7
    contano tori, misure di grano   ED 1   4   7   10
    [they count bulls, measures of wheat]
PN PN 39, 2
    bag-woman donna dalle molte buste ED   2   4   8   10
    [*donna-borsa* woman of many bags]
PN PS 93, 2
    li fa stridere così forte non   ED   2   3   7 8   10
    [he makes them screech so strongly I]

Like the *ottonario*, the *decasillabo* is configured as a plain yet highly rhythmicized metre in *prugni*. The examples above show a few of its embodiments in rhythmical patterns of trochaic (*PN GD* 66) and anapaestic (*PN PN* 53) memory, as well as heterodox configurations (*PN PN* 41; *PN PN* 56; *PN MG* 88).

On the whole, the use of the *endecasillabo* is quantitatively less significant but still crucial. As previously mentioned, the reinterpretation of this module is important in the context of Italophone translingual poetry, as it pinpoints the ways in which the experience of moving across languages has the potential to infuse novel rhythmical possibilities within one of the most central and iconic metres of the Italophone poetic tradition. The portions of text above provide a picture of the main uses of the *endecasillabo* in *prugni*. Overall, triple-stressed patterns of iambic, anapaestic, and dactylic memory prevail (*PN PS* 97; *PN PN* 47; *PN PS* 102), although if necessary a multiplication of stresses may occur in order to comply with broader accentual dynamic (*PN PN* 39; *PN PS* 93). Significantly, the *endecasillabo* often occurs in openings and other liminal or marked positions (see above *PN PS* 97; 47). Morphologically speaking, Pumhösel frequently inflects the metre in binary articulations that contain one caesura. Irregular patterns, which are extensively peppered with double stresses as well as with multilingual inserts, are widely attested. In general, in the use of the *endecasillabo*, Pumhösel amplifies the element of collision that already emerges as a generative force in other metres in a specific way: that is, the more conventional the rhythm of the *endecasillabo*, the more it is immersed in anti-poetic and mobile language. This stylistic collision is also amplified by the frequent non-compliance of metre and syntax.

On the whole, long lines are relatively rare in *prugni* (12.88%). In the majority of cases, they represent isolated inserts in horizontally dry compositions, while in one sole poem, *simmetria assurda* [absurd symmetry] (*PN PN* 65), they are configured as the prevailing module. This poem is part of the section *prugni*, and consists of a metaphorical encounter with the father that occurs in the branches of the plum tree. Within the verse, the plum tree acts once again as an element of connection between past and present. I transcribe an excerpt below:

PN PN 65, 12–15
   deve chiedere aiuto ormai quando i bottoni sono piccoli
   troppi calli sulle dita rigide ma ancora
   sale sul prugno e sullo stesso albero
   salgo anch'io e ci fermiamo sullo stesso ramo

VL	1	3		6		8	9		12	14	16
VL	1	3			7		9			13	
ED	1		4			8		10			
VL	1	3		6				10	12		

[he needs to ask help now while the buttons are small | too many corns on the rigid fingers and yet | he still climbs the plum tree and I | climb too and we rest on the same branch]

Pumhösel's long line enjoys a constitutive rhythmical complexity as well as a linguistically plain articulation. Significantly, the long line occurs in a text that embodies the difficulties of establishing a linear communication with the father. Within the context of Pumhösel's semantics of brevity, then, the impossibility of saying is not embodied by a dryness of the verse, but rather by an uncommon dilation of it.

On the whole, the metrical analysis demonstrates that Pumhösel inflects metres in both regular and irregular configurations, without a particular convergence towards conventional patterns. Her distinctive employment of metres embodies an overarching element of tension which, together with synaesthetic movements and the occurrence of transitional imagery, supports her in foregrounding transformation, mobility, and interconnectedness. As such, rhythmical dissonance plays an important role in the book, and is created by Pumhösel within two main trajectories. On the one hand, the poet introduces an element of tension by infusing her verse with heterodox rhythmical articulations. In these cases, the presence of double stresses, hybrid pauses, and collisions between metre and syntax creates a defamiliarizing effect within the diction. Secondly, she allows regular rhythmical articulations to interact with an anti-poetic, plain, and material use of language. Returning to Pumhösel's reflections on poetry writing, it is apparent that these two trajectories support her in enhancing the identification between physical movement and the practice of versification. As the author herself explains:

Si è parlato anche della bocca come passaggio, cammino di parole che dal dentro vanno fuori, e pensavo che il cammino è una cosa molto importante anche in poesia perché il passo in qualche modo determina il ritmo. Il passo determina il ritmo a seconda dell'emozione, dell'angoscia, dell'ansia, della felicità, diventa più veloce, più lento, più ritmico in qualche modo.

[There was also talk of the mouth as a passage, as a path of words which go outwards from the inside, and I was thinking that the path is also a very important thing in poetry, because the stride in some way determines the rhythm. The stride determines the rhythm according to emotion, anguish, anxiety, happiness, it becomes faster, slower, more rhythmical in a certain way.][62]

This physical and mobile nature of rhythm impacts the formal and metrical articulation of *prugni*. On this basis, I argue that in *prugni*, Pumhösel introduces a distinctive transient rhythm, which she uses to further materialize her ever-evolving physical and linguistic movement. In the following and final section, I will analyse the productive intersection of these trajectories and the composite and mobile use of language in the self-anthology.

Touching, Glancing, Hearing, Feeling: A Transitional Language

The treatment of language in *prugni* is overall extremely dynamic. Two main aspects foreground its employment. First of all, crucial spaces of linguistic innovation are realized by the author through the many occurrences of transitional imagery. Moreover, in *prugni* Pumhösel experiments with linguistic mobility, in particular through the employment of multilingual inserts, neologisms, and technical-scientific vocabulary. All these aspects support the poet in infusing her diction with movement, and in amplifying her focus on transformation. The focus on movement also emerges through her use of spatial indexicality. These aspects are explored in the paragraphs that follow.

First of all, transitional imagery manifests within different trajectories in *prugni*. Metalinguistic allusions represent one of the most fertile trajectories in expressive terms. As explained in the first section, Pumhösel, like other translingual authors, demonstrates an understanding of language that is first and foremost material, and thus grounded in the physical qualities of signifiers. This understanding stems directly from her translingual experience, and in particular from the most exophonic parts of that experience. In fact, for Pumhösel, the experience of speaking from the outside of a language is a liberating and profoundly generative one. More specifically, the act of speaking and writing in a language other than her mother tongue generates a distance that contributes to her physical and synaesthetic sensing of words, as she explains: '[...] guardo ogni parola da tutti i lati, tocco, tasto, non sono mai molto sicura' [I look at every word from all sides, I touch, I tap, I am never very sure].[63] This distinctive perception of language filters into her poems, where words and verses are frequently depicted as both objects that can be touched, manipulated, and recombined, and as autonomous bodies that free themselves from the desires of the poet. In these latter cases, Pumhösel uses animations of language as tools to foreground an overturning of agency in the creative process, shifting from the human to the non-human. The metalinguistic and metapoetic occurrences of both kinds are numerous, so I transcribe below the most representative examples:

> i versi liberati giocano con il filo [the freed verses play with the thread] (*PN LP* 22, 7); Appena uscite dalla penna | le parole gridano aiuto [as soon as they leave the pen | words cry for help] (*PN SM* 82, 1–2); si nasconde proprio lì sotto il mio verso [it hides there below, my verse] (*PN PN* 34, 3;) La poesia mi salta addosso quando | sto per metterla nella lavastoviglie [Poetry jumps on

me when | I am about to put it in the dishwasher] (*PN GD* 66, 1–2); [...] con l'anemometro | si potranno misurare anche i versi | liberi il messaggio sarà sempre | diverso [...] [with the anemometer | one could also measure free | verse the message will always be | other] (*PN LP* 25, 9–11); parole si spostano formano | metafore strofe che durano | giusto il tempo di una lettura | all'alba rientrano tutte in ordine [some words move | they form | metaphors stanzas which last | only the time of a reading | at dawn they all return to their place] (*PN SM* 80, 6–9); Il pipistrello non vede, ma sopravvive | grazie alla poesia. Produce | ultrasuoni e aspetta l'eco, le rime [the bat does not see, but survives | thanks to poetry. He produces | ultrasounds and waits for the echo, the rhyme] (*PN LP* 21, 1–3)

As the excerpts show, words, lines, and verses in *prugni* are the result of mechanical, scientific, and natural processes. The poet's process is that of a simple *passeur*, able to collect on paper the direct emanations of matter; an artisan, who builds her verse manually, line by line; a scientist, who allows chemical reactions to produce poetry; and eventually a bat, who uses her poetry to eat and thus to live. This attitude resonates considerably with the notion of 'storied matter', introduced by Serenella Iovino and Serpil Oppermann within the context of material ecocriticism.[64] This notion alludes to the idea that narratives and stories are inscribed in matter itself, and as such in landscapes, objects, and bodies alike. Pumhösel shows herself to be drawn to the unveiling of these narrative qualities of matter, and attempts, through an extremely receptive posture and a continuous process of subtraction and erosion of subjectivity, to allow the referential world to speak, and in particular to liberate that which is perceived as marginal and peripheral. This understanding of poetry as the unveiling of something that is already inherent within matter is inscribed in many of the foundational metaphors of *prugni*. It is present, for instance, in the allusion to bioluminescence that entirely occupies the first section. Bioluminescence is a scientific phenomenon in which a body transforms chemical energy into electrical energy and subsequently produces light. The allusion to this process allows Pumhösel to depict the surfacing of verses on the page as a luminous pulse that emanates from bodies and landscapes themselves, and in turn to delegate the act of poetry writing to matter itself. These dynamics confirm the emergence in Pumhösel's poetry of a subject that departs from postmodern fragmentation, and approaches instead an ecocentric and transindividual terrain, one that is centred on the continuous transition from inside to outside, past to present, human to non-human. In this way, the animation of language works towards corroborating ecocentric trajectories.

Transitional imagery is developed in a further series of personifications, in particular botanical ones, and in frequent embodiments of metamorphosis. These further illuminate the mutual embeddedness of the human and non-human, and of different objects and elements. Moreover, transitional imagery foregrounds the interrelationship between past and present, especially in the occurrence of figures related to the author's childhood such as the plum tree, the snow, and the river. Here I transcribe some of the most notable examples of both personifications and metamorphoses in *prugni*:

i viticci di una vicia selvatica | mi riconoscono come un possibile | sostegno a cui allacciarsi [the tendrils of a vicia selvatica | recognise me as a possible | support to cling to] (*PN BL* 4, 3–5); Un raggio di sole si inginocchia | e viene ingoiato dall'erba (*PN PN* 41, 1–2) [a ray of sunshine kneels | and is swallowed by the grass]; La grappa di prugne | conserva di ogni frutto | la biografia e brucia | dalla voglia di | raccontarle [the plum brandy | preserves of every fruit | the biography and burns | from the desire to tell] *PN PN* 46); le slitte aspettano l'inverno [the sleighs wait for winter] (*PN PN* 47, 4); mentre il prugno volge lo sguardo | verso l'interno e conta i propri anelli [while the plum tree turns its gaze | inward and counts its own rings] (*PN PN* 49, 12–13); Sono del gatto | le impronte sul cuscino. | Anche esso spera [The prints on the pillow | belong to the cat. | It too hopes] (*PN HK* 123); di notte è chiaro | il linguaggio degli odori | nel sottobosco [the language of scents | is clear at night | in the underbrush] (*PN HK* 138); finché il freddo dura, la | neve ricorda [while the cold lasts, the | snow remembers] (*PN HK* 142).

★ ★ ★ ★

[...] io so | che devo aprire gli occhi e smettere | di essere volpe [I know | I have to open my eyes and stop | being a fox] (*PN BL* 7, 4–7); ho visto con mani di vento | e ramo di prugno (*PN PN* 44, 1–2) [I saw with hands of wind | and branch of plum tree]; Ho ingoiato un nocciolo e subito | l'ho dimenticato. Ma ora di notte | le mie braccia diventano rami, | i piedi radici [I swallowed a pit and suddenly | I forgot. But now at night | my arms become branches | my feet roots] (*PN PN* 53, 2–4); Nelle piogge | primaverili fiorirono anche le sue | macchie di ruggine [In the spring | rains its rust stain | blossomed too] (*PN PN* 64, 2–3, 4–6); Poi, però, dal fruttivendolo | ho visto un'arancia [...] Girandola ho visto il francobollo | fermo sulla buccia [then, though, at the fruit shop | I saw an orange [...] Turning it I saw the stamp | still on the skin (*PN GD* 67, 4–10); un'ortensia per | un chiodo arrugginito | cambia colore [a hydrangea | with a rusty nail | changes colour] (*PN HK* 131).

By making plants talk and letting rust flourish, Pumhösel highlights transformation as a governing mechanism within the environment, with the double intention of shifting attention from the subject to the matter and unveiling the multiple stories that the matter conceals. All of these elements contribute to an increased focus on in-betweenness and a projection of the poet's gaze well beyond the human sphere.

From a strictly linguistic point of view, *prugni* is an extremely composite work. On the whole, the mobile qualities of its language respond to the poet's need to perform transitivity and transparency with respect to the reality observed. At the same time, the language of *prugni* also foregrounds an accelerated polysensoriality. The analysis of frequencies allows Pumhösel's taste for a plain and anti-literary diction, as well as her focus on metalinguistic tropes and synaesthesia, to emerge. In fact, among the most frequent words are substantives such as *parola* [word] (27), *verso* [verse] (20), *poesia* [poem] (10), and *pagina* [page] (7), and verbal forms such as *vedere* [to see] (13), *sentire* [to hear] (8), *volere* [to want] (20) and *sapere* [to know] (18). The frequency lists also underline the insistent presence of a number of keywords mostly related to the non-human realm, such as *prugno* [plum tree] (19), *terra* [land] (13), *ramo* [branch] (13), *vento* [wind] (12), *neve* [snow] (12), *foglia* [leaf] (12), *aria* [air] (11), and *luna* [moon] (7).⁶⁵ Finally, the lists record the important presence of temporal determinants, and in particular ones that allude to synchrony such as *quando* [when] (15) and *mentre* [while] (15).

On the other hand, Pumhösel infuses her verse with a series of linguistic innovations — primarily through the use of multilingual inserts and the introduction of a series of neologisms — which commonly introduce a bridge between the first and second languages. The use of multilingual inserts is related to a need to mobilize the diction, and in Pumhösel it often accompanies the discourse on in-betweenness and on the generative force of the experience of physical and linguistic movement. A very representative example is provided in this famous short poem that I have transcribed in its entirety below.

alla frontiera	[*at the border*
il *Mond* digrigna i denti	the Mond grinds his teeth
li fa stridere così forte non	he makes them screech so strongly I
riesco a dormire mentre egli	cannot sleep while he
cresce incontro alla Buona	grows towards the Good
Speranza e la speranza aumenta	Hope and the hope increases
finché non è piena ma la luna	until it is full but the moon
in tedesco è maschile e al suo	is masculine in German and
interno sta un uomo io sono	it has a man in it I am
più a sud qui la luna è donna	further south here the Luna is woman
e alla frontiera se rimani sveglio	and at the border if you stay awake
si trasforma in ermafrodita	she becomes hermaphrodite
mentre grandina silenzi contro	while she throws sharp silence against
il vuoto il troppo scontato	the void the too familiar
ogni volta che colpisce	each time the point is
un bersaglio il dolore rimane	struck the pain remains
fresco a lungo e non riesco	long fresh and I cannot
a dormire perché lei	sleep because she
non vuole (*PN PS* 93)	does not let me.]

The poem *alla frontiera* [at the border] embodies the transformative nature of the experience of movement by making visible the effects of the process of translanguaging. In fact, Pumhösel uses the double allusion to the moon in German (*Mond*) and Italian (*luna*) to depict the reverberations of the act of physical and linguistic crossing. While performing a passage, the moon not only changes position but also gender (*Mond* is a masculine noun while *luna* is a feminine one). The poet focuses as such on fluidity, and on overcoming borders through movement.

On other occasions, the multilingual insert, regularly accompanied by explanatory notes, facilitates the unfolding of flash-backs and the materialization of the past. This is the case in the poem *il tempo* cited earlier, wherein the appearance of the chocolate Krampus enacts the race *à rebours* which unfolds in the following lines. The majority of multilingual inserts occur in the titles. For instance, the titles of *ursprung* [origin] (*PN LP* 23), (*Beipacktext*) [package insert] (*PN PS* 99), and (*Heimweh? / Fernweh?*) [homesickness and nostalgia for a faraway place] (*PN BL* 11) all identify semantic nodes that the poet prefers to allude to in her mother tongue. Multilingual titles and inserts also extend beyond German, as is the case in *Hommage à Charles A. Brown*

(*PN PN* 42) and *ai primi numeri. in memoriam* [to the first numbers. in memoriam] (*PN PS* 102). In almost all cases, further occurrences of multilingual inserts in *PN* allude instead to intertextual references and onomastic inserts, such as *Mandel'štam* and *Majakovskij* (*PN LP* 33) and *Puškin* (*PN GD* 73).

A second path through which Pumhösel performs linguistic mobilization is represented by neologisms, including the synaesthetic *olfattiche* (*PN PN* 63), which, as Negro points out, 'riunisce in sè i sensi della vista e dell'olfatto' [combines within itself the senses of sight and smell].[66] In fact, linguistic transformation, and in particular the transition from first to second language, is conveyed not only through the explicit German inserts mentioned above, but also through a compositional wordplay that is common in Pumhösel's mother tongue, and that filters into the Italophone verse of *prugni*. For instance, the author frequently dismantles and recomposes language in neo-formations such as *scientifica | mente* (*PN BL* 6), *in | dietro* (*PN MG* 86, 4–5) and *de-co-ra-re* (*PN MG* 88). These marked forms foreground the diction on a morphological level, and intensify the play on words.

Finally, I must mention Pumhösel's use of technical-scientific language in *prugni*, which is so abundant as to act as a mechanism in internal translanguaging. Below I have transcribed some important occurrences, especially from botanical vocabulary:

> [...] un equiseto di palude soltanto [only a marsh horsetail] (*PN BL* 9, 1–3); infine — come l'avena | fatua — anch'io cerco [eventually — like the avena | fatua — I try too] (*PN BL* 10); appartiene alla famiglia degli olmi | montani (e forse non lo sa) [it belongs to the family of wych | elms (and perhaps it doesn't know)] (*PN BL* 19, 6–7); con le pietre variegate | foderate di muschio | prostrato [with marbled stones | lined with prostrate | moss] (*PN LP* 27, 7–12); un ragno | delle paludi argironeta credo si chiami [a diving bell spider | argyroneta I believe it's called] (*PN LP* 28, 3–5); nemmeno un verso soltanto | l'ombra di un nome selenite forse [not even one line only | the shadow of a name selenite perhaps] (*PN SM* 80, 11–15); la pietra infine | si riveste di muschio | e felce dolce [eventually the stone | is clothed in moss | and sweet fern] (*PN HK* 161).

Almost all occurrences are highlighted by the poet through the use of italics, and are consequently viewed as marked transitional segments in the diction. On the whole, the trajectories that foreground Pumhösel's use of language allow us to conceptualize the translingual verse as a space of contact, and, even more importantly, eventual liberation enacted through constitutive movement.

This recognition of Pumhösel's use of language must close, as in the case of Hajdari, with a few considerations regarding indexicality, and in particular on the use of verbs of movement and spatial deixis. Like the case of Hajdari, the analysis of verbs of movement reveals a quantitative projection towards linear movement and crossing, with a very high frequency of verbs such as *andare* [to go] (11), *tornare* [to come back] (11), *cadere* [to fall] (8), and *passare* [to pass] (8). A fine-grained analysis of occurrences confirms the attention given to the semantic sphere of crossing, already identified by D'Alessandro as foundational in Pumhösel's works.[67] The conspicuous investment in verbs and expressions of transition confirms the poet's desire to infuse the representation of space with an idea of movement, as well as to illuminate the generative effect of dwelling within the transitional.

Finally, the use of spatial deixis and of demonstrative adjectives in particular allows different configurations of proximity and distance to emerge with respect to Hajdari's case. On the whole, deixis that expresses proximity is surprisingly rare. I have collected all the occurrences below:

> *questa circostanza* la sfrutto [I exploit this circumstance] (*PN BL* 1, 6); tutte *queste cose* insieme [all of these things together] (*PN PS* 105, 4–6); Con *questi strumenti* mi chiedo che cosa | si potrebbe fare oggi... [I wonder what one could do | with these instruments today] (*PN LP* 26, 8–9); si sa che una rosa è una rosa è una [...] ma *questa* | è di plastica [we know a rose is a rose is a rose is a [...] but this one | is made of plastic] (*PN GD* 70, 1, 3–4); [...] dal fruttivendolo | ho visto un'arancia [...] 'Me ne dia un chilo' — ho detto | 'e mi ci metta anche *questa*!' [at the fruit shop | I saw an orange [...] 'I'll take a kilo,' I said, | 'and add this one too!'] (*PN GD* 67, 4–5, 11–12); la notte afosa di *questo* | spietato *agosto* fiorentino [a sultry night in this | merciless Florentine August] (*PN GD* 73, 12–13).

In fact, it is evident that spatial referents converge more so on notions of distance:

> ... *quella piccola luce* [that small light] (*PN BL* 6, 4); come *quella volpe* si affanna [how that fox struggles] (*PN BL* 8, 5); e non so chi incolpare per *quel rospo* [and I don't know who to blame for that toad] (*PN BL* 9, 10); ... *quel muscolo* superstar parola [that organ superstar word] (*PN BL* 14, 2); a *quelle* sue *foglie* asimmetriche [to those typical asymmetric leaves] (*PN BL* 19, 3); a *quel corso* | d'acqua lento [...] su *quei cuscini* | in *quel letto* a poco [to that slow | water- | course [...] on those pillows | in that bed slowly] (*PN LP* 27, 8–9, 16–17); *quel piccolo campo* non rende ma forse [that small field is barren but maybe] (*PN PN* 34, 3); sta un prugno — ma non è *quello* con il nido [...] oggi *quella casa* si chiama Casa di Keats [...] proprio in *quel luogo* nell'ombra [a plum tree rests — but it is not that one with the nest [...] today that house is called Keats House [...] right in that place in the shade] (*PN PN* 42, 5, 9, 11); come su *quei rami* che continuano [like on those branches which continue] (*PN PN* 50, 3); ... È *quella* | l'immagine di casa... (*PN PN* 56, 2) [It is that | the image of home]; *quella stessa soddisfazione*... [that same satisfaction] (*PN PN* 60, 3); E a *quel vetro* ti aggrappi [and to that window you cling] (*PN MG* 87, 12); a *quella centrifuga*, forza [to that centrifugal force] (*PN PS* 105, 8).

This configuration reveals the centrality of the idea of distance, intended not as a means of disengaging from the environment, but rather as a generative force and a lens through which to elaborate novel epistemological spaces. Distance filters images and objects, which are portrayed in their transition from past to present, a transition which entails another transformation.

Spatial indexicality thus unveils the polarization of objects and bodies across past and present, and at the same time emphasizes their interconnections and ever-evolving natures. While spatial indexicality often marks a reverse path towards landscapes of childhood, the latter are also constantly immersed, through a continuous process of movement and transformation, in a framework of environmental connectedness, which the translingual verse both foregrounds and embodies.

Notes to Chapter 3

1. Barbara D'Alessandro, 'Scavalcare l'orizzonte: movimento e transitorietà in Barbara Pumhösel', *Studi interculturali*, 3 (2014), 161–80 (p. 162).
2. See D'Alessandro, p. 162.
3. Silvia Rosa, 'Quella precaria sensazione di equilibrio. Intervista a Barbara Pumhösel', *Poesia del nostro tempo*, 2019 <https://www.poesiadelnostrotempo.it/intervista-a-barbara-pumhoesel/>.
4. Among her most famous titles are Barbara Pumhösel and Anna Sarfatti, *Amore e pidocchi* (Turin: EDT, 2007); Barbara Pumhösel, *La principessa Sabbiadoro* (Milan: Giunti, 2007); *La voce della neve* (Milan: Rizzoli, 2013).
5. See in particular Barbara Pumhösel, 'La frontiera li attraversa: appunti sulla poesia transculturale austriaca', in *I colori sotto la mia lingua: scritture transculturali in tedesco*, ed. by Eva-Maria Thüne and Simona Leonardi (Rome: Aracne, 2009), pp. 151–70.
6. Apart from *prugni*, Pumhösel has also published the collection *in transitu* (Osimo: Arcipelago Itaca, 2016) and *Un confine in comune* (Rome: Ensemble, 2021).
7. See for instance her collaboration with the online fanzine *El Ghibli: Rivista di letteratura della migrazione*, <http://www.el-ghibli.org/>.
8. See 'VII° Seminario italiano degli scrittori e delle scrittrici migranti' <http://www.sagarana.net/scuola/seminario7/seminario1.html> [accessed 12 October 2016].
9. For the notion of translocal see Scott Slovic, 'Translocalità: la nozione di luogo nell'ecocritica contemporanea', in *Ecocritica: la letteratura e la crisi del pianeta*, ed. by Caterina Salabè (Rome: Donzelli, 2013), pp. 27–42.
10. See D'Alessandro.
11. See Alice Loda, 'Eco-Pusterla: A Semantic-Stylistic Analysis of Bocksten', *Incontri. Rivista europea di letteraura italiana*, 35.1 (2020), 99–115 (pp. 101–08) <http://doi.org/10.18352/incontri.10337>; Alice Loda, 'Gli animali nel primo Pusterla: una lettura di "Il dronte" e "L'anguilla del Reno"', *California Italian Studies*, 10.1 (2020), 1–18.
12. See on this point Maria Antonietta Grignani, *Lavori in corso: poesia, poetiche, metodi nel secondo Novecento* (Modena: Mucchi, 2007), p. 121.
13. See in particular Lawrence Buell, *The Environmental Imagination: Thoreau, Nature Writing, and the Formation of American Culture* (Cambridge, MA: Harvard University Press, 1996), pp. 7–8; J. Scott Bryson, *Ecopoetry: A Critical Introduction* (Salt Lake City: University of Utah Press, 2002), pp. 1–2. Both studies are cited in my articles Loda, 'Eco-Pusterla', p. 102; Loda, 'Gli animali nel primo Pusterla', pp. 5–6.
14. Pumhösel, *prugni*.
15. Grazia Negro, 'La leggerezza profonda dell'In-der-Welt-sein: la poetica degli oggetti in Barbara Pumhösel', *Kúmá*, 13 (2007), p. 7 <http://www.disp.let.uniroma1.it/kuma/archivio.html> [accessed 3 December 2013].
16. Serenella Iovino, 'Loving the Alien. Ecofeminism, Animals, and Anna Maria Ortese's Poetics of Otherness', *Feminismo/s*, 22 (2013), 177–203.
17. Iovino, pp. 179–80.
18. Iovino, p. 184.
19. For this debate see Aaron M. Moe, *Zoopoetics: Animals and the Making of Poetry* (Lanham, MD: Lexington Books, 2013), pp. 17–18.
20. Iovino, p. 189.
21. Iovino, p. 192.
22. Iovino, p. 201.
23. 'VI° Seminario italiano degli scrittori e delle scrittrici migranti' <http://www.sagarana.net/scuola/seminario6/seminario4.html> [accessed 22 June 2016].
24. 'VI° Seminario italiano degli scrittori e delle scrittrici migranti'.
25. Grazia Negro, 'Simmetrie asimmetriche tra umano e natura', in *prugni*, by Barbara Pumhösel (Isernia: Cosmo Iannone, 2008), pp. 149–54 (p. 153).
26. Among the authors explicitly mentioned in *prugni* are Ernst Jandl, Osip Mandelstam, Vladimir Mayakovsky, Bertolt Brecht, William Carlos Williams, Rainer Maria Rilke, Karl Krolow, Wisława Szymborska, Alexander Pushkin, John Keats, and Ted Hughes.

27. On Kristeva's notion of intertextuality see 'Problèmes de la structuration du texte', in *Théorie d'ensemble* (Paris: Seuil, 1968), pp. 297–316 and *Desire in Language: A Semiotic Approach to Literature and Art* (New York: Columbia University Press, 1980), especially pp. 36–63.
28. Susanna Lidström and Greg Garrard, '"Images Adequate to Our Predicament": Ecology, Environment and Ecopoetics', *Environmental Humanities*, 5.1 (2014), 35–53 (p. 49).
29. Clive Scott, 'Translating the Nineteenth Century: A Poetics of Eco-Translation', *Dix-neuf*, 19.3 (2015), 285–302 (p. 286) <https://doi.org/10.1179/1478731815Z.00000000083>.
30. Scott, p. 291.
31. 'VI° Seminario italiano degli scrittori e delle scrittrici migranti'.
32. Tawada, 'From Mother Tongue to Linguistic Mother', p. 142.
33. Tawada, 'From Mother Tongue to Linguistic Mother, p. 143.
34. The collection includes 122 unpublished poems, and 48 previously published in the timeframe 1998–2007.
35. Negro, 'Simmetrie asimmetriche tra umano e natura', p. 149.
36. Negro, 'Simmetrie asimmetriche tra umano e natura', p. 149.
37. Negro, 'Simmetrie asimmetriche tra umano e natura', p. 150.
38. Rosa.
39. Negro, 'Simmetrie asimmetriche tra umano e natura', p. 151.
40. In the quotations from the book, the sections are abbreviated as follows: *bioluminescenze BL, lezioni di poesia LP, prugni PN, guadare GD, simmetrie mancine SM, la maniglia di ghiaccio MG, poesie sparse PS* e *haiku HK*. Individual poems are indicated by an abbreviated mention of the book (*PN*) followed by an abbreviation of the section, then by a number which reflects its order of appearance in the book as well as by an indication of the line numbers where relevant.
41. Rosa.
42. Rosa.
43. Following the author's note on the text (*PN*, pp. 155–57), the timing of their respective compositions is roughly as follows: *MG* 2000, *GD* 2004, *PN* I 2005, *SM* 2005–2006, *PN* II 2007, *PS* 1998–2007.
44. For the general structure of poems see Figures A.3 and A.4 in the Appendix.
45. Rosa.
46. Lecomte, *Ai confini del verso*, p. 20.
47. See also Negro, 'La leggerezza profonda dell'In-der-Welt-sein'.
48. This translation has been revised by Lucia Moon.
49. Rosa.
50. See Negro, 'La leggerezza profonda dell'In-der-Welt-sein'. On the mobilization of the representation of Eve see also Pumhösel's short story 'Il bacio', *El Ghibli*, 44 (2014) <http://www.el-ghibli.org/il-bacio/> [accessed 21 May 2017].
51. Rosa.
52. Eva Taylor, 'Su due fiumi. — Scrittura bilingue e autotraduzione. Tra riva e sentiero — le poesie sul fiume Erlauf di Barbara Pumhösel', *Arcipelago Itaca. Letterature, visioni ed altri percorsi*, 5 (2011), 179–80.
53. See Charles Armitage Brown, *Life of John Keats*, ed. by Dorothy Hyde Bodurtha and Willard Bissell Pope (London: Oxford University Press, 1987).
54. See Stefano Colangelo, 'Haiku e altre piccole tempeste', in *Culture allo specchio: arte, letteratura, spettacolo e società tra il Giappone e l'Europa*, ed. by Wada Tadahiko and Stefano Colangelo (Bologna: Emil, 2012), pp. 116–29 (p. 120).
55. See Joan Giroux, *The Haiku Form* (Rutland, VT: Tuttle, 1974); Kenneth Yasuda, *Japanese Haiku: Its Essential Nature and History* (North Clarendon, VT: Tuttle, 2011).
56. For the circulation of the haiku see in particular Yoshinobu Hakutani, *Haiku and Modernist Poetics* (New York: Palgrave Macmillan, 2009); René Etiemble, 'Sur une bibliographie du "haiku" dans les langues européennes', *Comparative Literature Studies*, 11.1 (1974), 1–20. The genre arrived in Italy from France; then, through D'Annunzio's mediation, it surfaced in the works of many authors including Corrado Govoni, Umberto Saba, and Giuseppe Ungaretti (see Colangelo; Giorgio Sica, 'Come perle intorno ad un filo. Breve storia dell'Haiku nella poesia

italiana', *Esperienze letterarie*, 30.1 (2005), 113–32). For the Germanophone context see Maria Teresa Morreale, *Fuga verso un 'altrove': l'haiku in lingua tedesca* (Palermo: Società grafica artigiana, 1981).
57. See Scott, pp. 286–87.
58. The use of the tricolon as a foregrounding figure has been noted by Taylor in *gedankenflussabwärts*: 'le liste, per lo più a tre elementi (già in Ursprung, ma anche in Erlauf ecc.) costituiscono una figura stilistica che ritorna' [lists, mostly with three elements (already present in Ursprung, but also in Erlauf etc.), constitute a stylistic figure that keeps returning]. Taylor, 'Su due fiumi', p. 180.
59. For the *Stabreim* see Ursula Isselstein, 'Breviario di metrica tedesca', in *La poesia tedesca del Novecento*, ed. by Ursula Isselstein and Anna Chiarloni (Turin: Einaudi, 1990), pp. 423–65.
60. Andrea Afribo, *Poesia contemporanea dal 1980 a oggi. Storia linguistica italiana* (Rome: Carocci, 2007), p. 23.
61. Loda, 'Eco-Pusterla', p. 105; Loda, 'Gli animali nel primo Pusterla', p. 13.
62. 'VII° Seminario italiano degli scrittori e delle scrittrici migranti'.
63. 'VI° Seminario italiano degli scrittori e delle scrittrici migranti'.
64. See Serenella Iovino and Serpil Oppermann, *Material Ecocriticism* (Bloomington: Indiana University Press, 2014).
65. For a mapping of the most frequently occurring words see Table A.2 in the Appendix.
66. Negro, 'Simmetrie asimmetriche tra umano e natura', p. 153.
67. D'Alessandro.

CHAPTER 4

Hybridity and Dynamism in Hasan Atiya Al Nassar's Verse

Al Nassar's Iraqi-Italian Poetic Journey

Analysing the work of Hasan Al Nassar means first of all returning to the framework of exile poetry. The author was born in Nasiriyah in 1954, and moved to Italy as part of the Iraqi diaspora, following the establishment of Saddam Hussein's regime.[1] The poet recalls his escape, via Baghdad and Damascus towards Rome, in one of his scholarly works: 'Salii sull'aereo con pochissime cose, sapendo che molto probabilmente non avrei mai più visto l'Iraq e, che se fosse stato scoperto in qualche modo il mio tentativo di fuga, sarei stato sicuramente ucciso. Ce l'ho fatta. Dai primi anni '80 vivo in Italia' [I boarded the plane with very few things, knowing that most likely I would never see Iraq again, and that, if my attempt to escape had been uncovered, I would certainly have been killed. I made it. Since the early 1980s I have been living in Italy].[2] Flaviano Pisanelli and Laura Toppan, in their monograph dedicated to Italophone translingual migrant poets, have mapped the different phases of Al Nassar's journey in Italy, and in particular of his life in Florence, where he moved a few years after his displacement.[3] While I would refer readers to their study for a detailed biographical account, it is necessary to recall here that Al Nassar, who had graduated with a degree in Literature from the University of Baghdad and had begun a robust writing career well before his exile, was able to rebuild his scholarly trajectory in Italy, completing a Bachelor's degree in Literature at the University of Florence and then a Doctorate in History at the University of Naples, and in parallel beginning to employ the Italian language for his literary writings. As Pisanelli and Toppan explain, Al Nassar's time in Italy was extremely troubled, due to economic difficulties as well as the pain caused by his separation from his family, with whom in large part he never reunited after his departure.[4] Living in Italy as a political refugee from 1983 onwards, Al Nassar began quite early on to collaborate with journals and cultural associations and to build his literary path, experimenting with different genres, though poetry remained his constant and major commitment.[5] The author died in Florence in 2017. His works of poetry were awarded several prizes and have been the object of several analyses, in Italy and abroad.

In order to contextualize Al Nassar's work, it is necessary to recall three main aspects that are central to its development, namely: the distinctive positioning of Iraqi authors within the landscape of Italophone translingual migrant poetry; the dimension of collectivity and resistance that commonly foregrounds their works; and the particular ways in which Al Nassar approaches and inhabits the experience of literary translingualism. As Mia Lecomte explains, the first surfacing of Italophone works by Iraqi migrant authors dates back to the 1970s, and must be considered in relation to the significant displacement of Middle Eastern intellectuals towards Europe and America, as a result of troubled political situations, persecutions, and conflicts.[6] More specifically, Lecomte recalls that a very early influx of Iraqi citizens into Italy was made up of students, artists, and writers who found refuge there. Among the earliest poetic voices to emerge within the Italophone scene are, for instance, Thea Laitef and Fawzi Al Delmi, both of whom were very influential authors for Al Nassar. The presence of the Iraqi community in Italy consolidated progressively throughout the 1980s.[7] In parallel, the Italophone production of Iraqi-Italian translingual authors increased significantly, presenting a notable internal variety, but also a series of important common traits that will allow me to identify some collective trajectories in the following paragraphs.[8]

In editorial terms, a very important step in collecting and memorializing the poetics of Iraqi-Italian authors is represented by the publication in 1998 of the anthology *Quaderno mediorientale I: Iraq*, in the *Cittadini della poesia* series edited by Mia Lecomte in collaboration with Francesco Stella.[9] This anthology collects a selection of poetic works by Laitef, Al Delmi, and Al Nassar, and as such facilitates the tracing of a comparative line through these three crucial Iraqi-Italian poetics. Despite the fact that these three poetics all demonstrate highly original traits, on examination some important common aspects emerge. The first is indubitably the centrality and pervasiveness of the critical category of exile within the verses. In the essay that opens the book, Pino Blasone argues that exile has existed at the very core of contemporary Arabic poetry since the beginning of the nineteenth century.[10] Significantly, many of the exiled poets whom the scholar mentions in his introduction, including Gibràn Khalìl Gibràn, Badr Shakir al Sayyàb, Adonis, and Sa' di Yùsuf re-emerge abundantly within the verses of Laitef, Al Delmi, and Al Nassar in the form of intertextual presences.[11] Moreover, Al Nassar himself speaks about al-Sayyàb, Yùsuf, and Adonis as three very influential authors for the development of his own work.[12] This is an important aspect, because it allows me to identify the presence of exile in the poetry of Iraqi-Italian translingual authors, and in the work of Al Nassar in particular, as not only the translation of an individual and personal trauma into verse, but also the reverberation and mediation of a collective trauma. The primary element of resistance that informs these verses eventually materializes across this double trajectory.

In one of my previous studies, I identified a series of further tropes that emerge from the work of translingual Iraqi-Italian authors, and I maintain these to be crucial tropes to keep in mind when first approaching the qualities of Al Nassar's poetics.[13] All of these tropes are, of course, related to the central question of exile, and in large part they stem directly from it. The first of these tropes relates to the pervasiveness of movement and crossing-related imagery within the verses. In fact, the works of the three authors mentioned above foreground a poetic space that is constitutively multiple and that abundantly merges past and present, dream and reality, fear and joy, Iraq and Italy. This aspect led me in turn to identify a strong theme of contrapuntality in these works, which is particularly evident in the use of indexicality, and above all in the mobile employment of spatial deixis, proper names, and toponyms. As such, contrapuntal dynamics are confirmed to perform a foundational function in the literary surfacing of the experience of exile, according to a trajectory famously traced by Edward Said.[14]

A second common feature that I identified within the poems is the strong sense of communal belonging, visible in the overarching centrality of the collective dimension. The act of poetry writing is interpreted first and foremost as a political and civil mission, and more especially as a means of advocating for the displaced community. This aspect is even more significant in this context, as it comes from poets who have experienced extensive silencing and censorship. Al Nassar himself explains: 'Ho iniziato a scrivere e a pubblicare molto giovane: avevo tra i diciassette e i diciotto anni e ho cominciato pubblicando racconti [...] Più volte sono stato interrogato dalla censura a causa dei miei racconti' [I started writing and publishing when I was very young: I was between seventeen and eighteen years old and I started publishing short stories [...] I was repeatedly interrogated by censors because of my stories].[15] Lecomte recalls that this collective vocation is particularly strong in the poetics of the so-called 'generazione di Baghdad' [Baghdad generation], to which Al Delmi and Laitef belong, and which was notorious for promoting an idea of culture and of literary writing that was 'militante, progressista e innovatrice' [militant, progressive, and innovative].[16] These dynamics led me to identify the pervasiveness of the idea of resistance in the works of Iraqi-Italian authors, a quality that manifests itself even within the innermost components of versification, as I shall discuss.

A third common element that I identified within the poetics of Iraqi-Italian authors is the prominence of the expressive and generative action of the mother tongue, and of its literary tradition, within the versification in the second language.[17] In the second chapter of the current study I explained that, in the case of Hajdari, the mother tongue and its literary tradition take some time to be reconstructed and reconfigured within the novel linguistic-semantic horizon of the double verse. On the contrary, in the works of Iraqi-Italian translingual authors, and Al Nassar in particular, the Arabic poetic tradition manifests itself immediately within the Italophone diction. Its presence in Al Nassar's work is also related to a specific positioning regarding the practice of translanguaging, which I shall discuss later in this section. In any case, the presence of the Arabic poetic tradition is felt heavily in the verses of Iraqi-Italian translingual authors, and is inscribed, for instance, in their reinterpretation of classical forms and genres, such as the long song *qasīda* and the short poem *ghazal*.[18] Further traces of this tradition are visible on the prosodic and figurative level. In fact, the verses of all three poets demonstrate a crucial sensitivity to accentual dynamics, repetitions, and the rhythmicization of line components, and they show a preference for measures wherein metre and syntax comply, all of which constitute central aspects within classical as well as modern and contemporary Arabic poetry.[19] These dynamics are extremely relevant to Al Nassar's work, and in the following sections I will trace their emergence within the deepest formal and linguistic articulations of his translingual verse.

To conclude this introductory discourse, a few lines must be dedicated to Al Nassar's interpretation of translingualism, and particularly to his use of the Italian language, a process which was anything but easy, especially in the years immediately following his displacement. Among all the authors whose works are investigated herein, Al Nassar is a poet in whose works and interventions the pain of writing in a second language, and the wound generated by the forced separation from the mother tongue, emerge clearly. In terms of poetic practice, the separation was never completed, as Al Nassar continued to write in Arabic in parallel to his translingual activity, but he did so without the opportunity to devise an audience for his mother-tongue productions. In fact, Pisanelli and Toppan stress that, for Al Nassar, the change of language was determined first and foremost by the need to be read, something that was extremely difficult otherwise, especially in the first phase of exile: 'negli anni in cui arriva in Italia, l'autore si rende conto del grosso problema editoriale che investe la pubblicazione di opere in versione bilingue e di uno scarso interesse per la produzione letteraria araba contemporanea. Inoltre non trovando traduttori dall'arabo, inizia a scrivere in italiano per essere letto' [in the years that he first arrives in Italy, the author realizes the major editorial problem that affects the publication of works in bilingual editions, and the scarce interest in contemporary Arabic literary production. Moreover, finding no one who would translate from Arabic, he begins writing in Italian in order to be read].[20] With time, Al Nassar's positioning with respect to the Italian language changed significantly. In fact, in a later interview, the author explained: 'a volte scrivo direttamente in italiano, altre in arabo e poi mi autotraduco in italiano' [sometimes I write directly in Italian, other times I write in Arabic and then I self-translate into Italian].[21] Thus his self-translational process is partly interrupted in late phase, in which Italian becomes a more direct and unmediated means of expression. However, his relationship with the Italian language will remain a very complicated one, and this confirms Lecomte's argument that translingualism per se cannot be analysed without acknowledging the incredibly broad spectrum of perceptions of the second language and of the mother tongue, with the latter in particular ranging from being recognized 'come un'opportunità in continua evoluzione' [as an ever-changing opportunity] to being viewed 'come l'ultimo baluardo di sè a cui non si è disposti a rinunciare' [as the last fortress of the self that one is not willing to renounce].[22]

In conclusion, Al Nassar finds in the second language both a barrier and a space of hope. This ambivalence towards the translingual experience, and its intermingling with the exilic condition, is highlighted with particular strength by another Iraqi-Italian author, Laitef, who explains:

> Si tratta di una lotta vitale con la lingua... Per un esule, significa strappare il bavaglio dell'incomunicabilità. Fonte di diffidenza, isolamento o avversione. Per il poeta e il narratore, farsi mediatore della Coscienza. È come fare breccia

in una parete, attraverso la quale filtri la luce che annuncia il cielo, io spero, della libertà.

[It is about a vital struggle with the language... For an exile, it means ripping off the gag of incommunicability, source of distrust, isolation, or aversion. For the poet and the narrator, it means becoming a mediator of Consciousness. It is like breaking through a wall, through which you filter the light that announces the heavens — I hope — of freedom].[23]

As I shall illustrate, in Al Nassar's translingual works, the contrapuntality of his experience notably emerges through the coexistence of poems characterized by the heavy workings of the mother tongue and its tradition, and other verses wherein the Italian language is accessed in more transitive and less mediated ways. The analysis that develops in the following sections pinpoints the surfacing of these complex and fluid dynamics in one of Al Nassar's major books: *Roghi sull'acqua babilonese*.

Fire, Water, Stone: Hasan Al Nassar's *Roghi sull'acqua babilonese*

Al Nassar authored three poetry books: *Poesie dell'esilio*, *Roghi sull'acqua babilonese*, and *Il labirinto*.[24] The books are deeply interrelated on a formal-semantic level. *Roghi*, which is the primary object of my analysis, consists of twenty-six poems written entirely in free verse, and represents a synthesis of roughly twenty years of translingual poetic activity, collecting texts previously published in periodicals and anthologies, as well as other volumes.[25] As such, it is an ideal terrain on which to map the qualities of Al Nassar's translingual poetic journey.

Within Al Nassar's poetics, Pisanelli and Toppan have identified three aspects that are all embodied in the translingual verse of *Roghi*.[26] First of all, they recognize the pain of separation as a central element in the author's poetic exploration. This overarching pain leaves the body and the verse as the only presences that can possibly survive within the exilic reality. Secondly, the scholars identify within Al Nassar's works the pivotal role of memory, and in particular of the dialectic past–present, arguing that 'l'esilio si esprime nella continua rimemorazione di luoghi, persone, attimi, che si intrecciano con il presente dell'autore, con la sua nuova lingua, con la città di Firenze' [exile is expressed in the continuous remembrance of places, peoples, moments, which are intertwined with the author's present, with his new language, with the city of Florence].[27] This aspect nourishes the configuration of the critical category of exile as a profoundly dialogic one, and one that is firmly embedded in a collective trajectory. Third, Pisanelli and Toppan recognize the constitutive contrapuntality of Al Nassar's verse, which emerges in *Roghi* even in the oxymoron of the title, playing on the semantically opposite poles of fire and water. In fact, contrapuntality surfaces in *Roghi* not only in the double unfolding of Iraqi-Italian spatial trajectories, but also in the play on oppositions (dream–reality, exile–home, individual–collective), which, as I shall explain, is also reflected in the formal and metrical profile of texts. The coexistence of these binary categories constitutes a central juncture in the book. Significantly, Pisanelli and Toppan argue that 'le due culture, i due paesaggi, le due lingue, i due ritmi sono sempre presenti sincronicamente nel momento della creazione letteraria' [the two cultures, the two landscapes, the two rhythms are always synchronously present in the moment of literary creation].[28] This constitutive contrapuntality does not mean that Al Nassar's verse is built on a rigid system of dichotomies. On the contrary, contrapuntality is a quality that allows the poet to develop a fluid gaze on the realities he observes, and to infuse his translingual verse with the same fluidity.

On the whole, *Roghi* consists of a journey in which the subject — who is frequently decentred and pluralized by means of a polyphonic play on voices — is engaged in a perpetual movement that does not seem to envisage a possible conclusion or resolution. As I shall discuss, this movement is textually embodied by the long poem, the form that dominates the collection. The landscapes that the subject visits are dusty, dry, and evanescent, and their representations are peppered with an important set of metaphors, which contribute to the foregrounding of deformative trajectories. Non-human elements are either hostile (fire, cold, sand, wind) or redemptive (water), and they are frequently revealed to possess a multilayered polysemantic nature. Fire, for instance, not only performs the function of consuming matter, but is also seen as a powerful agent of transformation and hence as a generative actor. Similarly, water is a stable and salvific element, but it may also allude synaesthetically to the journey (particularly when the subject finds himself on the seashore contemplating or remembering experiences of passage), or it may represent an impassable barrier (in particular when different embodiments of the rain intervene to separate the subject and his thoughts from the outer world). The presence of these elements supports the poet in his interrogation of movement and introduces a collective and more-than-human trajectory into his verse. Nonetheless, it is important to anticipate that, in Al Nassar's poetry, exile is depicted as a suffocating experience, from which, in the end, no one is saved: the ultimate meaning of the human trajectory is instead sought in the resistance to a common condition of pain, and therefore in the acceptance and continuation of the journey itself.

From a structural point of view, the collection is undivided and, unlike the other two self-anthologies included herein, it is not broken into sections. Among the twenty-six texts that constitute the book, six are drawn from the anthology *Quaderno mediorientale*, seven from the volume *Poesie dell'esilio*, two appeared in periodical publications, and twelve are published therein for the first time.[29] In the case of previously published poems, the order of appearance varies significantly with respect to the first redactions. In particular, Al Nassar tends to bring forward poems that were located towards the end of previous works. Nonetheless, the examination of textual histories reveals that Al Nassar is the most conservative among the three poets studied herein. In fact, variants in *Roghi* are minor, and tend mostly to involve punctuation and graphical aspects. In addition, Al Nassar seems interested in a few cases in reworking the division of stanzas (*RG* 3; *RG* 20; *RG* 22), an aspect which, as I shall explain, plays an important role in the articulation of his long poems. Moreover, in the book the author tends to recompose groups of hemistiches that were spread over two lines in previous editions (*RG* 4; *RG* 5; *RG* 15; *RG* 16). Only in one case does Al Nassar intervene significantly in the text's structure, eliminating the close of the composition (*RG* 22). Other minor variants involve lexical aspects that strive to assuage the polarization of the previously mentioned contrasting semantic fields that abundantly inform the book.

Over the following sections, I will analyse the formal, metrical-rhythmical, and linguistic profile of the self-collection. Specifically, in the first section, I will address the articulation of textual geographies within the book, and expand on the structure and significance of the long poems, which are the most frequent form in the collection. As noted by Silvana Grippi,[30] Al Nassar's long poems foreground a profoundly contrapuntal nature, and are reminiscent of the Arabic long heterometric song the *qasīda*. Because of these fluid qualities, the analysis of this form is particularly important in illuminating dynamics of hidden metre and metrical hybridization. In the second section, I will analyse the occurrence of metres in the self-anthology, with particular attention paid to a series of central measures.[31] The analysis will also expand on the distinctive rhetorical and rhythmical profile of the book, highlighting the unfolding of impactful processes of metrical hybridization that are traceable, for instance, in the polyphonic articulation of texts and in the alternation of voices therein. The final section is dedicated to lexical values, and particularly to the emergence of a language of pain in Al Nassar's translingual verse. This section also closely examines the contrapuntal embodiments of space and movement that emerge from *Roghi*'s verse.

Poetic Forms: Passage and Hybridity in Al Nassar's Long Poems

In terms of progression, Al Nassar's versification strategies do not undergo a radical mutation over time, remaining instead quite steady, similarly to those of Pumhösel. Nonetheless, a less direct relationship with the mother tongue is noticeable particularly in the more recent verses, those that appear for the first time in *Roghi*, and that likely correspond to compositions written directly in Italian, outside of dynamics of self-translation.[32]

Structurally, the book is entirely shaped around the distinctive form of the long poem. Before engaging in a close description of the foundational values of this specific form in the self-anthology, I must discuss its function as a space of encounter and dialogue between the literary traditions through which Al Nassar moves. In fact, in *Roghi* the long poem is configured primarily as a space in which formal and imaginative devices that stem directly from classical Arabic poetry may surface, devices that are then reinvented and translated into the fluid and contrapuntal articulation of the translingual verse.

As I have mentioned, the employment of extended compositions in *Roghi* supports the author in portraying the unfolding of the human experience as an everlasting journey, and in embodying the centrality of movement. From a stylistic point of view, Al Nassar's long poems are characterized by extreme variety, and they frequently present alternations of lyrical-elegiac, descriptive-reflective, and epic-narrative insertions. Moreover, the long compositions show a constant projection towards a collective dimension, primarily materialized through polyphonic rhythmical strategies and a multiplication of utterances. As previously mentioned, these features all have much in common with the classical Arabic long song the *qasīda*. According to Roger Allen, the traditional *qasīda* is a polythematic and monometric long poem that originates in the oral tradition of the pre-Islamic era, and embodies a journey that is above all a 'confrontation with the unknown'.[33] Together with the *qitah* — a short form that Allen believes originated before the *qasīda* — and the *ghazal*, this form represents a fundamental module within classical Arabic poetry, and one that received wide critical fortune. In terms of structure, Suzanne Pinckney Stetkevych recalls that the *qasīda* conventionally witnessed a tripartite development, composed of an elegiac prelude (*nasib*), an account of a desert journey (*rahil*), and an argumentative conclusion (*gharad*) in the form of praise, satire, invective, or elegy.[34] On the whole, the *qasīda* enjoyed an extraordinary transnational dissemination, being translated and inflected in many different languages, and as such configuring itself as a world poetry form.[35] The traditional form was obviously transformed over the centuries and across its numerous translingual interpretations, adhering less and less to the original conventions. Nonetheless, some tropes, such as the form's primary function of embodying movement and passage, have been largely maintained.[36] In his long poems, Al Nassar recuperates this latter function even though he radically renounces other conventional aspects that the classical form entails, such as the final expression of fulfilment and salvation. While the dialogue with the *qasīda* in *Roghi*'s poetics should not be overestimated, the influence of the semantics of this form is significant. More broadly, the presence of a net of entanglements with Arabic poetry within the translingual verse allows me to conceptualize Al Nassar's works as crucial spaces of resistance to physical and linguistic displacement, and as such to illuminate a generative 'minor' presence of the mother tongue and its tradition within the innermost substance of the versification in the second language.

In terms of internal articulation, in *Roghi* Al Nassar's long poems are extremely vertically extended, with almost half of the compositions exceeding fifty lines in length.[37] The poet does not demonstrate an attraction towards regular patterns, and stanzas are most often of uneven lengths. The semantic unit of the stanza represents a fundamental component in the development of Al Nassar's long compositions. As I shall demonstrate, the poet employs partitions to perform a crucial contrastive function that stresses the play on opposites that permeates the book, as well as to embody linear movement and plastic transformation. Syntactically, their most frequent configuration is end-stopped, and it is notable that enjambment is never used to enchain them. While all these factors identify stanzas as self-contained autonomous segments, a series of iterative devices such as repetitions and other sound iterations intervenes to increase cohesion across them.

Remarkably, *Roghi* contains just one example of a short composition. A close look at this undivided poem allows us to uncover some of the foundational qualities of *Roghi*'s articulation of individual stanzas, and to preliminarily reveal some of the inflections of linguistic distance that emerge within the book:

Silenzio
Verrà da me il silenzio:
il silenzio che entra nelle vesti dei morti.
L'istante era povero
(abbandonato e ferito)
ed i nostri cieli stranieri.
Fuggiremo alla ricerca della
Rivoluzione,
ha gridato il vento,
e i nostri ultimi giorni
hanno urlato, feriti. (RG 1)

[*Silence*
It will come to me, the silence:
the silence that enters through the vestments of the dead.
The moment was wretched
(forsaken and wounded)
and our skies foreign.
We will run away in search of the
Revolution,
the wind shouted,
and our last days
cried too, wounded.]

The poem above, *Silenzio* [Silence] is the first in order of appearance in *Roghi*.[38] Despite its introductory positioning, it prefigures the conclusion of the journey, as well as a progressive loss of voice of the subject, whose body and days are dissolved in the final escape of the wind: *fuggiremo alla ricerca della | Rivoluzione, | ha gridato il vento* [we will run away in search of the | Revolution, | the wind shouted]. Structurally, the composition is made up of three syntactical sentences and built around a series of marked sound identities, related in particular to iterations of whispered tones (*silenzio* [silence] 1, 2; *istante* [instant] 3; *nostri* [our] 5, 8). The transformational nature of the text is inscribed in the shift from the individual to the collective (see the transition from the singular *Verrà* [it will come] 1 to the plural *Fuggiremo* [we will run away] 6), and in the portrayal of a final transformation and dissolution. These transitions are foregrounded by rhythmical contrapuntality, by the presence of a choral rhythm, embodied by the prevailing solemn anapaest, and by a more rapid and irregular rhythm that introduces the direct speech of the wind. Personification is a central figure in this text. More generally, transitional imagery is employed in *Roghi* to allude to deformation and mutation, as well as to highlight movement as an impactful force within more-than-human balances, and one that significantly dominates the central subject.

The analysis of this poem facilitates the articulation of a number of considerations regarding the effects of linguistic distance in Al Nassar's verse. As previously discussed, it is known that translingual authors are prone to developing a transitive and material relationship with the second language, which is reflected in a play on the subtraction and isolation of words, as in the case of Pumhösel's and of Hajdari's early works, for instance. In Al Nassar, the emergence of a material and bodily relationship with the language is largely attested, but it does not correspond to a surfacing of transparency and brevity in the diction (with the exception of a phenomenological employment of the short line, which I will examine later). Rather, the second language appears to be substantially mediated by a central rhetoricizing function of the hidden mother tongue, which appears particularly active on a syntactical-metrical level due to self-translational dynamics, and is extremely powerful in all stages of Al Nassar's translingual experience. While the search for a transitive quality within the Italophone diction may surface occasionally (for instance in the selection of adjectives and in the development of linear figures such as the simile), on the whole the poet builds from the beginning of his translingual experience a dense rhetorical filter between signifier and signified, one that he is determined to maintain. This filter is enhanced by the occurrence of a series of devices, such as inversions and repetitions, which allow Al Nassar to increment figurative density and raise the literariness of the diction. More specifically, the inversions create a dissonance within the diction that deliberately augments the distance between signs and matters, while repetitions allow the contrapuntality of Al Nassar's translingual verse to emerge, and simultaneously allude to the impossibility of embodying reality through words. It is within this multiplicity and these distinctive tensions that the strongest expressive marks of Al Nassar's translingual verse eventually surface.

The book also presents one example of a prosimetrum, *Ombre scure (nella vita del sig. Hasan Atiya Al Nassar)*, which is placed towards the end. The prosimetrum, which may be reminiscent of the Arabic *maqamat*, occurs in other translingual works by Iraqi-Italian authors, such as Younis Tawfik's novel *La straniera*.[39] Its articulation in *Roghi* is distinctive.

> Prima di svegliarmi, in quei giorni, ho scoperto l'ora Zero, porti per i villaggi e città mai viste prima, ufficiali di guerra e pantaloni sazi di coltelli e polvere da sparo. E il mio cuore! Il mio cuore traboccava paura e timidezza come di fronte a un nuovo amore. [...]
>
> > Ho visto sacerdoti
> > uscire dalla croce
> > del Messia
> > verso la bara di legno.
> > La Morte dondola
> > come una collana sopra il petto. (RG 24)

[In those days, before waking up, I discovered the zero hour, ports in villages and cities never seen before, war officials and trousers filled with knives and gunpowder. And my heart! My heart overflowed with fear and shyness, as though encountering new love. [...]

> I saw priests
> leaving from the cross
> of the Messiah
> towards the wooden coffin.
> Death hangs
> like a necklace on the breast]

Generally, as the excerpt shows, Al Nassar uses prose inserts to allow the subject to investigate both reality (with a strong attention to space) and the self (with a reflective aim). Poetry inserts, on the other hand, are characterized by regular and paced rhythms, and perform a mostly lyric-elegiac function, or else take on the role of epilogues which sometimes open up to expressionist tones (*ho visto sacerdoti | uscire dalla croce* [I saw priests | coming out of the cross] 1, 2).

The remaining compositions of *Roghi* are all long poems. A good indication of the mobile qualities of this form can be drawn from an examination of the function of stanzas. I have mentioned above that stanzas are treated in *Roghi* as syntactically autonomous segments. On the whole, Al Nassar makes three main uses of them. First, in a majority of cases, the poet alternates them contrastively, to foreground transitions between different genres and styles, focal points, or past and present landscapes. This contrastive use of stanzas has the effect of infusing the verse with contrapuntality and fluidity, and thus of drawing attention to the composite nature of the journey. Second, Al Nassar sometimes makes dynamic use of stanzas, expanding and retracting them to mark a linear progression. In these cases, the material unfolding of the articulation of stanzas embodies the journey itself. Finally, the author may employ stanzas in a plastic fashion, deforming them to allude to the alteration and transformation of the matter that occurs through the experience of movement and the performance of passage. In the following paragraphs I will provide a few examples of each of these functions, placing them in relation to the general formal and semantic values of *Roghi*.

One significant contrastive employment of stanzas is that which is related to the alternation of genres and styles, as well as to a sudden change in focal point:

> I nostri alberi sfiancati dal ghiaccio dei morti:
> più feroce è questa paura
> nel lampo ti ho vista come cielo pregno di pietre
> non dovresti levare il tuo fuoco
> sopra i vetri della casa che è mia
>
> > Mi copre il freddo di ghiaccio
> > e nell'amore tu sei
> > il mio alloggio isolato. (*RG* 22, 1–13)
>
> [Our trees flattened by the weight of the dead:
> this fear is fiercer
> in a glimpse I saw you, a sky thick with stones
> you should not raise your flames
> above the windows of that house which is mine
>
> > The ice cold covers me
> > and in love you are
> > my secluded shelter.]
>
> Boschi seguono la tua ombra, e donne tra le zagare.
> Ti innalzi là, dove sorgono le città dell'estate,
> dove baci di fanciulla diventano inni sacri.
>
> È donna d'anima. È tra i figli uccisi, è tra i figli vivi.
> Già l'alba le porta lacrime (e ancora lontana è la notte). (*RG* 16, 1–5)

> [Woods follow your shadow, and women amongst the florets.
> You rise there, where summer's cities bloom,
> where maidens' kisses are sacred hymns.
>
> She is woman. She is with the murdered children, she is with the living children.
> Already dawn brings her to tears (and the night is still far).]

In the first example, taken from the long composition *Le città nude* [The naked cities] (*RG* 22), stanzas mark a passage from a narrative diction to an elegiac and suspensive one, which identifies a refrain. The transition is made visible through the shift from the collective (*noi*) to the individual (*io*) and, more visibly, through the graphical dislocation of one stanza to the right of the page. In general, dislocations of entire stanzas are frequent in Al Nassar's verse, and they are most often associated with choral inserts and refrains. In a previous study, I noted that dislocation is common in the verse of Iraqi-Italian authors, and can be interpreted as a sign of formal hybridization.[40] In fact, as Allen points out, classical Arabic metre pays specific attention to segments and portions of lines, such as feet and hemistiches. The latter may be graphically separated on the page by a blank space or vertically organized in couplets. With due caution, then, the dislocation of lines and entire stanzas by Iraqi-Italian poets can be read in relation with this graphical-semantic sensing of linear components that is typical of Arabic poetry.[41] In *Roghi*, these entanglements are used to introduce an element of rhythmical dissonance, and they often support the composite and dialogic development of the compositions. In the following excerpts, taken from the poem *Roghi* (*RG* 16), punctuation and rhythm highlight a change in focal point, foregrounding an alternation of voices, and separating the allocution from a more suspensive descriptive insert. This double rhythmical unfolding also characterizes the rest of this composition more generally.

A final contrastive use of stanzas engages with a sudden mutation of referential marks, and as such unveils the contrapuntality of the past and present trajectories within which the subject constantly moves:

> Nuvole d'Iraq
> e contadini analfabeti.
> Le barche sono pronte,
> il deserto tranquillo, cammelli sollevano
> i nomi degli uccisi.
> Sono caduti i bombardieri,
> sono caduti
> sul lato destro della collina,
> e questo è un silenzio,
> questa, una notte verde,
> e i fazzoletti non sono più bianchi
> come li vidi ieri mattina.
>
> Poiché l'Ora del mattino ha adottato
> un vuoto massacro dell'ora e del giorno in cui
> si cadrà in Arno,
> su Firenze

> che sorgendo dall'ombra degli avi
> ha dato a questa verde notte
> il filo
> dell'Aurora:
> un abito di luce.
> E la città è frantumata
> una seconda volta. (*RG* 21, 34–56)

> [Clouds of Iraq
> and illiterate peasants.
> The boats are ready,
> the desert quiet, camels raise
> the names of the murdered.
> They fell — the bombers,
> they fell
> on the right side of the hill,
> and this is silence,
> this, a green night,
> and the handkerchiefs are no longer white
> like they were yesterday morning.
>
> Because the Hour of the morning adopted
> an empty massacre of the hour and the day on which
> we fall into the Arno,
> on Florence
> which, rising from the shade of ancestors,
> gave to this green night
> the thread
> of the aurora:
> a dress made of light.
> And the city is shattered
> a second time.]

The above excerpt includes two central verses from the long poem *La città che rimane* [the city that remains] (*RG* 21). The contrapuntal allusion to Iraq and Italy, past and present, is marked by the change of stanzas. These dynamics allow Al Nassar to develop a double, ambivalent, and fluid gaze on the reality that is first observed and then embodied within his translingual verse.

There are two further crucial expressive employments of stanzas in the book, and they are related to the poet's need to embody dynamicity and plasticity respectively within his compositions. On the one hand, stanzas may be stretched or restricted so as to allude to the complexity of movement and passage. On the other, partitions may be treated as plastic units that foreground transformation and deformation:

> Qui.
> Alle tende dei beduini
> come lupo si ferma la Notte.
>
> Questa è la forza dell'amore che penetra
> Queste sono le tavole della morte.
> Questa è la mancanza di vino che blocca la memoria
> Questo è un filo di sangue

> È FISCHIO DI VENTO CATTURATO
> [...]
>
> LA TUA CROCE:
> ERBA SUL CIGLIO DEL SENTIERO.
> Appoggiamoci alla candela dell'amore.
> Cantando YA ROHI AL GARIBAH
> Ya rohi al garibah...
> O ANIMA MIA STRANIERA ! ! ! (*RG* 11, 6–14; 32–37)
>
> [Here.
> By the Bedouin tents
> night rests like a wolf.
>
> This is the force of love that enters
> These are the tables of death.
> This is the lack of wine that blocks memory
> this is a thread of blood
>
> IT IS A CAPTURED BREATH OF WIND
> [...]
>
> YOUR CROSS:
> GRASS ON THE EDGE OF THE PATH
> Let's lean against the candle of love.
> Singing YA ROHI AL GARIBAH
> Ya rohi al garibah...
> OH MY FOREIGN SOUL ! ! !]
>
> Il rifugio, compagna d'esilio,
> ci abbandona dopo la notte della sconfitta
>
> I giorni vili s'insinuano
> nelle pieghe dell'animo sospeso,
> e di nuovo ascoltiamo le grida dei morti
>
> Dalle città soffocate dall'aria
> si leva il silenzio che ci ha perseguitati,
> le nostre mani non posseggono che armi giocattolo,
> armi che non feriscono neanche granelli di polvere... (*RG* 4, 1–9)
>
> [The refuge, companion in exile,
> abandons us after the night of defeat.
>
> Vile days plant themselves
> in the creases of our waiting soul,
> and again we listen to the cries of the dead
>
> The silence that haunted us rises
> from cities suffocated by air,
> our hands carry only toy weapons,
> weapons that could not hurt a speck of dust...]

The first example, drawn from *Corona sull'acqua dell'amore* [Crown on the water of love] (*RG* 11), demonstrates a focus on the composite nature of movement, which is enhanced by the alternation of stanzas of different lengths, and foregrounded by different graphical inflections and multilingual inserts. This trajectory governs the entire articulation of the long poem. In the second case, taken from *Esilio* [exile] (*RG* 4), deformative processes emerge from the progressive plastic expansion of stanzas. The latter mimetically accompanies the incorporation of the subject into the exiled community and thus marks the transition from individual to collective intention.

This excursus through the structural characteristics of Al Nassar's poems has allowed some distinctive aspects to emerge. First and foremost, it has underlined the contrastive, dynamic, and plastic employment of stanzas as a critical quality in the shaping of Al Nassar's long poems. Some of these functions comply with the semantics of the classical *qasīda*, whose prosodic memory is mobilized and reinvented by Al Nassar through his translingual verse. From the *qasīda*, which acts as a hidden metre in the book, Al Nassar borrows a crucial engagement with the notion of passage as a transformative experience. On the whole, textual morphologies contribute to complicating the path of the subject, whose mission is to inhabit, perform, and translate movement. The pain of linguistic displacement and the resistance to it that is performed within the poems leaves abundant traces within the diction in the form of contrapuntal marks, perhaps the most impactful that we have encountered so far on a formal-semantic level.

Metre and Hidden Metre

In the long journey of *Roghi*, Al Nassar uses and combines a wide range of metres. Apart from some exceptions, his texts, while quite extensive, vertically speaking, tend towards horizontal conciseness. Long lines, though semantically crucial when they do occur, are quantitatively rare. At the micro-level of the line, the identification between metre and syntax is still strong, but may be interrupted by enjambments and figures that occasionally break the compactness that is normally articulated.

Type	Count	Percentage
BS	17	1.02%
TS	63	3.80%
QS	113	6.81%
QN	127	7.65%
SN	167	10.06%
ST	213	12.83%
OT	186	11.20%
NO	158	9.52%
DS	138	8.31%
ED	116	6.99%
VL	362	21.8%
Total	1660	100%

TABLE 4.1 Types of lines in *RC*

Table 4.1 records the occurrence of metres within the book. As the mapping shows, measures from the *bisillabo* to the *senario* are both quantitatively and qualitatively significant (29.34% of occurrences). In fact, short measures play a central role in the verticalization of the diction, which is pivotal within the articulation of long poems. As such, the occurrence of short metres engages with dynamics of juxtaposition and the phenomenological deconstruction of the reality observed, dynamics which intervene extensively throughout the book. When employed at the edges of stanzas or of compositions, and in the openings in particular, short lines often foreground allocutions, which are extremely common in *Roghi*:

```
RG 5, 197–201
    Guardali:                BS   1
    pastori,                 TS        2
    ubriachi,                QS              3
    servi scacciati,         QN   1              4
    randagi come noi...      ST        2         4       6
    [Look at them: | shepherds, | drunks, | outcast servants, | wandering like us...]
RG 6, 8–10
    Il regno dei morti       SN        2                 5
    si muove verso una valle OT        2         4              7
    luminosa,                QS              3
    [The reign of the dead | moves towards a bright | valley,]
RG 11, 7–9
    Qui.                     BS   1
    Alle tende dei beduini   OT              3                  7
    come lupo si ferma la Notte.  DS         3         6               9
    [Here. | By the Bedouin tents | night rests like a wolf.]
RG 12, 85–87
    Il suo lamento           QN                   4
    non lascia               TS        2
    una goccia di pianto.    ST              3              6
    [His lament | does not leave | a drop of tears.]
RG 21, 68–69
    E tu, Firenze                  QN   2         4
    stai adesso tornando dai cespugli, DS 2            5              9
    tornando senza aver avuto figli  ED  2         4       6      8      10
    [And you, Florence | are returning now from the thicket, |
    returning without having given birth]
RG 1, 6–7
    Fuggiremo alla ricerca della   DS         3                 7      9
    Rivoluzione,                   QN             4
    [We will run away in search of the | Revolution,]
```

In numerous cases, even with short measures, metre complies with syntax. The end-stopped configuration of the line is most favoured by Al Nassar, as it enhances the focus on segments, which is a central preoccupation in his translingual practice (*RG* 5, 11). The excerpts also demonstrate the aforementioned deconstruction of the syntactical phrase by means of the short line, which is a frequent configuration (*RG* 12, 25). On the whole, the longitudinal disposition of the phrasal components, as identified by the short measure, has the effect of slowing down the diction and introducing suspension, a function that is maintained whether short measures occur at the closes (*RG* 5) or within the bodies of the compositions (*RG* 12; *RG* 25). Short lines can also be inserted into the diction so as to increase or decrease the syllabic progression, and thus support plastic and dynamic needs (*RG* 11). Finally, they may result from an enjambment (*RG* 6). Generally, enjambments and inversions have the effect of fragmenting the pace.

Within the landscape of short metres, the *senario* (10.06%) deserves to be explored in more detail because of its significant rhythmical action throughout the book. On the whole, this metre is a highly musical one, and is frequently employed serially to create cohesion and introduce parallelisms and iterations. Moreover, it performs the important function of foregrounding accentual dynamics within long poems:

> *RG* 24, 35–37
>   E come un bambino   SN   2   5
>   volevo difendere   SN   2   5
>   il mio paradiso   SN   2   5
>   [And like a child | I wanted to defend | my paradise]
> *RG* 12, 100–01
>   L'aria schiaccia l'aria.   SN   1   3   5
>   L'acqua schiaccia l'acqua.   SN   1   3   5
>   [Air crushes air. | Water crushes water.]
> *RG* 6, 6
>   è l'ombra che cresce   SN   1   2   5
>   [it is the shadow that grows]
> *RG* 8, 28
>   Tutto è ormai entrato   SN   1   2   3   5
>   [Everything has entered now]
> *RG* 25, 70
>   come giavellotto.   SN   1   5
>   [like javelin.]

The above examples display some of the most frequently occurring inflections of the *senario*. The double pulsation, with a polarization of accents at the edges of lines, is the dominant configuration. Generally, this inflection supports binary articulations which are particularly prominent in the self-anthology from an accentual point of view. The first excerpt above demonstrates the occurrence of a dactylic-like version of the *senario*, which may extend to entire blocks of lines (*RG* 24, 35–37). Ternary developments and trochaic-like configurations are generally quite rare (*RG* 12). Irregular patterns are present, and they still imply a rhythmical insistence on the openings of lines, though here the multiplication of pulsations and the occurrence of double stresses suggest more visibly issues of fragmentation, tension, and mobility (*RG* 6, 8).

Lines of medium length (from the *settenario* to the *novenario*, 33.55% in total) are the core metres of *Roghi*, and the entire collection is shaped around their governing rhythmical values. Moreover, these metres of medium length are the spaces in which polyphonic dynamics and rhythmical entanglements with the mother tongue emerge with more clarity. As usual, the *settenario* is configured as a central phonosemantic unit within the verse. On the whole, this is Al Nassar's favourite metre and is notably the most frequently occurring metre in the collection (12.83%):

RG 5, 109						
il nostro pallore e	ST		2		5	6
[our pallor and]						
RG 6, 19						
battito che gridava	ST	1				6
[rhythm that shouted]						
RG 8, 2						
Nubi spingono lacrime	ST	1		3		6
[Clouds bear tears]						
RG 8, 16						
l'ho ignorato e l'ignoro.	ST			3		6
[I have ignored it and I ignore it.]						
RG 11, 37						
O ANIMA MIA STRANIERA ! ! !	ST	1			4	6
[OH MY FOREIGN SOUL ! ! !]						
RG 11, 39						
irando con i lupi.	ST		2		5	6
[raging with the wolves.]						
RG 11, 47						
La febbre ti schiaffeggia.	ST		2			6
[the fever strikes you.]						
RG 13, 28						
Dal principio al principio.	ST			3		6
[From beginning to beginning.]						
RG 19, 45						
E così siamo noi,	ST			3	4	6
[And so we are,]						
RG 25, 61						
loro, i bimbi dell'isola,	ST	1		3		6
[them, children of the island,]						

Among the conventional inflections of the *settenario*, the anapaestic one is by far the most common (*RG* 8, 13, 25). Within the dialogic articulation of Al Nassar's compositions, this rhythmical inflection generally comes to identify collective utterances and is frequently found in refrains.[42] Despite the fact that regular inflections of the metre are well attested, the *settenario* expresses the height of its rhythmic potential in irregular and highly dissonant inflections, which are extremely common (*RG* 5; *RG* 6: *RG* 8; *RG* 11; *RG* 19). On the whole, in both regular and irregular configurations, a binary and strongly caesuraed scansion seems to prevail (*RG* 11; *RG* 13; *RG* 25). This aspect is significant, as it once again underlines the centrality and autonomy of linear segments in the metrical unfolding of *Roghi*, and as such allows the generative prosodic function of the mother tongue to further emerge. Figuratively, the *settenario* is also the preferred ground in which transitional imagery surfaces and unfolds (*RG* 6; *RG* 11). Finally, the metre is significantly concerned with processes of metaphorization and sound iterations (*RG* 11; *RG* 25).

A similar discourse can be elaborated for the *ottonario* (11.20%) and the *novenario* (9.52%). The former measure is quantitatively more prevalent, yet the latter still performs a central rhythmical function:

RG 4, 45						
Ma NOI, compagna d'esilio,	OT	2	4		7	
[but WE, companion in exile,]						
RG 5, 6						
io cominciai a svanire	OT		4		7	
[I began to vanish]						
RG 5, 64						
col suo abito di cenere	OT		3		7	
[with its dress of ashes]						
RG 8, 11						
in quest'ora, amore mio,	OT		3		7	
[in this hour, my love,]						
RG 10, 37						
Essa portava una rosa,	OT	1	4		7	
[She brought a rose,]						
RG 23, 22–24						
guerra dei ragazzi sciolti,	OT	1		5	7	
guerra delle zone fredde,	OT	1		5	7	
[war of unfettered youth, | war of the cold zones,]						

* * * * *

RG 4, 35						
e raccolgo i resti e le ombre	NO		3	5		8
[and I gather the remains and the shadows]						
RG 4, 16						
Le nuvole dell'inquietudine.	NO	2				8
[The clouds of turmoil.]						
RG 5, 145						
odore incrostato sul nero	NO	2		5		8
[scent encrusted on black]						
RG 22, 35						
alle mie luci e alle mie tenebre.	NO		4			8
[for my light and my darkness.]						
RG 11, 130						
Chi solleva ora questa notte?	NO		3 4			8
[Who lifts this night now?]						
RG 12, 114						
Canto dei poetici lupi,	NO	1		5		8
[Song of poetic wolves,]						
RG 12, 33						
boschi — o mia patria — io canto solo.						
	NO	1	4		6	8
[Woods — oh my homeland — I sing alone.]						
RG 22, 34						
perché gli anni sono veleno	NO	2	3	5		8
[because years are poison]						

The most frequently occurring inflections of the *ottonario*, which may also appear with dactylic (*RG* 4; *RG* 10) and trochaic-like rhythms (*RG* 23), contain two main pulsations (*RG* 5; *RG* 8). A multiplication and scattering of stresses is rare overall within the octosyllabic measure, and when it does occur, it occurs in topical and liminal positions such as the openings of stanzas. On the other hand, the *novenario* sees a prevailing triadic development, with particular attention paid to the third, fourth, and fifth position (RG 4; RG 5; RG 12). A multiplication of stresses may intervene in order to accelerate the pace in poems characterized by a high degree of expressive tension (RG 11; RG 12; RG 22). Finally, it is also possible to find the *novenario* in binary articulations, in which the two pulsations are most often infused at the edges of lines (RG 4; RG 22).

While metres of medium length are relevant because of their rhythmical values, medium-long measures such as the *decasillabo* (8.31%) and the *endecasillabo* (6.99%) are the places in which metrical hybridization and exchanges with the mother tongue, including ritual repetitions and multilingual inserts, become more visible. Morphologically, the *decasillabo* follows the same trajectories as medium-short lines, being inflected in patterns with two or three prevailing pulsations. The *endecasillabo* demonstrates an extremely composite rhythmical profile, which reflects its central phonosemantic function:

RG 2, 17–18
    ed io ho perso tutte le mie forze.   DS   3   5   9
    volevo inoltrarmi in una nuvola   DS 2   5   9
    [and I have lost all my strength. | I wanted to enter a cloud]

RG 5, 30
    io sento che è acqua paradisiaca,   ED 2   4 5   10
    [This is heavenly water, I feel,]

RG 11, 121
    perché scarsa è la luce del cuore   DS 2 3   6   9
    [because scarce is the light of the heart]

RG 13, 60
    Dove Hasan Al Nassar. un testardo,   DS 1   3   6   9
    [Where Hasan Al Nassar. a stubborn,]

RG 13, 100
    da anni io sono solo con il mio nome, ED 1   4   6   10
    [for years I have lived alone with my name,]

RG 13, 105
    Annuso i sogni miei disordinati   ED 2   4   6   10
    [I sniff my messy dreams]

RG 14, 23
    la statura dell'uomo si china   DS   3   6   9
    [the stature of man bends down]

RG 12, 144–46
    Una rosa non ama un'altra rosa,   ED   3   6   10
    un inferno non ama un altro inferno, ED   3   6   10
    una patria non ama un'altra patria.   ED   3   6   10
    [One rose does not love another rose, | one hell does not love another hell, | one homeland does not love another homeland.]

RG 11, 22
    Apro l'estate annegata di stelle,   ED 1   4   7   10
    [I open the summer drowning in stars,]

RG 21, 44
    e i fazzoletti non sono più bianchi   ED   4   7   10
    [and the handkerchiefs are no longer white]
RG 22, 19
    per noi pietra è il pane, pugnale l'acqua. ED 2 3 5 8 10
    [for us bread is a stone, water a dagger.]
RG 25, 26
    Amarezza, mare, amore, miraggio   ED   3   5   7   10
    [Sourness, sea, love, mirage]

As the examples show, the *decasillabo* often appears in rhythmical couplets (RG 2). Among its conventional inflections, the anapaest is the most significant (RG 14), although here, as compared to the *settenario*, the anapaest is less related to collective instances, and may be rhythmically more fluid, especially through a multiplication of stresses in the openings (RG 11; RG 13). In the different inflections of the *endecasillabo*, Al Nassar traces composite rhythmical trajectories. As the examples show, the anapaestic and dactylic development is prevalent, and the poet demonstrates an attraction for ternary articulations (RG 12; RG 11; RG 21). However, the measure is also open to highly expressive configuration primarily achieved through a reduplication or multiplication of stresses (RG 3; RG 5; RG 21; RG 22) and other deformative processes. Finally, the *endecasillabo* often occurs in crucial positions, appearing in particular toward the borders of poems, where it imparts a grounding pace to the compositions, and maybe employed to raise the literariness of the diction (RG 14).

Long lines (21.8% in total) complete the picture of *Roghi*'s metres. They often see a binary and strongly caesuraed articulation that once again highlights the substantial autonomy of hemistiches and linear segments:

RG 16, 6–11

    Sii tranquilla, poiché sentieri d'acqua s'aprono
    nella foresta del tuo cuore.
    Sii tranquilla ora che tra Baghdad e i tuoi occhi
    s'incendiano gli anni orfani,
    e le trascorse stagioni sono più belle del passo degli usignoli,
    perchè tu sei il canto che sgorga, l'inno della collina.

VL		3		6	8	10	12	
NO			4		8			
VL		3	4			9	12	
OT	2			5	7			
VL			4		7		12	15	20
VL	2			5		8	10	15	

[Be still, for paths of water may open | in the forest of your heart. | Be still now that the orphan years burn | between Baghdad and your eyes, | and spent seasons are more graceful than the nightingale's step, | because you are the song that flows, the hymn of the hill.]

The excerpt above is taken from the long poem *Roghi* [Fires] (RG 16). Hemistiches appear herein as substantially autonomous segments. This autonomy is confirmed by a comparison with previous versions of the text, contained in *Quaderno mediorientale*, in which the hemistiches are graphically separated.[43] In the version contained in the self-anthology, Al Nassar recomposes the long lines by recoupling the hemistiches, an operation that nonetheless retains their substantial rhythmical autonomy.

On the whole, Al Nassar's long lines are extremely rhetoricized and infused with a high degree of literariness, and as such they escape any transition to a plain or prosaic practice. Rhythmical cohesion across the long lines is primarily achieved through accentual dynamics and the related attention to isochronism:

RG 2, 29–34

> Mi fanno male le città che si avvolgono su se stesse
> come un turbine
> E colpi segreti che si muovono nell'animo.
> Mi sforzo con la mia tristezza
> per spingere i sassi che vagano verso il cuore
> tormento degli anni, e le rovine dell'esilio

VL			4		8	11	16
QS		3					
VL	2		5		9	13	
NO	2			6	8		
VL	2		5		8	13	
VL	2		5		9		

[They hurt me — the cities that are wrapped around themselves | like a whirlwind | And secret forces that move in the soul. | With sadness I strive | to push the stones that roam towards my heart | torment of years, the ruins of exile]

RG 13, 46–47

> Allora il tuo nome era per me come un sentiero nella foresta
> e adesso sei un albero solo che teme la notte,

VL	2	5	9		13	18
VL	2	5	8	11	14	

[To me your name was, once, like a path through the forest; | now you are a solitary tree that fears the night]

RG 16, 4–5

> È donna d'anima. È tra i figli uccisi, è tra i figli vivi.
> Già l'alba le porta lacrime (e ancora lontana è la notte).

VL		2	4	6	8	10	13	15
VL	1	2		5	7	10	13	16

[She is woman. She is with the murdered children, she is with the living children. | Already dawn brings her to tears (and the night is still far)]

RG 19, 38–39

> Così lontana è la terra, quella che ci ha generati?
> Così lontana quella sabbia d'estate che ci bruciò?

VL	2	4	7	9		12	15
VL	2	4		8	11		16

[Is it so distant, the land that birthed us? | Is it so distant, that summer sand that burned us?]

RG 22, 40–41

> Da piazza Santissima Annunziata fino alla chiesa di San Marco
> ci incorona l'autobus pubblico con il suo fumo
>
> | VL | | 2 | | 5 | | 9 | 11 | | 14 | | | 18 |
> |---|---|---|---|---|---|---|---|---|---|---|---|---|
> | VL | | | 3 | 5 | | 8 | | | 14 | | | |

[From piazza Santissima Annunziata to the church of San Marco | the public bus crowns us with its fumes]

Long lines may be composed of equal hemistiches (for instance, two *novenari* in RG 2, 29 and two *settenari* in RG 19, 380), though the caesura more often identifies segments of different length. Ternary articulations are rare but do still occur (RG 16, 4). On the whole, the diction is fast-paced, and rhythmical congruence involves the openings in particular.

In the case of Al Nassar's *Roghi*, the analysis of metres must be complemented by a specific discourse on two features that dramatically impact the verse on a rhythmical level: polyphony and repetitions. Polyphony emerges as one of the main characteristics of the collection, and is deeply inscribed in the rhythmical substance of verses. In fact, in Al Nassar's poems, diverse voices are not only often identified by dislocation or other graphical expedients, but they may also be associated with different sets of rhythmical conventions. This use complies with a dialogic employment of prosody that Shemtov has inscribed within the framework of metrical hybridization.[44] The examples of polyphonic uses of rhythm are numerous within the self-anthology.

RG 1, 74–86

> Incapace di raccontare il coraggio sui prati,
> o anche O bella ciao!
> E il popolo ora non avanza più con fiori rossi.
>
> Morto sulla strada
> l'uomo che conservava i nostri inni perduti.
> Senza un ieri
> che diventasse passato.
> Morto sulla strada.
> E all'acqua irakena
> si appiccica il colletto della sua camicia.
> LA TEMPESTA HA ZANNE.
> STRAPPA *LA* PIOGGIA DEI POVERI.
>
> ... Ya rohi al garibah ...
>
> | VL | | | 3 | | | | 8 | | 11 | | 14 | |
> |---|---|---|---|---|---|---|---|---|---|---|---|---|
> | SN | 1 | | 3 | | 5 | | | | | | | |
> | VL | | 2 | | 4 | | | 8 | | 10 | | 12 | 14 |
> | SN | 1 | | | | 5 | | | | | | | |
> | VL | 1 | | | | | 6 | 8 | 9 | | | 12 | |

QS 1		3				
OT 1			4	7		
SN 1			5			
SN	2		5			
VL	2		6		12	
SN	3		5			
OT 1			4	7		
OT 1		3		7		

[Unable to recount the bravery on the fields, | or even to sing *O bella ciao!* | The people no longer carry red flowers. | He who kept our lost hymns | Is dead on the street. | Without a past | which would become history. | Dead on the street. | And the collar of his shirt sticks | to Iraqi water. | THE STORM HAS FANGS | IT RIPS THE RAIN OF THE POOR]

RG 13, 7–17

Da una sponda all'altra traiamo naufraghi.
I pastori se ne vanno verso le dimore del tramonto
e noi siamo nella risolutezza giovani,
la canizie è sopra le nostre gioie fragili.
In occasione di ogni assenza ho cercato datteri
che spazzassero la tua ferita:
osserverò nel desiderio una candela
che solleva il giorno dal buio
(e l'oscurità appartiene al mio silenzio).

ED	3	5	8				
VL	3		7	9		13	17
VL	3			10	12		
VL	3	5	8	10	12		
VL		4	8		11	13	
DS	3			9			
VL		4	8		12		
VL		5	7		11		

[We tow the survivors from one shore to another. | The shepherds leave for their sunset abodes | and, in our resolve, we are young; | dotage hovers over our fragile joys. | With every absence I searched for dates | to clean your wound: | with longing, I will look at a candle | that lifts the day from darkness | (and darkness belongs to my silence).]

RG 13, 16–17

Perciò il tremore salta un'altra volta nel mio corpo.
Rivolge la parola a ciò che resta delle trecce della notte.

VL	2	4	6	8	10	14	
VL	2		6	8	10	14	18

[Thus the tremor invades my body once more. | It speaks to the threads of night that remain]

In the first example, again taken from *Corona sull'acqua d'amore* [Crown on the water of love] (*RG* 11), the differentiation between four voices is mirrored not only in the graphical aspects and the division of stanzas, as we have seen, but also in multilingual dynamics, syllabic extensions, and, more subtly, linear pulsations. In the second example, the passage from an individual to a collective voice is foregrounded by the alternation of rhythmical inflections. The poet uses the iambus for the individual utterance and the anapaest for the collective one. While the use of the anapaest for the collective utterances is not surprising, the identification of the fast-paced iamb with the individual voice in *Roghi* occurs especially in the sharpest, most rage-filled, and most expressive instances. As such, on a further level, prosodic ambiguity underpins dynamics of exclusion and inclusion, estrangement and alienation, and is sometimes but not always dissolved upon entrance into the rhythmic collective and shared dimension.

A second rhythmical pillar of the collection resides indubitably in the expressive use of repetition, which occurs in the book with and without *variatio*. In a previous study, I discussed the centrality of iterative dynamics within the Arabic poetic tradition and shed light on their expansive use by Iraqi-Italian authors.[45] The presence of repetitions in *Roghi*, which constitutes Al Nassar's ultimate stylistic signature, can thus be conceptualized as a further sign of the emergence of the hidden metre.

The typologies of iterative devices are extremely abundant in the book. Repetitions may be employed in sequence or may be placed in related openings and closes located at significant distances from each other, increasing in the latter cases the formal-semantic circularity of the long poems. They can also be used as a method of establishing identities between stanzas, opening a dialogue between segments that the self-sufficiency of partitions and the end-stopped configurations seem rather to deny. On a more fine-grained level, sets of anaphors may enhance the phenomenological decomposition of the phrase that has been demonstrated to be recurrent in *Roghi*. Some of the most crucial uses of the figure are exemplified below:

> Fra lei e la grande città le mappe del mondo.
> <u>Monti, campi d'erba, foreste nel cielo</u>
> ed alberi sulle pianure.
> [...]
> Adesso fra il suo paese e la grande città
> <u>ci sono monti e campi d'erba e foreste nel cielo</u>. (*RG* 3, 1–3, 34–35)

[Maps of the world lie between the big city and her. | Mountains, fields, forests in the sky | and trees on the plains. [...] Now between her country and the big city | there are mountains and fields and forests in the sky.]

> <u>Lei</u> entra nel presente,
> [...]
> È <u>lei</u> che entra nella Guerra
> [...]
> <u>Lei</u> è quel bianco che ha perso il suo segreto (*RG* 15, 1, 25, 38)

[She enters into the present | [...] It is she who enters the war | [...] She is that white that has lost its secret]

E come un bambino
volevo difendere
il mio paradiso
dal confine dei castelli
<u>di</u> legno,
<u>di</u> rabbia,
<u>di</u> pianto
o <u>di</u> quel vento
che fa crollare un fiore... (*RG* 24, 43)

[And like a child | I wanted to defend my paradise | from the border | of wood, | of raging, | of crying | castles | or of that wind | that makes a flower crumble...]

<u>GUERRA</u>.
<u>Guerra</u> del cielo più alto,
<u>guerra</u> della terra,
<u>guerra</u> dell'acqua,
<u>guerra</u> del sangue,
<u>guerra</u> dei ragazzi perfetti,
<u>guerra</u> dei ragazzi sbagliati,
<u>guerra</u> dei ragazzi sciolti,
<u>guerra</u> delle lettere scritte nel profondo della notte,
<u>guerra</u> delle zone fredde,
<u>guerra</u> della sabbia che bussa alla porta di ferro,
<u>guerra</u> di truppe animose,
<u>guerra</u> di soldati corrosi e senza volto
che occupano il fiume,
occupano il male,
occupano il bicchiere dell'acqua.
<u>GUERRA</u>. (*RG* 23, 15–31)

[WAR | war of highest sky, | war of the soil, | war of water, | war of blood, | war of perfect youth, | war of mistaken youth, | war of unfettered youth, | war of letters written in the depth of night, | war of the cold zones, | war of the sand that knocks at the iron door, | war of spirited troops, | war of corroded and faceless soldiers | who occupy the river, | who occupy evil, | who occupy this glass of the water, | WAR.]

It is clear that iterative dynamics contribute to the identification of phonosemantic nodes within the long compositions, and act as elements of cohesion therein. This trajectory is enhanced when identical repetitions involve a set of key words, as in the following example:

l'ansia, come d'<u>esilio</u>, scorre da un regno sconosciuto
portando, portando i segreti delle ragazze agli specchi
o verso pietre, a volte porta i nomi degli amanti, a volte porta
i nomi dell'<u>esilio</u>
adesso l'<u>amore</u> non entra nell'inquietudine del tuo cuore
tremo per i golfi oscuri, come quelli che ritornano da te
con le vele del <u>mare</u>
dai confini dell'oriente distrutto fino all'occidente esploso
abbiamo dovuto entrare nel <u>mare</u>, per nascondere le isole
della <u>paura</u> e della sconfitta. (*RG* 4, 57–66)

[anguish, like exile, flows from an unknown kingdom | bringing, bringing the secrets of the girls in the mirror | or towards stones, sometimes it carries the names of lovers, sometimes it carries | the names of exile | love not does not enter the restlessness of your heart | I tremble across the dark gulfs, like those that return to you | with the sails of the sea | from the borders of the East, destroyed, to the exploded West | we have had to enter the sea, to hide the islands | of fear and of defeat.]

The excerpt, taken from the long poem *Esilio* [exile] (*RG* 4), which consists of sixty-six lines in total, demonstrates the multiple emergences of a series of key words, which travel through the entire body of the text. Among the repeated terms are the thematic words *esilio* [exile] (1, 10, 40, 45, 57, 60), *amore* [love] (11, 21, 55, 61), *città* [city] (6, 29, 49), *paura* [fear] (10, 51, 66), *fuoco* [fire] (22, 23), *cuore* [heart] (55, 61), *mare* [sea] (63, 65), and *ombra* [shadow] (19, 26, 35). This type of iteration may be supported by the metrical articulation.

The play on repetitions extends beyond a simple or linear use of anaphora. Al Nassar also insists on other liminal iterative figures, such as epistrophe and anadiplosis, which connect the ends of lines and the ends and beginnings of lines respectively. Moreover, the author demonstrates a notable sensitivity toward double iterative figures, such as symploce, which combines anaphora and epistrophe; epanadiplosis, which consists of the repetition of a word or syntagma at the beginning and at the end of a line or phrase; and epizeuxis, in which words or groups of words are repeated in rapid succession. All these figures contribute to the intensification of rhythmical and formal-semantic identities, corroborating a process of hyperbolic and almost obsessive reprise that also makes visible the resistant action of the mother tongue within the translingual verse:

> vederti portare la patria sulla testa
> come un cappello da sole
> [...]
> non abbiamo soffitti
> che ci riparino dal sole, (*RG* 5, 131–32, 138–39)
>
> [seeing you carry your homeland on your head | like a sunhat [...] we have no roof | to shelter us from the sun]
>
> Abbiamo declinato
> il prato verso la sabbia,
> e la sabbia verso il fiume,
> e il fiume verso i pesci e i gabbiani. (*RG* 9, 7–10)
>
> [We have pushed | the pasture towards the sand | and the sand towards the river, | and the river towards the fish and the seagulls]
>
> L'aria schiaccia l'aria.
> L'acqua schiaccia l'acqua.
> La terra schiaccia la terra. (*RG* 12, 100–02)
> [Air crushes air. | Water crushes water. | Soil crushes soil.]
>
> Le nostre mani sono nella carne del corpo
> e il corpo della carne è nelle nostre mani, (*RG* 13, 77–78)

[Our hands are in the flesh of the body | and the body of the flesh is in our hands]

e <u>tu, tu</u> sii tranquilla (*RG* 16, 24)

[and <u>you, you</u> be still]

<u>portando, portando</u> i segreti delle ragazze agli specchi (*RG* 4, 28)

[bringing, bringing the secrets of the girls in the mirrors]

The poet favours double and circular figures, as they support him in infusing circularity into the diction and increasing the syntactical closure of both stanzas and lines. Often these are combined with chiasmi and inversions (*RG* 13). Linear repetitions, and *geminatio* in particular, increase the emphasis on phonosemantic nodes and are often used to foreground allocutions. Finally, liminal figures, especially those that occur at the ends of lines, tend to substitute or perfect rhymes (*RG* 5).

A different level of iteration involves hybrid figures of non-identical repetition. In the context of *Roghi*, repetition with *variatio* is a crucial device, as it supports the poet in embodying deformative-expressionist trajectories that constitute an important semantic juncture within the collection. For instance, paronomastic dynamics, whose inflections include polyptoton and figura etymologica, are often used to embody a heightened level of linguistic pain, where the relation between word and matter is marked by incommunicability. In this sense, the abundance of non-identical iterations possesses an even stronger semantic value with respect to identical repetitions, as it identifies a swerve, a liminal and contrapuntal tension, that mimetically alludes to the complexity of the experience of languaging in exile.

Alla stazione i ferrovieri <u>non l'han vista</u>,
<u>non la vide</u> nessuno dei passeggeri (*RG* 3, 7–8)

[At the station the railwaymen have not seen her, | none of the passengers have seen her]

<u>tremarono</u> le pagine ultime del libro
e <u>tremasti</u> anche tu. (*RG* 5, 195–97)

[they trembled — the final pages of the book — | and you trembled too.]

<u>l'ho ignorato</u> e <u>l'ignoro</u> (*RG* 8, 17)
[I have ignored it and I ignore it.]

è l'ultimo <u>marinaio</u> meridionale
che il <u>mare</u> non rammenta, (*RG* 5, 34–35)

[he is the last southern sailor | who the sea does not remember]

È rimasto <u>addormentato</u>
come <u>dormono</u> (*RG* 19, 29–30)

[He remained asleep | like [the dead] sleep]

un <u>sogno</u> fresco
sulla mensa del <u>sonno</u>. (*RG* 11, 30–31)

[a new dream | on the sleep's table]

Cresce <u>rossa la rosa</u>
nello spazio del cuore. (*RG* 24, 22–23)

[The rose grows red | in the space of the heart]

<u>Palmeti, come pianeti</u>, come costellazioni, di fuoco (*RG* 4, 53)

[Palm groves, like planets, like constellations, of fire]

In conclusion, both articulations of repetition allow Al Nassar's complex relationship with language and the contrapuntal tension that foregrounds his translingual verse to emerge. On the one hand, the centrality of these figure within *Roghi*'s verse demonstrates that the rhythmical values of the mother tongue perform a pivotal function within the translingual diction; on the other, this centrality foregrounds the complexity of the experience of moving and writing across languages and cultures.

Linguistic Deformation and Mobile Trajectories

It is now clear that Al Nassar's translingual verse is characterized by a series of mobilizing, transformative, and deformative tensions. This aspect is also reflected in the lexical choices. First of all, out of the three authors whose works are investigated herein, Al Nassar is the one who attempts most consistently, and right from the beginning of the translingual experience, to access literariness and to infuse rhetorical density into his work. As I have explained, this process is realized primarily through rhythmic strategies and repetitions, but it is also inscribed in the lexical values that emerge from the texts. On a quantitative level, the frequency list foregrounds the recurrence of a series of key words, which configure themselves as critical phonosemantic marks.[46] Among the most frequently recurring terms are, for instance, *guerra* [war] (51 occurrences), *acqua* [water] (46), *amore* [love] (36), *fuoco* fire (32), *terra* [land] (32), *città* [city] (30), *mare* [sea] (19), and *corpo* [body] (19). There is also a high frequency of terms that allude to temporal determinants, such as *notte* [night] (35) and *giorno* [day] (29). Finally, a prominent space is given to pronominal deixis, with *nostro* [ours] (86), *mio* [my] (68), *suo* [her/his/its] (57), and *tuo* [your] (52) all among the ten most recurrent words.

In previous sections, I have mentioned that *Roghi* marks the emergence of a language of pain, as becomes clear from a close analysis of metalinguistic and metapoetic inserts. Compared to Hajdari and Pumhösel, Al Nassar inserts fewer allusions to the acts of talking and writing into his verse. When he does so, the actions of talking and writing are often unfinished, or performed by non-human actors, or related to ideas of separation and deformation. As such, poems foreground dynamics of enduring, rather than performing, the experience of languaging.

Mi hai chiesto | di scrivere il giorno dopo [you asked me | to write the day after] (*RG* 25; 19–20); E NELLA NOTTE È STATA SCRITTA LA FERITA [AND OVERNIGHT THE WOUND HAS BEEN WRITTEN] (*RG* 10, 42); Anni senza calici d'amore che li scrivano [Years without goblets of love to write them] (*RG* 11, 53); dove la notte scrive il mio silenzio e la mia siccità [where the night writes my silence and my drought] (*RG* 22, 15); Chi scriverà, a me o a te, queste righe in ritardo? [Who will write, to me or you, these late lines?] (*RG* 17, 19); Sono così lontani i giorni nei quali volevamo scrivere | i nostri nomi? [Are they so distant, the days when we hoped to write | our names?] (*RG* 19, 42–43); prima di incidere una sola parola, | fuoco [before engraving one single word | fire] (*RG* 12, 15–16); Ho scritto sul fazzoletto — amore quando torni — | balbetto [I wrote on a handkerchief — my love, when will you return — | I stammer] (*RG* 12, 51–52); dove su Shatra si spezza il cielo | dove ridico le parole [where sky breaks on Shatra | where I retell the words] (*RG* 13, 58–59); e parlo con il mare, | parlo con la taverna che mi scaccia via, | con l'aria che dorme lontano dalle finestre del mio sonno [and I speak with the sea, | I speak with the tavern that drives me away | with the air that sleeps far from the window of my dreams] (*RG* 13, 102–04).

In *Roghi*, the subject is rarely found engaging with the spoken or written word. The gestures of both speaking and writing are frequently approached, yet they are often unachieved. As the excerpts show, these gestures are often suffered through, delegated to other moments, or even performed by elements themselves (*RG* 10; *RG* 11; *RG* 19; *RG* 17; *RG* 22). When the subject is involved in the communicative process, the dialogue may be enacted without a clear interlocutor (*RG* 13), thus enhancing the focus on the impossibility of saying (*RG* 12; *RG* 13). In this sense, it is significant that one of the very few moments in which Al Nassar captures the subject's act of writing evokes a makeshift setting, and refers to a brief note written on a *fazzoletto* [tissue], while the central subject is caught in the act of *balbettare* [stammering] (*RG* 12). Within these metalinguistic inserts we thus find consistent allusions to aphasia and, once again, attempts to draw nearer to something that is constantly kept in a distant and unreachable location. On the whole, the only way in which communication is fully possible is through the deformative act of screaming, which is embedded in the numerous inflections of the verb *gridare*. We find this verb in highly metaphorical inserts such as *e gridava in me un'esplosione* [and an explosion was screaming in me] (*RG* 4, 12); *le nostre bocche gridano* [our mouths scream] (*RG* 9, 4); *ma quando grida uno di noi* [but when one of us screams] (*RG* 11, 100); *Dal deserto esco gridando il tuo nome* [I come out of the desert screaming your name] (*RG* 13, 53); *con il rantolo dell'impaurito, gridiamo all'incursione* [with the gasp of the fearful, we scream at the encroachment] (*RG* 18, 63). In lexical-semantic terms, then, communication is reduced to a powerfully disfiguring and rage-filled gesture. Overall, the major direction in which the metalinguistic inserts move is thus not towards linearity, but rather towards rupture and distortion.

It is worth lingering on the further dynamics of linguistic mobilization that more broadly comply with the polyphonic, deformative, and expressionist tropes that are central to the poetic profile of *Roghi*. These include, for instance: the use of multilingual inserts; the use of ellipses, anacoluthon, and other strategies that enhance indeterminateness; the metaphorical use of verbs including parasynthetic forms; the deviant use of prepositions that do not usually accord with the verbs to which they are connected; and finally the foregrounding of words through the overabundant use of inversions. Transcribed below are examples of some of these features:

> Appoggiamoci alla candela dell'amore. | Cantando YA ROHI AL GARIBAH | Ya rohi al garibah ... | O ANIMA MIA STRANIERA ! ! ! [Let's lean against the candle of love. | Singing YA ROHI AL GARIBAH | Ya rohi al garibah... | OH MY FOREIGN SOUL ! ! !] (*RG* 11, 34–37); Non ha detto che il verziere di Zamil | è un martire che i missili hanno distrutto [He did not say that the orchard of Zamil | is a martyr destroyed by missiles] (*RG* 13, 64–65); cercheremo il segno di Alhaj Hannon Atiya | nella kufia dei lavoratori a giornata [we will look for signs of Alhaj Hannon Atiya | in the kufia of the day labourers] (*RG* 18, 108–09).

★ ★ ★ ★ ★

> Spine stanno sui pori della mano [Thorns lodge in the pores of the hand] (*RG* 2, 26); I rivoltosi di vasi di fiori [flowerpots insurgents] (*RG* 12, 1); e la terra come i compagni è stanca [and the soil, like the comrades, is tired] (*RG* 4, 41); e quando l'estate parte [and when summer leaves] (*RG* 4, 32); Apro l'estate annegata di stelle [I open the summer drowning in stars] (*RG* 11, 22); irando con i lupi [raging with the wolves] (*RG* 11, 39); ti porgo a bere [I give you to drink] (*RG* 18, 18); E balzano i piccioni dall'erba [and the pigeons leap from the grass] (*RG* 18, 20); Per questo porto ripetendo | l'obbrobrio della morte [For this I carry, repeating | the shame of death] (*RG* 12, 3–4); Abbiamo declinato | il prato verso la sabbia, | Per questo i nostri sogni | sono inseriti sciolti (*RG* 9, 9–12) [We have declined | the pasture for the sand | for this our dreams | are inserted unleashed]; si affratella alla Virtù [fraternises with Virtue] (*RG* 6, 12).

★ ★ ★ ★ ★

> rosse rose [roses, red] (*RG* 5, 122); costumi dei neri anni [customs of the years, dark] (*RG* 7, 21); ci fa paura della donna asceta la rabbia [she scares us — the ascetic woman — her rage] (*RG* 11, 64); a lui offriamo dell'olivo il ramo [the branch of the olive tree, to him we offer it] (*RG* 11, 101); e noi siamo nella risolutezza giovani [and, in our resolve, we are young] (*RG* 13, 9)

The first set of excerpts foregrounds the use of multilingualism. Transliterations from Arabic are often employed to support polyphonic articulations and to identify refrains (*RG* 11). In other occurrences, multilingualism is related mostly to onomastic and toponomastic inserts (*RG* 13; *RG* 18) and may be signalled graphically through the use of capital letters or italics (*RG* 11; *RG* 13). Significantly, Al Nassar never provides translations of multilingual inserts, nor does he provide footnotes or glossaries. As such, with respect to the textual taxonomies identified by Brioni, he appears to be quite an irrelative case, as the mother tongue is not only domesticated within the depths of the translingual diction, but is also allowed to speak in its material and musical values, without any preoccupation with translating its meaning.

The following suite of excerpts identifies a forceful and translational use of language and structures (verbs in particular), which denotes Al Nassar's desire to apply pressure to the semantic boundaries of the second language, and as such to remould it from the inside. Finally, the last examples demonstrate the action of inversions, which play an important role in corroborating the combinatory and deformative processes of *Roghi*. Evidently, these have consequences not only from a syntactical point of view, but also for the detection and illumination of a series of key words and semantic nodes.

In the use of language, other processes also reveal themselves to be pervasive, such as the presence of a harsh and overabundant metaphorization and the recurrence of transitional figures such as personification. Metaphors, especially expressionistic ones, represent the core of *Roghi*'s transformative nature, and infuse the verse with imaginative tension. On the other hand, personifications also act as important elements of more-than-human entanglement, as well as language reinvention.

> duro come polvere della tristezza (a volte) [hard like the dust of sadness (sometimes)] (*RG* 4, 56); vederti portare la patria sulla testa | come un cappello da sole [seeing you carry your homeland on your head | like a sunhat] (*RG* 5, 131–32); né il giardino o i nostri vermi alleati (*RG* 13, 76 [neither the garden nor our allied worms]; Annuso i sogni miei disordinati [I sniff my messy dreams] (*RG* 13, 105); Chi spegnerà le lucciole nella casa oltre il fiume? [Who will turn off the fireflies in the house across the river?] (*RG* 17, 18); Questa, una notte verde: | spara rondini di luce [This, a green night: | it shoots swallows of light] (*RG* 21, 2–3).

★ ★ ★ ★ ★

> Respirano le spiagge nelle tenebre [the shores breathe in darkness] (*RG* 4, 17); IL MATTINO SERRA | LE TENDE DELL'ALBA [THE MORNING LOCKS | THE CAMP OF DAWN] (*RG* 10, 40–41); come lupo si ferma la Notte [night rests like a wolf] (*RG* 11, 9); La febbre ti schiaffeggia [the fever strikes you] (*RG* 11, 47); LA TEMPESTA HA ZANNE. | STRAPPA LA PIOGGIA DEI POVERI [The storm has fangs. | It rips the rain of the poor] (*RG* 11, 84–85); Nel mio corpo dorme la notte [In my body night sleeps] (*RG* 13, 67); sono quelli che infilano una vela | nel cuore dell'inferno [they are the ones who put a sail | in the heart of hell] (*RG* 18, 10–11); prima che rotoli il mattino (*RG* 18, 78) [before morning comes] ; L'acqua tace [the water falls silent] (*RG* 21, 32); spunterà dal cuore della terra [it will sprout from the heart of the land] (*RG* 24, 18).

Metaphors are one of the spaces in which words have the greatest potential to take on concepts that remain inexpressible outside of distortive processes (see for instance *vederti portare la patria sulla testa | come un cappello da sole* [seeing you carrying your homeland on your head | like a sunhat] *RG* 5). On the other hand, rather than indicating forms of binding between human and non-human as is the case in Pumhösel, personifications seem to support dynamics of plastic transformation and contact in Al Nassar.

I have mentioned above that *Roghi* is a collection substantially built on contrasts and oppositions. This quality emerges in the treatment of spatial indexicality as well. Spatial indexicality is abundant, and is particularly visible in expressions of proximity, which the various inflections of the demonstrative adjective *questo* [this] embrace. Below I provide a mapping of the most central occurrences within the book:

> in un angolo di *questa terra* possiedo il mare [in a corner of this land I own the sea] (*RG* 13, 33); Avanzeranno, dunque, in *questa parata* [They will advance,

thus, in this parade] (*RG* 13, 39); si innalzerà un'altra stella da *questo sentiero* [another star will rise from this path] (*RG* 17, 21); Era *questa* la *strada* del riccio [this was the street of the burr] (*RG* 18, 45); *Questa* è la *spiga* della terra [this is the sheaf of the land] (*RG* 20, 6); e che sarà rivestita *questa casa* che crolla [and that this crumbling house will be covered] (*RG* 21, 27); Conosce *questo corpo* l'amore? [Does this body know love?] (*RG* 26, 1); *Questo* è il *campo* del cuore [this is the field of the heart] (*RG* 18, 24); Chi solleva ora *questa notte*? [Who now raises this night?] (*RG* 11, 130); distruggerò *questo tormento* [I will destroy this torment] (*RG* 13, 41); Chi visiterà la tua casa in *questo esilio*? [who will visit your home in this exile?] (*RG* 13, 42); *questo brivido* segreto nel corpo [this secret quiver within the body] (*RG* 18, 7); Sono *questo rovesciamento* [They are this reversal] (*RG* 18, 8, 38); *questo* è l'*eterno* che lieto dorme [this is the eternal that softly sleeps] (*RG* 20, 7); *Questo* è un *silenzio* [this is a silence] (*RG* 21, 1); più feroce è *questa paura* [this fear is fiercer] (*RG* 22, 2); e *questa nudità* penetra [and this nudity pierces] (*RG* 5, 17).

The occurrences of *questo* in the excerpts above perform two distinct functions. On the one hand, they may either foreground an idea of home (*RG* 13; *RG* 20; *RG* 21; *RG* 26) or reinforce a focus on movement and the journey itself (*RG* 13; *RG* 17; *RG* 18). On the other hand, they may converge on intangible elements, as is demonstrated by the second block of references. The latter group of occurrences is the largest, and further stresses the location of the subject within metaphorical spaces. The treatment of temporal referents as matter, which can be seen in the opening example (*RG* 11), is a very interesting one in this regard. The occurrences of the adjective *quello* [that] are comparatively rarer, and are mostly used to foreground the past.

> Lontani sono *quei momenti* portati dalla leggerezza del vento [Far are those moments carried on the lightness of the wind] (*RG* 2, 25); costruite su *quegli anni* morti [built on those dead years] (*RG* 4, 30); Cammina di nascosto in *quel suo corpo* accogliente [it lies hidden in that warm body of hers] (*RG* 13, 27); *quel pallore* [that pallor] (*RG* 14, 18); in *quell'ora* del mattino [at that hour of the morning] (*RG* 14, 29); *quel bianco* da cui si sono allontanati [that white from which [the skies] departed] (*RG* 15, 41); E vorrei vederti un'altra volta in *quella strada* [and I would like to see you again in that street] (*RG* 17, 23); E persino l'ultima riga di *quel paese* [and even that country's last border] (*RG* 18, 12); noi in *quell'oro* ritorniamo [in that gold we return] (*RG* 18, 86); il giornale in quei giorni [in those days, the newspaper] (*RG* 19, 13); o di *quel vento* [or of that wind] (*RG* 24, 42); E *quel corpo* che fece gemere il passerotto [and that body that made the sparrow weep] (*RG* 26, 27).

As emerges from the analysis developed across the preceding paragraphs, *Roghi*'s diction shows important points of contact with metaphorical expressionism and the descriptive categories that Contini introduced in order to critically approach it.[47] This trait is confirmed by the significant emergence of a focus on action within the book, visible in the recurrence of verbal forms. Significantly for my discourse, the verse of *Roghi* is richly peppered with verbs of movement. Comparing the occurrences that emerge from the concordances to Patrizia Violi's taxonomy, Al Nassar seems to prefer verbs that allude to linear movement, just as the other two authors do, rather than forms that allude to transformation. In fact, among the most frequently occurring are *portare* [to carry] (29 occurrences), *entrare* [to enter] (27), *venire* [to come] (15), *uscire* [to go out] (14), *cadere* [to fall] (11), *fuggire* [to escape] (11), and *passare* [to pass] (10), although forms such as *crescere* [to grow] (4), *emigrare* [to emigrate] (4), and *allungarsi* [to stretch] (2) are also attested. The taste for unusual and literary words leads Al Nassar to also employ verbs such as *giungere* [to reach] (2), *balzare* [to jump] (1), *estendere* [to extend] (1), *insinuarsi* [to insinuate oneself] (1), *salpare* [to weigh anchor] (1), and *zampillare* [to gush] (1). Within his use of verbs of movement, dynamic forces prevail over plastic and modelling ones. On the whole, this could be seen as a counterpoint to the focus on transformation that is conveyed through other devices such as metaphor and personification. In the same way that deixis anchors texts to the referential world and to metaphorically distorted spaces, verbs of movement support the depiction and celebration of a perpetual linear movement. In conclusion, the lexical analysis shows the depth of Al Nassar's translingual operation, and confirms, through the surfacing of a constitutive contrapuntality, that movement and transformation are fundamental forces in *Roghi*.

Notes to Chapter 4

1. For a reconstruction of the historical circumstances see Charles Tripp, *A History of Iraq* (Cambridge: Cambridge University Press, 2007), esp. pp. 186–276. On the Iraqi diaspora see Ibrahim Sirkeci, 'Iraqi International Migration: Potentials for the Postwar Period', *Population Review*, 43.1 (2004), 37–49; Géraldine Chatelard, 'Migration from Iraq between the Gulf and the Iraq Wars (1990–2003): Historical and Sociospacial Dimensions', *University of Oxford, Centre on Migration, Policy and Society*, 2009 <http://www.compas.ox.ac.uk/publications/working-papers/wp-09-68/#c221> [accessed 25 August 2013]; Scott Anderson, 'The Iraqi Diaspora', *Aperture*, 198 (2010), 68–79.
2. Hasan Atiya Al Nassar, *La letteratura dell'esilio: il caso iracheno* (Milan: CUSL, 1996), pp. 12–13.
3. See Pisanelli and Toppan, pp. 183–94.
4. See Pisanelli and Toppan, p. 184.
5. Al Nassar contributed to the Lebanese journal *Al-Menfiyon* and played an active role in associations such as 'Lega degli scrittori, giornalisti e artisti democratici iracheni'. From the late 1990s, with fellow poet and scholar Fawzi Al Delmi, he was the editor of the section on Arabic and Persian poetry for the Italian journal *Semicerchio. Rivista di poesia comparata* <http://semicerchio.bytenet.it/> [accessed 23 April 2020]. During those years, he reviewed the works of Adonis (18 (1998), pp. 88–90; 19 (1998), pp. 91–93), Mahmud Darwish (24–25 (2001), pp. 105–06), Nizar Qabbani (18 (1998), p. 86), Barakat Salim (19 (1998), p. 93), and Aziz al-Samawi (20–21 (1999), p. 157).
6. Mia Lecomte, *Di un poetico altrove*, p. 117.
7. For a mapping of influxes see Colombo and Sciortino, *Gli immigrati in Italia*, p. 29; Macioti and Pugliese, *L'esperienza migratoria*, p. 31.
8. In an article published in 2015, by cross-referencing data available in the Basili database with those provided by Francesco Cosenza in his bibliographic mapping *Letteratura nascente e dintorni: bibliografia aperta* (Milan: Biblioteca Dergano-Bovisa, 2011), I identified eleven authors of Iraqi origin who published literary works in Italian in the timeframe 1995–2003. For details see Loda, '"Dolce era la notte": Iraqi and Iranian Poets in Italy', p. 107.
9. *Quaderno mediorientale I*.
10. Pino Blasone, 'Salvaci dall'esilio dell'afasia!', in *Quaderno mediorientale I: Iraq* (Florence: Loggia de' Lanzi, 1998), pp. 7–15.
11. See Blasone.
12. Pisanelli and Toppan, p. 280.

13. See Loda, '"Dolce era la notte": Iraqi and Iranian Poets in Italy'.
14. See Said.
15. Pisanelli and Toppan, p. 278.
16. Lecomte, *Di un poetico altrove*, p. 117.
17. See Loda, '"Dolce era la notte": Iraqi and Iranian Poets in Italy', pp. 110–20.
18. See Loda, '"Dolce era la notte": Iraqi and Iranian Poets in Italy', pp. 111–13.
19. For an overview see Roger Allen, 'Poetry', in *An Introduction to Arabic Literature* (Cambridge: Cambridge University Press, 2000), pp. 65–132.
20. Pisanelli and Toppan, p. 186.
21. Pisanelli and Toppan, p. 278.
22. Lecomte, *Di un poetico altrove*, p. 123.
23. Thea Laitef, *Lontano da Baghdad* (Rome: Sensibili alle foglie, 1994), p. 88.
24. Hasan Atiya Al Nassar, *Poesie dell'esilio* (Florence: DEA, 1991); *Roghi sull'acqua babilonese*; *Il labirinto* (Florence: La Penultima, 2013). *Il labirinto* was then issued in a second edition (Pallare: Matisklo, 2015) and in a third posthumous edition, revised and expanded (Rome: Ensemble, 2018). This latter volume contains a critical introduction by Edoardo Olmi and a foreword by Marco Incardona. The collection includes Al Nassar's poems emerged as a part of the activities of the Florentine literary collective *Affluenti*, which holds a very active and prominent presence in the contemporary italophone literary scene.
25. Excerpts from the second book, which is the object of my analysis, are referred to within this chapter with the abbreviation *RG*, followed by the number of the poem in order of appearance, and by the indication of line numbers where relevant.
26. See Pisanelli and Toppan, pp. 183–94.
27. Pisanelli and Toppan, p. 186.
28. Pisanelli and Toppan, p. 189.
29. *Quaderno mediorientale I*; Al Nassar, *Poesie dell'esilio*.
30. See in particular the review of *Roghi* in Silvana Grippi, 'Edizioni DEA: Hasan Atiya Al Nassar' <http://www.deapress.com/culture/letteratura/14774-edizioni-dea-hasan-atiya-Al Nassar.html> [accessed 28 February 2020].
31. Shemtov, 'Metrical Hybridization'.
32. See Pisanelli and Toppan, p. 278.
33. Allen, p. 128.
34. Suzanne Pinckney Stetkevych, *Early Islamic Poetry and Poetics* (Farnham: Ashgate, 2009), p. 13.
35. See for instance Stefan Sperl and Christopher Shacke, *Qasīda Poetry in Islamic Asia and Africa* (New York: Brill, 1996).
36. The function of the *qasīda* of embodying passage and its conservation in time has been at the centre of scholarly attention. See for instance Jaroslav Stetkevych, *The Zephyrs of Najd: The Poetics of Nostalgia in the Classical Arabic Nasib* (Chicago, IL: University of Chicago Press, 1993); Suzanne Pinckney Stetkevych, *Reorientations: Arabic and Persian Poetry* (Bloomington: Indiana University Press, 1994).
37. For a comprehensive mapping, see Figure A.5 in the Appendix.
38. *Silenzio* is one of the texts that is reproposed in various editions without variants. Al Nassar constantly places the composition in strategic positions, for instance in the middle of *Poesie dell'esilio* and at the end of his sylloges in *Quaderno Mediorientale I*.
39. Younis Tawfik, *La straniera* (Milan: Bompiani, 1999). On Tawfik's use of the prosimetrum and the entanglements with the form of *maqamat* see M. Cristina Mauceri, '*La straniera* di Younis Tawfik: un dialogo tra due culture', *Italian Studies in Southern Africa/Studi d'italianistica nell'Africa australe*, 16.1 (2003), 8–25; Rosanna Morace, *Letteratura-mondo italiana* (Pisa: Edizioni ETS, 2012), pp. 191–218.
40. Loda '"Dolce era la notte": Iraqi and Iranian Poets in Italy', p. 115.
41. See Allen, pp. 74–75, 120, 210. See also Julie Scott Meisami, 'Arabic and Persian Concepts of Poetic Form: Divergences in Interrelated Poetic Systems', in *Proceedings of the 10th Congress of the International Comparative Literature Association, New York (1982)*, ed. by Anna Balakian and James Wilhelm (New York: Garland, 1985), pp. 146–55.

42. This use is not surprising, as in the classical tradition, the anapaest is the metre of choral poetry. See Lucia Athanassaki and Ewen Lyall Bowie, *Archaic and Classical Choral Song: Performance, Politics and Dissemination* (Boston, MA: De Gruyter, 2011).
43. *Quaderno mediorientale I*, pp. 63–64.
44. See Shemtov, 'Metrical Hybridization'.
45. Loda, ' "Dolce era la notte": Iraqi and Iranian Poets in Italy', pp. 113–15.
46. See the list of most frequent occurring words in the Appendix, Table A.3.
47. See Contini.

CONCLUSION

This book has examined in depth the foundational qualities of the translingual verse, as they emerge from the works of Gëzim Hajdari, Barbara Pumhösel and Hasan Atiya Al Nassar. I have begun with a theoretical exploration of a series of critical notions, which has allowed me to conceptualize literary translingualism as a trajectory, one that travels expansively over space and time and identifies a varied realm of intersections. The critical exploration of a series of travelling concepts, such as resistance, distance, rhythm and movement, has enabled me to identify some of the constitutive forces that shape the translingual experience, within and beyond an Italophone literary field. More specifically, I have observed how dynamics of resistance operate within the translingual verse in active opposition to monolingualizing pressures, countering binary and non-fluid understandings of languages and cultures. Furthermore, I have pinpointed that linguistic distance infuses the translingual verse with a groundbreaking and transformative tension and has the effect of recasting the perception of the outer reality and the experience of language for the authors. Finally, a critical exploration of the concept of rhythm has allowed me to foreground the ways in which contrapuntal dynamics are inscribed in the innermost formal-semantic qualities of the translingual verse. The notion of rhythm has also been connected to physical movement and trajectories of mobility, according to an entanglement that the authors themselves commonly point out. On a broader scale, the articulation of a critical discourse has enabled me to intersect stylistic methodologies with cultural theory and to assert the significance of a close approach to texts in the context of translingual and migrant writing.

In the three chapters dedicated to Hajdari, Pumhösel and Al-Nassar, respectively, I have comprehensively explored the qualities of their translingual verse. This analysis has allowed me to identify a series of common features as well as substantial differences in the emergence and development of the authors' translingual paths. Important differences surface from the authors' distinctive interpretations of translingualism, which hold important connections with the diverse circumstances of their migration to Italy. Hajdari inhabits translingualism by developing a double language. The surfacing of this double language is extremely significant if considered in light of the colonial and postcolonial dynamics that historically permeate the relationship between Italy and Albania. The double language is a strictly antihierarchical instrument, and it foregrounds the mutual embeddedness of Albanian and Italian, based on their rhythmical encounter. As such, its articulation embodies a radical mobilization of power relationships and opens novel linguistic spaces, which are infused with relationality and fluidity. Meanwhile, Pumhösel interprets translingualism as an act of radical liberation, one that allows her to get closer to words and their material qualities and to deepen her discourse on more-than-human entanglements. As such, Pumhösel explores the generative force of linguistic distance, which she cultivates as an empowering tool. Finally, Al Nassar reacts to his forced migration by developing a language of pain, one which expressionistically marks his translingual verse. In his poems, the translingual verse is used as a tool to actively resist from within the experience of exile.

In terms of diachronic transformation of the translingual verse, the experiences of the three authors are distinctive. This is visible, for instance, in the poets' positioning with respect to the mother tongue and its literary tradition as well as in the evolution of this positioning over time. For Hajdari, the entanglements with the Albanian poetry tradition vary considerably in parallel to the progress of the translingual experience. While the entanglements are erased in an early translingual phase, the poet devises a path toward their progressive recuperation, which culminates in the vigorous contrapuntality of the last epic phase. Once Hajdari governs his translingual verse and concludes his theoretical excavation into body and exile, his verse begins to open and to demonstrate its transmediterranean nature in full. This is a path towards an assertive dimension that Andrea Gazzoni has traced, more broadly, in Hajdari's whole literary path, and one that he connects to the progressive increase in physical distance from Albania.[1] Notably, for Pumhösel and Al-Nassar, the relationship with the tradition of the mother tongue does not undergo a significant transformation over time. Pumhösel's dialogue with the Germanophone tradition is mostly visible in her use of intertextuality as well as in prosodic and lexical memories. However, this dialogue is immediately diluted and complicated within a verse that firmly rejects any national affiliation. On the contrary, Al Nassar allocates to the first language and its tradition a central generative force. This force also stems from the practice of self-translation and, more generally, from the poet's positioning with respect to his linguistic displacement. In fact, Al Nassar approaches the second language out of non-choice, in response to the need of being read and building an audience in Italy. In the most mature phases of his translingual practice, the author partly abandons the practice of self-translation, but he maintains on the whole an extremely close relationship with the mother tongue and its tradition. This relationship is used in his verse as an active instrument to resist the lacerating experience of physical and linguistic displacement.

In terms of textual geographies, Hajdari, Pumhösel and Al Nassar's poems present extremely variegated profiles. Nonetheless, contrapuntality and fluidity emerge as radical forces in the verses of all three authors. Hajdari's favourite module is the quatrain. Notably, this is a central structure in Albanian popular and epic poetry, and it is a common structure within the Italophone tradition as well. Hajdari inflects his quatrain differently according to the progression of his translingual experience. More specifically, he employs it in short poems in the first Albanian phase, retracts it in his early translingual works, and returns to it in the long compositions of the last epic phase. Through his double language, the increasing entanglements with the Albanian poetry tradition and the progressive morphological merging of Albanian and Italian, Hajdari rhythmically reinvents a structure that connects the two literary traditions across which he moves. Pumhösel's treatment of textual geographies goes decidedly in another direction. First, poetic forms in her verse perform a material function, and their concrete nature supports the development of an ecocentric trajectory. Second, her poems are shaped toward a constitutive brevity, and they emerge from a generative process of carving and subtraction. Both aspects, and the latter in particular, explain Pumhösel's attraction to the haiku. The engagement with the haiku holds many layers of significance in the context of Pumhösel's translingual writing. For example, the form is used by the author to strengthen the transnational trajectory and the semantics of interconnectedness that her verse identifies. Meanwhile, Al Nassar designs a very specific trajectory with his use of poetic forms. Since his early translingual works, he demonstrates an attraction for the long poem, which he maintains over time. Al Nassar's long poems have a distinctive structure, and they allocate a central expressive role to the stanzas, which are used to embody contrast, movement, and plastic distortion. Because of their entanglements with the long song *qasīda*, as well as their fluid metrical and linguistic profile, the long poems are configured as the main product of contrapuntal and dialogic translingual forces.

On a metrical level, all three poets move across the fluid boundaries of the free verse. Their works commonly foreground an attraction for accentual isochronism, which is one of the hidden effects of their first languages within the translingual verse. Hajdari and Al Nassar use rhythm in dialogic ways, thereby increasing the polyphonic dynamics in their verse. As such, they strictly engage with the process of metrical hybridisation conceptualized by Vered Shemtov.[2] Both poets tend to associate slow rhythms with a collective voice and fast articulations to an individual one. Notably, the employment of iconic metres of the Italophone tradition, such as the *settenario* and the *endecasillabo*, is significant for all the authors. In particular, the *settenario* is a central module, and it is chosen chiefly for its agile sensual qualities. In Hajdari's poems, the occurrence of this metre can be placed in relation to the extensive dissemination of its homologue in Albanian popular and epic poetry. In Pumhösel, the high occurrence of *settenario* is instead impacted by the formal requirements of the haiku. Al Nassar uses the module mostly to impress a ground pace on his long poems and to reinforce accentual trajectories. Furthermore, in inflecting the *endecasillabo*, the most famous metre in the Italophone tradition, the authors reach some of the highest levels of metrical fluidity. The dynamics of mobilization of this metre emerge not only in the many multilingual inflections of it but also, and most centrally, in the distinctive rhythmical qualities that it comes to assume as an effect of the process of translanguaging. Both Hajdari and Al Nassar tend to employ the *endecasillabo* to enhance the literariness of their texts, and they place it in strategic positions, such as at the edges of compositions and verses. On the contrary, Pumhösel inserts the *endecasillabo* within her system of plain and anti-lyrical diction, thus employing it as a means for establishing contrastive tensions in the diction.

On the whole, the examination of lexical values revealed an important degree of reinvention of the second language. This is manifested by the authors' use of multilingual inserts, calques, and neologisms. These spaces of transformation of language, which Gianfranco Contini expansively discussed within the context of metaphorical expressionism,[3] play an important role in the authors' translingual works, where they are consistently accompanied by metaliguistic inserts. For Hajdari, an embodiment of pain and cruelty in language-related imagery characterizes the early translingual phase. With time, the author releases this tension and begins to build, rather, on the generative effect of moving across languages. Pumhösel is the one author who expands most copiously on the metalinguistic discourse. In her poems, language itself takes life and power, often subjugating and controlling the human sphere. This is a dimension that Pumhösel shares with other translingual authors, such as Yoko Tawada.[4] While in all the three authors' works we find the idea of being written, submerged and dominated by language, it is only in Pumhösel that this idea becomes a trope, one which foregrounds an ecocentric and anti-anthropocentric trajectory. In Al Nassar's verse, only a small number of poems explicitly allude to language, and they rely in these cases on a sharp metaphorisation and a constitutive distortion. As such, talking is most often related to the act of screaming, an aspect that embodies a linguistic wound that cannot be soothed.

Finally, the analysis reveals that representations of movement are central in the authors' verses. The attention to movement is inscribed, first, into a fluid use of indexicality. For Hajdari and Al Nassar, spatial deixis results in a play on oppositions and marks the contrastive unfolding of past and present scenes. For Pumhösel, referential marks mostly foreground an understanding of the world as a system that is in perpetual movement. All the authors point frequently to the interchangeability of spatial and temporal referents. As such, days, nights, and hours are intensively inhabited and travelled. This contributes to increasing and complicating the discourse on movement, especially considering Violi's conceptualization of the latter as a sum of subject, space and temporality.[5] The use of verbs of movement is consistently significant in the authors' works, and overall it defines linear trajectories rather than plastic transformation. Finally, the experience of physical and linguistic crossing emerges in the abundance of transitional imagery, which is recurrent in all the authors' works, and central in Pumhösel's, where it foregrounds more-than-human interconnections.

In conclusion, this research on the translingual verse has discussed the radical transformative power that physical and linguistic movement holds in the process of versification. Translingual migrant poetics not only embody novel and fertile poetic ecologies but also perform a pivotal function in devising more inclusive and fluid ideas about the world in which we are all immersed. While future analyses on this theme are desirable, I hope that this book has contributed by acknowledging movement and contact as crucial generative forces in the contemporary literary space and, hopefully, in its progressive historicization.

Notes to the Conclusion

1. Gazzoni, 'Una terra scritta dall'esilio'.
2. Shemtov, 'Metrical Hybridization'.
3. Contini, pp. 89–105.
4. See Yoko Tawada, 'Portrait of a Tongue', in *Yoko Tawada's Portrait of a Tongue: An Experimental Translation by Chantal Wright*, by Chantal Wright and Yoko Tawada (Ottawa: University of Ottawa Press, 2013), pp. 35–144.
5. Violi, p. 85.

BIBLIOGRAPHY

'VI° Seminario italiano degli scrittori e delle scrittrici migranti' <http://www.sagarana.net/scuola/seminario6/seminario4.html> [accessed 22 June 2016]

'VII° Seminario italiano degli scrittori e delle scrittrici migranti' <http://www.sagarana.net/scuola/seminario7/seminario1.html> [accessed 12 October 2016]

7 poeti del Premio Montale, Roma 1997: Laura Maria Gabrielleschi, Gezim Hajdari, Gabriella Pace, Biagio Salmeri, Oliver Scharpf, Francesca Traina, Sebastiano Triulzi (Milan: All'insegna del pesce d'oro, 1998)

AFRIBO, ANDREA, *Poesia contemporanea dal 1980 a oggi: storia linguistica italiana* (Rome: Carocci, 2007)

AL NASSAR, HASAN ATIYA, *Il labirinto* (Florence: La Penultima, 2013; 2nd edn, Pallare: Matisklo, 2015; 3rd edn, Rome: Ensemble, 2018)

—— *La letteratura dell'esilio: il caso iracheno* (Milan: CUSL, 1996)

—— *Poesie dell'esilio* (Florence: DEA, 1991)

—— *Roghi sull'acqua babilonese* (Florence: DEA, 2003; 2nd edn, 2004)

ALLEN, ROGER, 'Poetry', in *An Introduction to Arabic Literature* (Cambridge: Cambridge University Press, 2000), pp. 65–132

ANDERSON, SCOTT, 'The Iraqi Diaspora', *Aperture*, 198 (2010), 68–79

ANDORNO, CECILIA, *Linguistica testuale: un'introduzione* (Rome: Carocci, 2003)

ARMATO, FRANCESCO, *Premiata Compagnia delle poete* (Isernia: Cosmo Iannone, 2013)

ARNDT, SUSAN, DIRK NAGUSCHEWSKI, and ROBERT STOCKHAMMER, eds, *Exophonie: Anders-Sprachigkeit (in) der Literatur* (Berlin: Kadmos, 2007)

ATHANASSAKI, LUCIA, and EWEN LYALL BOWIE, *Archaic and Classical Choral Song: Performance, Politics and Dissemination* (Boston, MA: De Gruyter, 2011)

BAKHTIN, MIKHAIL MIKHAILOVICH, *Speech Genres and Other Late Essays*, ed. by Michael Holquist and Caryl Emerson, trans. by Vern W. McGee (Austin: University of Texas Press, 1986)

BAL, MIEKE, *Travelling Concepts in the Humanities: A Rough Guide* (Toronto: University of Toronto Press, 2012)

BARTHES, ROLAND, *Mythologies* (Paris: Éditions du Seuil, 1957)

BASILI, 'Banca Dati sugli Scrittori Immigrati in Lingua Italiana, University of Rome La Sapienza', <http://www.disp.let.uniroma1.it/basili2001/> [accessed 10 August 2013]

BAYNHAM, MIKE, and TONG KING LEE, *Translation and Translanguaging* (New York: Routledge, 2019)

BHABHA, HOMI K., *The Location of Culture* (London: Routledge, 1994)

BLASONE, PINO, 'Salvaci dall'esilio dell'afasia!', in *Quaderno mediorientale I: Iraq* (Florence: Loggia de' Lanzi, 1998), pp. 7–15

BOND, EMMA, and DANIELE COMBERIATI, eds, *Il confine liquido: rapporti letterari e interculturali fra Italia e Albania* (Nardò: Besa, 2013)

—— 'Narrare il colonialismo e il postcolonialismo italiani: la "questione" albanese', in *Il confine liquido: rapporti letterari e interculturali fra Italia e Albania*, ed. by Emma Bond and Daniele Comberiati (Nardò: Besa, 2013), pp. 7–30

BOUCHANE, MOHAMED, *Chiamatemi Alì*, ed. by Carla De Girolamo and Daniele Miccione (Milan: Leonardo, 1991)

BOUCHARD, NORMA, 'Reading the Discourse of Multicultural Italy: Promises and Challenges of Transnational Italy in an Era of Global Migration', *Italian Culture*, 28.2 (2010), 104–20

BREGOLA, DAVIDE, *Il catalogo delle voci: colloqui con poeti migranti* (Isernia: Cosmo Iannone, 2005)

BRIONI, SIMONE, *The Somali Within: Language, Race and Belonging in Minor Italian Literature* (Oxford: Legenda, 2015)

BROWN, CHARLES ARMITAGE, *Life of John Keats*, ed. by Dorothy Hyde Bodurtha and Willard Bissell Pope (London: Oxford University Press, 1987)

BRYSON, J. SCOTT, *Ecopoetry: A Critical Introduction* (Salt Lake City: University of Utah Press, 2002)

BUELL, LAWRENCE, *The Environmental Imagination: Thoreau, Nature Writing, and the Formation of American Culture* (Cambridge, MA: Harvard University Press, 1996)

BUFFONI, FRANCO, ed., *Ritmologia. Atti del convegno 'Il ritmo del linguaggio. Poesia e traduzione'. Università degli Studi di Cassino, Dipartimento di linguistica e letterature comparate. 22–24 Marzo 2001* (Milan: Marcos y Marcos, 2002)

BURNS, JENNIFER, *Migrant Imaginaries: Figures in Italian Migration Literature* (Bern: Peter Lang, 2013)

BURNS, JENNIFER, and CATHERINE KEEN, 'Italian Mobilities', *Italian Studies*, 75 (2020), 1–15 <https://doi.org/10.1080/00751634.2020.1744862>

CANAGARAJAH, SURESH, 'Codemeshing in Academic Writing: Identifying Teachable Strategies of Translanguaging', *The Modern Language Journal*, 95.3 (2011), 401–17 <https://doi.org/10.1111/j.1540-4781.2011.01207.x>

CHATELARD, GÉRALDINE, 'Migration from Iraq between the Gulf and the Iraq Wars (1990–2003): Historical and Sociospacial Dimensions', *University of Oxford, Centre on Migration, Policy and Society*, 2009 <http://www.compas.ox.ac.uk/publications/working-papers/wp-09-68/#c221> [accessed 25 August 2013]

COLANGELO, STEFANO, 'Fonomanzie: appunti preliminari sul plurilinguismo poetico', *Quaderna*, 2 (2014), 1–17

—— 'Haiku e altre piccole tempeste', in *Culture allo specchio: arte, letteratura, spettacolo e società tra il Giappone e l'Europa*, ed. by Wada Tadahiko and Stefano Colangelo (Bologna: Emil, 2012), pp. 116–29

COLOMBO, ASHER, and GIUSEPPE SCIORTINO, *Gli immigrati in Italia* (Bologna: Il Mulino, 2004)

—— 'Italian Immigration: The Origins, Nature and Evolution of Italy's Migratory Systems', *Journal of Modern Italian Studies*, 9.1 (2004), 49–70 <https://doi.org/10.1080/1354571042000179182>

CONTINI, GIANFRANCO, 'Espressionismo letterario', in *Ultimi esercizî ed elzeviri: 1968–1987* (Turin: Einaudi, 1988), pp. 41–105

COSENZA, FRANCESCO, *Letteratura nascente e dintorni: bibliografia aperta* (Milan: Biblioteca Dergano-Bovisa, 2011)

CRECCHIA, ANTONIO, 'Prefazione', in *Antologia della pioggia*, by Gëzim Hajdari (Santarcangelo di Romagna: Fara, 2000), pp. 7–18

D'ALESSANDRO, BARBARA, 'Scavalcare l'orizzonte movimento e transitorietà in Barbara Pumhösel', *Studi interculturali*, 3 (2014), 161–80

DE LUCA, BERNARDO, 'Per una verifica del verso accentuale', *L'Ulisse*, 16 (2014), 20–31

DE MAURO, TULLIO, *Storia linguistica dell'Italia unita* (Rome-Bari: Laterza, 1991)

DELEUZE, GILLES, and FÉLIX GUATTARI, *Kafka: pour une littérature mineure* (Paris: Éditions de Minuit, 1975)

DI GIANVITO, SARA, *In balia delle dimore ignote: la poesia di Gëzim Hajdari* (Nardò: Besa, 2015)
DIONISOTTI, CARLO, *Geografia e storia della letteratura italiana* (Turin: Einaudi, 1971)
DOWLING, SARAH, *Translingual Poetics: Writing Personhood under Settler Colonialism* (Iowa City: University of Iowa Press, 2018)
EDWARDS, NATALIE, *Multilingual Life Writing by French and Francophone Women: Translingual Selves* (New York: Routledge, 2020)
ETIEMBLE, RENÉ, 'Sur une bibliographie du "Haiku" dans les langues européennes', *Comparative Literature Studies*, 11.1 (1974), 1–20
FORSTER, LEONARD, *The Poet's Tongues: Multilingualism in Literature* (London: Cambridge University Press, 1970)
FORTUNATO, MARIO, and SALAH METHNANI, *Immigrato* (Rome: Teoria, 1990)
FRACASSA, UGO, 'Critica e/o retorica: il discorso sulla letteratura migrante in Italia', in *Leggere il testo e il mondo: vent'anni di scritture della migrazione in Italia*, ed. by Fulvio Pezzarossa and Ilaria Rossini (Bologna: Clueb, 2011), pp. 169–82
GARDINI, NICOLA, 'Amelia Rosselli e lo spazio della fuga', *Italianistica*, 2–3 (2002), 111–23
GAZZONI, ANDREA, 'Introduzione. Cantare nel sisma dell'esilio', in *Poesia dell'esilio: saggi su Gëzim Hajdari*, ed. by Andrea Gazzoni (Isernia: Cosmo Iannone, 2010), pp. 9–61
—— 'Nel tempo, in relazione, per frammenti: leggere due decenni attraverso Gezim Hajdari', in *Leggere il testo e il mondo: vent'anni di scritture della migrazione in Italia*, ed. by Fulvio Pezzarossa and Ilaria Rossini (Bologna: Clueb, 2011), pp. 119–218
—— ed., *Poesia dell'esilio: saggi su Gëzim Hajdari* (Isernia: Cosmo Iannone, 2010)
—— 'Una terra scritta dall'esilio: rappresentazioni e traduzioni dell'Albania nell'opera di Gëzim Hajdari', in *Il confine liquido: rapporti letterari e interculturali fra Italia e Albania*, ed. by Emma Bond and Daniele Comberiati (Nardò: Besa, 2013), pp. 137–48
GIOVANNETTI, PAOLO, *Modi della poesia italiana contemporanea: forme e tecniche dal 1950 a oggi* (Rome: Carocci, 2013)
GIOVANNETTI, PAOLO, and GIANFRANCA LAVEZZI, *La metrica italiana contemporanea* (Rome: Carocci, 2010)
GIROUX, JOAN, *The Haiku Form* (Rutland, VT: Tuttle, 1974)
GNISCI, ARMANDO, *Creolizzare l'Europa: letteratura e migrazione* (Rome: Meltemi, 2003)
—— *Via della decolonizzazione europea* (Isernia: Cosmo Iannone, 2004)
GOLDWYN, ADAM, '"Go Back to Homer's Verse": *Iliads* of Revolution and *Odysseys* of Exile in Albanian Poetry', *Classical Receptions Journal*, 8.4 (2016), 506–28
GRIGNANI, MARIA ANTONIETTA, *Lavori in corso: poesia, poetiche, metodi nel secondo Novecento* (Modena: Mucchi, 2007)
GRIPPI, SILVANA, 'Edizioni DEA: Hasan Atiya Al Nassar' <http://www.deapress.com/culture/letteratura/14774-edizioni-dea-hasan-atiya-al-nassar.html> [accessed 28 February 2020]
HAJDARI, GËZIM, *Antologia della pioggia* (Santarcangelo di Romagna: Fara, 2000)
—— *Bitter Grass*, trans. by Ian Seed (Bristol: Shearsman Books, 2020)
—— 'Breve panorama della poesia albanese dagli anni Trenta ad oggi', *Kúmá*, 3.1 (2002) <http://www.arbitalia.it/letteratura/hajdari_poesia_albanese.htm> [accessed 26 March 2017]
—— *Corpo presente* (Tirana: Botimet Dritëro, 1999)
—— *Erbamara* (Santarcangelo di Romagna: Fara, 2001)
—— *I canti del nizam* (Nardò: Besa, 2012)
—— *Maldiluna* (Nardò: Besa, 2005)
—— *Ombra di cane* (Frosinone: Dismisura, 1993)
—— *Peligorga* (Nardò: Besa, 2007)
—— *Poema dell'esilio* (Santarcangelo di Romagna: Fara, 2005)
—— *Poesie scelte (1990–2007)* (Nardò: Controluce, 2008)

―――― *Poezi të zgjedhura (1990–2007)* (Nardò: Besa, 2007)
―――― *Sassi contro vento* (Milan: Laboratorio delle Arti, 1995)
―――― *Spine nere* (Nardò: Besa, 2004)
―――― *Stigmata*, trans. by Cristina Viti (Bristol: Shearsman Books, 2016)
―――― *Stigmate* (Nardò: Besa, 2002)
HAJDARI, GËZIM, and GIULIA INVERARDI, 'Il poeta epico delle montagne maledette. Intervista a Gëzim Hajdari', *Comunicare letterature lingue*, 7 (2007), 299–312
HAJDARI, GËZIM, and ANITA PINZI, 'An Ode to Exile: In conversation with Gëzim Hajdari', *Warscapes*, 2013 <http://warscapes.com/conversations/ode-exile> [accessed 23 April 2019]
HAJDARI, GËZIM, and FRANCESCO ZURLO, 'Intervista in Workout', n.d.
HAKUTANI, YOSHINOBU, *Haiku and Modernist Poetics* (New York: Palgrave Macmillan, 2009)
IOVINO, SERENELLA, 'Loving the Alien. Ecofeminism, Animals, and Anna Maria Ortese's Poetics of Otherness', *Feminismo/s*, 22 (2013), 177–203
IOVINO, SERENELLA, and SERPIL OPPERMANN, *Material Ecocriticism* (Bloomington: Indiana University Press, 2014)
ISSELSTEIN, URSULA, 'Breviario di metrica tedesca', in *La poesia tedesca del Novecento*, ed. by Ursula Isselstein and Anna Chiarloni (Turin: Einaudi, 1990), pp. 423–65
KELLMAN, STEVEN G., *The Translingual Imagination* (Lincoln: University of Nebraska Press, 2000)
KHOUMA, PAP, *Io, venditore di elefanti*, ed. by Oreste Pivetta (Milan: Garzanti, 1990)
KIEMLE, CHRISTIANE, *Ways out of Babel: Linguistic and Cultural Diversity in Contemporary Literature in Italy: Exploring Multilingualism in the Works of Immigrated Writers* (Trier: Wissenschaftlicher Verlag Trier, 2011)
KRISTEVA, JULIA, *Desire in Language: A Semiotic Approach to Literature and Art* (New York: Columbia University Press, 1980)
―――― 'Problèmes de la structuration du texte', in *Théorie d'ensemble* (Paris: Seuil, 1968), pp. 297–316
LAITEF, THEA, *Lontano da Baghdad* (Rome: Sensibili alle foglie, 1994)
LAVEZZI, GIANFRANCA, *I numeri della poesia: guida alla metrica italiana* (Rome: Carocci, 2006)
LECOMTE, MIA, ed., *Ai confini del verso* (Florence: Le Lettere, 2006)
―――― *Di un poetico altrove: poesia transnazionale italofona (1960–2016)* (Florence: Cesati, 2018)
―――― *Sempre ai confini del verso* (Paris: Chemins de traverse, 2011)
LECOMTE, MIA, and LUIGI BONAFFINI, eds, *A New Map: The Poetry of Migrant Writers in Italy* (Los Angeles: Green Integer, 2007)
LERNER, GERDA, 'Living in Translation', in *Switching Languages: Translingual Writers Reflect on their Craft*, ed. by Steven G. Kellman (London: University of Nebraska Press, 2003), pp. 267–88
LIDSTRÖM, SUSANNA, and GREG GARRARD, '"Images Adequate to Our Predicament": Ecology, Environment and Ecopoetics', *Environmental Humanities*, 5.1 (2014), 35–53
LODA, ALICE, 'Corpo e tempo: Eros and Melancholy in Gëzim Hajdari's Transmediterranean Poetics', *Ticontre. Teoria, Testo, Traduzione*, 10 (2018), 137–67
―――― '"Dolce era la notte": Iraqi and Iranian Poets in Italy: Metrical-Stylistic Implications of Translingual Versification', *Italian Culture*, 33.2 (2015), 105–25
―――― 'Eco-Pusterla: A Semantic-Stylistic Analysis of *Bocksten*', *Incontri. Rivista Europea di Letteraura Italiana*, 35.1 (2020), 99–115 <https://doi.org/10.18352/incontri.10337>
―――― 'Exophonic Poetics in Contemporary Italy: Versification and Movement in the Works of Hasan Atiya Al Nassar, Barbara Pumhösel and Gëzim Hajdari' (unpublished doctoral thesis, University of Sydney, 2017)
―――― 'Gli animali nel primo Pusterla: una lettura di "Il dronte" e "L'anguilla del Reno"', *California Italian Studies*, 10.1 (2020), 1–18

Macioti, Maria Immacolata, and Enrico Pugliese, *L'esperienza migratoria: immigrati e rifugiati in Italia* (Rome-Bari: Laterza, 2010)
Manzi, Luigi, 'La notte straniera di Gëzim Hajdari. La luna e la melagrana', in *Poesia dell'esilio: saggi su Gëzim Hajdari*, ed. by Andrea Gazzoni (Isernia: Cosmo Iannone, 2010), pp. 317–21
Marazzini, Claudio, *Breve storia della questione della lingua* (Rome: Carocci, 2018)
Mattei, Alessandra, *La besa violata: eresia e vivificazione nell'opera di Gëzim Hajdari* (Rome: Ensemble, 2014)
Mauceri, M. Cristina, '*La straniera* di Younis Tawfik: un dialogo tra due culture', *Italian Studies in Southern Africa/Studi d'italianistica nell'Africa Australe*, 16.1 (2003), 8–25
―― 'La letteratura italiana della migrazione nei curricula universitari europei e nordamericani', in *Diaspore europee e lettere migrant: primo festival europeo degli scrittori migranti*, ed. by Armando Gnisci and Nora Moll (Rome: Edizioni interculturali, 2002), pp. 145–60
Mazak, Catherine, and Kevin Carroll, *Translanguaging in Higher Education: Beyond Monolingual Ideologies* (Bristol: Multilingual Matters, 2016)
Mazzoni, Guido, *Forma e solitudine: un'idea della poesia contemporanea* (Milan: Marcos y Marcos, 2002)
Meisami, Julie Scott, 'Arabic and Persian Concepts of Poetic Form: Divergences in Interrelated Poetic Systems', in *Proceedings of the 10th Congress of the International Comparative Literature Association, New York (1982)*, ed. by Anna Balakian and James Wilhelm (New York, 1985), pp. 146–55
Mengozzi, Chiara, *Narrazioni contese: vent'anni di scritture italiane della migrazione* (Rome: Carocci, 2013)
Menichetti, Aldo, *Metrica italiana: fondamenti metrici, prosodia, rima* (Padua: Antenore, 1993)
Meschonnic, Henri, *Critique du rythme: anthropologie historique du langage* (Lagrasse: Verdier, 1982)
―― *Poétique du traduire* (Paris: Verdier, 1999)
―― *Pour la poétique II* (Paris: Gallimard, 1963)
Moe, Aaron M., *Zoopoetics: Animals and the Making of Poetry* (Lanham, MD: Lexington Books, 2013)
Morace, Rosanna, 'Carmine abate', in *Letteratura-mondo italiana* (Pisa: Edizioni ETS, 2012), pp. 131–64
―― 'Carmine Abate: un mosaico identitario ricco per adozione', in *Il confine liquido: rapporti letterari e interculturali fra Italia e Albania*, ed. by Emma Bond and Daniele Comberiati (Nardò: Besa, 2013), pp. 98–116
―― *Letteratura-mondo italiana* (Pisa: Edizioni ETS, 2012)
Moretti, Franco, *Graphs, Maps, Trees* (London: Verso, 2005)
Morreale, Maria Teresa, *Fuga verso un 'altrove': l'haiku in lingua tedesca* (Palermo: Società grafica artigiana, 1981)
Negro, Grazia, 'La leggerezza profonda dell'In-der-Welt-sein: la poetica degli oggetti in Barbara Pumhösel', *Kúmá*, 13 (2007) <http://www.disp.let.uniroma1.it/kuma/archivio.html> [accessed 3 December 2013]
―― 'Simmetrie asimmetriche tra umano e natura', in *prugni*, by Barbara Pumhösel (Isernia: Cosmo Iannone, 2008), pp. 149–54
Otsuji, Emi, and Alastair Pennycook, 'Metrolingualism: Fixity, Fluidity and Language in Flux', *International Journal of Multilingualism*, 7.3 (2010), 240–54
Parati, Graziella, 'Introduction', in *Mediterranean Crossroads: Migration Literature in Italy*, ed. by Graziella Parati (Madison, NJ: Fairleigh Dickinson University Press, 1999), pp. 13–42

——— *Migration Italy: The Art of Talking Back in a Destination Culture* (Toronto: University of Toronto Press, 2005)
PARATI, GRAZIELLA, and MARIE ORTON, *Multicultural Literature in Contemporary Italy* (Madison, NJ: Fairleigh Dickinson University Press, 2007)
PASOLINI, PIER PAOLO, 'Nuove questioni linguistiche', in *Empirismo eretico* (Milan: Garzanti, 1995), pp. 5–24
PERLOFF, MARJORIE, *Unoriginal Genius: Poetry by Other Means in the New Century* (Chicago, IL: University of Chicago Press, 2010)
PIPA, ARSHI, *Albanian Folk Verse: Structure and Genre* (Munich: Trofenik, 1978)
——— 'Albanian Metrics', *Südost Forschungen*, 34 (1975), 211–33
PISANELLI, FLAVIANO, 'La Frontière invisible: la poésie italienne de la migration entre diglossie et 'dislocation', identité(s) et dépossession', *Italies*, 13.1 (2009), 487–507
——— 'Pour une "écriture plurielle": la littérature italienne de la migration', *Textes & contextes*, 2 (2008) <http://revuesshs.u-bourgogne.fr/textes&contextes/document.php?id=693> [accessed 19 October 2013]
PISANELLI, FLAVIANO, and LAURA TOPPAN, *Confini di-versi: frontiere, orizzonti e prospettive della poesia italofona contemporanea* (Florence: Firenze University Press, 2020)
POLEZZI, LOREDANA, 'La mobilità come modello: ripensando i margini della scrittura italiana', in *Studi europei e mediterranei*, ed. by Armando Gnisci and Nora Moll (Rome: Università degli Studi di Roma, La Sapienza, 2008), pp. 115–28
——— 'Questioni di lingua: fra traduzione e autotraduzione', in *Leggere il testo e il mondo: vent'anni di scritture della migrazione in Italia*, ed. by Fulvio Pezzarossa and Ilaria Rossini (Bologna: Clueb, 2011), pp. 15–33
——— 'Translation and Migration', *Translation Studies*, 5.3 (2012), 345–56
PUMHÖSEL, BARBARA, *in transitu* (Osimo: Arcipelago Itaca, 2016)
——— 'Il bacio', *El Ghibli*, 44 (2014) <http://www.el-ghibli.org/il-bacio/> [accessed 21 May 2017]
——— 'La frontiera li attraversa: appunti sulla poesia transculturale austriaca', in *I colori sotto la mia lingua: scritture transculturali in tedesco*, ed. by Eva-Maria Thüne and Simona Leonardi (Rome: Aracne, 2009), pp. 151–70
——— *La principessa Sabbiadoro* (Milan: Giunti, 2007)
——— *La voce della neve* (Milan: Rizzoli, 2013)
——— *prugni* (Isernia: Cosmo Iannone, 2008)
——— *Un confine in comune* (Rome: Ensemble, 2021)
PUMHÖSEL, BARBARA, and ANNA SARFATTI, *Amore e pidocchi* (Turin: EDT, 2007)
Quaderno africano I: Nigeria, Camerun, Eritrea (Florence: Loggia de' Lanzi, 1998)
Quaderno balcanico I: Albania, Bosnia (Florence: Loggia de' Lanzi, 1998)
Quaderno balcanico II: Albania, Bosnia, Croazia (Florence: Loggia de' Lanzi, 2000)
Quaderno mediorientale I: Iraq (Florence: Loggia de' Lanzi, 1998)
Quaderno mediorientale II: Iran (Florence: Loggia de' Lanzi, 2000)
QUAQUARELLI, LUCIA, 'Definizioni, problemi, mappature', in *Leggere il testo e il mondo: vent'anni di scritture della migrazione in Italia*, ed. by Fulvio Pezzarossa and Ilaria Rossini (Bologna: Clueb, 2011), pp. 53–64
ROMEO, CATERINA, 'Meccanismi di censura e rapporti di potere nelle autobiografie collaborative', *Between*, 5.9 (2015), 1–28
ROMITO, LUCIANO, and ANDREA TARASI, 'A Rhythmic-Prosodic Analysis of Italian L1 and L2', in *Prosodic and Rhythmic Aspects of L2 Acquisition: The Case of Italian*, ed. by Anna De Meo and Massimo Pettorino (Newcastle upon Tyne: Cambridge Scholars Publishing, 2012), pp. 137–52
ROSA, SILVIA, 'Quella precaria sensazione di equilibrio. Intervista a Barbara Pumhösel', *Poesia del nostro tempo*, 2019 <https://www.poesiadelnostrotempo.it/intervista-a-barbara-pumhoesel/>

Rosselli, Amelia, 'Metrical Spaces', trans. by Jennifer Scappettone, *Chicago Review*, 56.4 (2012), 37–43
—— 'Spazi metrici', in *L'opera poetica*, by Amelia Rosselli, ed. by Stefano Giovannuzzi (Milan: Mondadori, 2012), pp. 181–87
Said, Edward W., *Reflections on Exile and Other Essays* (Cambridge, MA: Harvard University Press, 2000)
Scego, Igiaba, *La nomade che amava Alfred Hitchcock = Ari raacato jecleeyd Alfred Hitchcock*, trans. by Zahara Omar Mohamed (Rome: Sinnos, 2003)
Schmid, Helmut, 'Improvements in Part-of-Speech Tagging with an Application to German', in *Natural Language Processing Using Very Large Corpora*, ed. by Susan Armstrong, Kenneth Church, Pierre Isabelle, Sandra Manzi, Evelyne Tzoukermann, and David Yarowsky (Dordrecht: Springer Netherlands, 1999), pp. 13–25 <https://doi.org/10.1007/978-94-017-2390-9_2>
—— 'Probabilistic Part-of-Speech Tagging Using Decision Trees', in *New Methods In Language Processing*, ed. by Daniel Jones and Harold Somers (London: Routledge, 2013), pp. 154–64
Scott, Clive, 'Translating the Nineteenth Century: A Poetics of Eco-Translation', *Dix-Neuf*, 19.3 (2015), 285–302 <https://doi.org/10.1179/1478731815Z.00000000083>
Segre, Cesare, 'Edonismo linguistico nel Cinquecento', in *Lingua, stile e società: studi sulla storia della prosa italiana* (Milan: Feltrinelli, 1991), pp. 369–96
—— 'La tradizione macaronica da Folengo a Gadda (e oltre)', in *Cultura letteraria e tradizione popolare in Teofilo Folengo. Atti del Convegno di studi promosso dall'Accademia Virgiliana e dal Comitato Mantova-Padania 77 . Mantova 15–16–17 ottobre 1977*, ed. by Mario Chiesa and Ettore Bonora (Milan: Feltrinelli, 1979), pp. 62–74
Shemtov, Vered, *Changing Rhythms: Towards a Theory of Prosody in Cultural Context* (Ramat-Gan: Bar-Ilan University Press, 2012)
—— 'Metrical Hybridization: Prosodic Ambiguities as a Form of Social Dialogue', *Poetics Today*, 22.1 (2001), 65–87
—— 'Prosody as Content, Ideology as Form: A New Approach to Prosodic Theory' (unpublished doctoral thesis, University of California–Berkeley, 2000)
Sibhatu, Ribka, *Aulò: canto-poesia dall'Eritrea* (Rome: Sinnos, 2004)
Sica, Giorgio, 'Come perle intorno ad un filo: breve storia dell'haiku nella poesia italiana', *Esperienze letterarie*, 30.1 (2005), 113–32
Sirkeci, Ibrahim, 'Iraqi International Migration: Potentials for the Postwar Period', *Population Review*, 43.1 (2004), 37–49
Slovic, Scott, 'Translocalità: la nozione di luogo nell'ecocritica contemporanea', in *Ecocritica: la letteratura e la crisi del pianeta*, ed. by Caterina Salabè (Rome: Donzelli, 2013), pp. 27–42
Sperl, Stefan, and Christopher Shacke, *Qasīda Poetry in Islamic Asia and Africa* (New York: Brill, 1996)
Spitzer, Leo, '*Der Unanimismus Jules Romains* im Spiegel seiner Sprache (Eine Vorstudie zur Sprache des französischen Expressionismus)', in *Stilstudien, II: Stilsprachen* (Munich: Hueber, 1928)
Stetkevych, Jaroslav, *The Zephyrs of Najd: The Poetics of Nostalgia in the Classical Arabic Nasib* (Chicago, IL: University of Chicago Press, 1993)
Stetkevych, Suzanne Pinckney, *Early Islamic Poetry and Poetics* (Farnham: Ashgate, 2009)
—— *Reorientations: Arabic and Persian Poetry* (Bloomington: Indiana University Press, 1994)
Stussi, Alfredo, *Introduzione agli studi di filologia italiana* (Bologna: Il Mulino, 2007)
Tawada, Yoko, 'From Mother Tongue to Linguistic Mother', trans. by Rachel McNichol, *Manoa*, 18.1 (2006), 139–43 <https://doi.org/10.1353/man.2006.0039>

—— '"Portrait of a Tongue"', in *Yoko Tawada's Portrait of a Tongue, An Experimental Translation by Chantal Wright*, by Chantal Wright and Yoko Tawada (Ottawa: University of Ottawa Press, 2013), pp. 35–144

TAWFIK, YOUNIS, *La straniera* (Milan: Bompiani, 1999)

TAYLOR, EVA, 'Su due fiumi. — Scrittura bilingue e autotraduzione. Tra riva e sentiero — le poesie sul fiume Erlauf di Barbara Pumhösel', *Arcipelago Itaca. Letterature, visioni ed altri percorsi*, 5 (2011), 179–80

TOPPAN, LAURA, 'La peligòrga di Gëzim Hajdari: "regina degli esuli in fuga"', *Italies*, 13 (2009), 243–60 <https://doi.org/10.4000/italies.2690>

TRIPP, CHARLES, *A History of Iraq* (Cambridge: Cambridge University Press, 2007)

VAJNA DE PAVA, SILVIA, 'La peligorga canta in italiano: la poesia di Gëzim Hajdari e i suoi apporti interculturali', in *Poesia dell'esilio: saggi su Gëzim Hajdari*, ed. by Andrea Gazzoni (Isernia: Cosmo Iannone, 2010), pp. 189–210

VENUTI, LAWRENCE, ed., *The Translation Studies Reader* (London: Routledge, 2000)

VICO, GIAMBATTISTA, *The New Science of Giambattista Vico* (Ithaca, NY: Cornell University Press, 1984)

VIOLI, PATRIZIA, 'La spazialità in moto: per una semiotica dei verbi di movimento', *Versus: quaderni di studi semiotici*, 73–74 (1996), 83–102

VORPSI, ORNELA, and ANTONIA PEZZANI 'Un oceano di distanza. Un'intervista a Ornela Vorpsi.', *Osservatorio Balcani e Caucaso*, 2007 <http://www.balcanicaucaso.org/aree/Albania/Un-oceano-di-distanza-36549> [accessed 14 October 2016]

WRIGHT, CHANTAL, 'Exophony and Literary Translation: What it Means for the Translator when a Writer Adopts a New Language', *Target*, 22.1 (2010), 22–39 <https://doi.org/10.1075/target.22.1.03wri>

—— 'Writing in the "Grey Zone": Exophonic Literature in Contemporary Germany' *German as a Foreign Language*, 9.3 (2008), 26–42

—— 'Yoko Tawada's Exophonic Texts', in *Yoko Tawada's Portrait of a Tongue: An Experimental Translation*, by Chantal Wright and Yoko Tawada (Ottawa: University of Ottawa Press, 2013), pp. 1–21

YASUDA, KENNETH, *Japanese Haiku: Its Essential Nature and History* (North Clarendon, VT: Tuttle, 2011)

YILDIZ, YASEMIN, *Beyond the Mother Tongue: The Postmonolingual Condition* (New York: Fordham University Press, 2011)

ZUBLENA, PAOLO, 'L'infinito qui: deissi spaziale e antropologia dello spazio nella poesia di Leopardi', in *La prospettiva antropologica nel pensiero e nella poesia di Giacomo Leopardi*, ed. by Chiara Gaiardoni (Florence: Olschki, 2010)

APPENDIX

FIG. A.1. Structure of poems in Gëzim Hajdari's *PS* (1). Column 1 (line count per poem) records the total number of lines in each poems. Column 2 (line count per stanza) indicates the number of stanzas in a poem (vertical axis) and the number of lines for each stanza (horizontal axis). Poems are identified by their number (in sequence) and the abbreviation of the section.

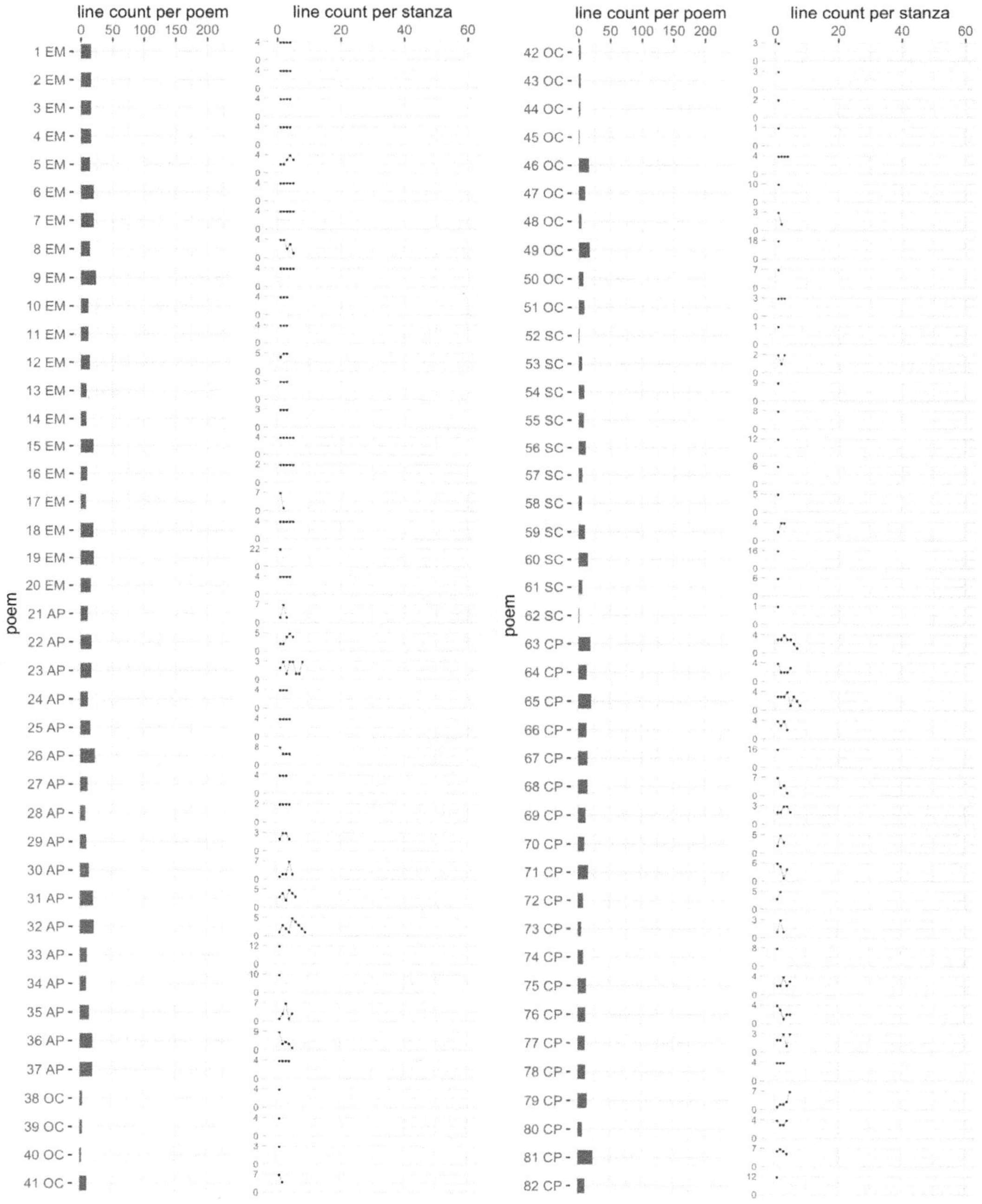

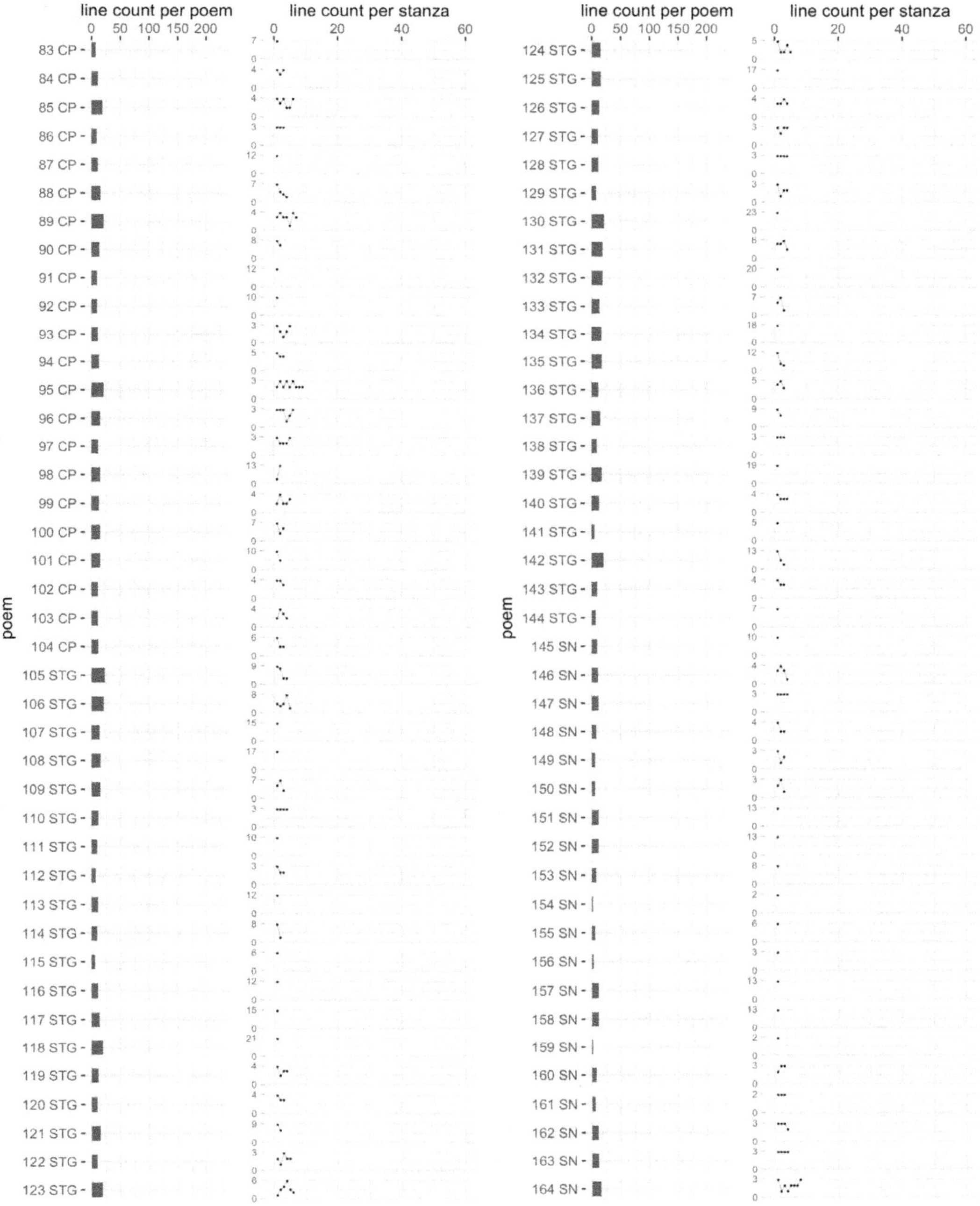
line count per poem
0 50 100 150 200
line count per stanza
0 20 40 60
poem
83 CP
84 CP
85 CP
86 CP
87 CP
88 CP
89 CP
90 CP
91 CP
92 CP
93 CP
94 CP
95 CP
96 CP
97 CP
98 CP
99 CP
100 CP
101 CP
102 CP
103 CP
104 CP
105 STG
106 STG
107 STG
108 STG
109 STG
110 STG
111 STG
112 STG
113 STG
114 STG
115 STG
116 STG
117 STG
118 STG
119 STG
120 STG
121 STG
122 STG
123 STG
line count per poem
0 50 100 150 200
line count per stanza
0 20 40 60
poem
124 STG
125 STG
126 STG
127 STG
128 STG
129 STG
130 STG
131 STG
132 STG
133 STG
134 STG
135 STG
136 STG
137 STG
138 STG
139 STG
140 STG
141 STG
142 STG
143 STG
144 STG
145 SN
146 SN
147 SN
148 SN
149 SN
150 SN
151 SN
152 SN
153 SN
154 SN
155 SN
156 SN
157 SN
158 SN
159 SN
160 SN
161 SN
162 SN
163 SN
164 SN

170 APPENDIX

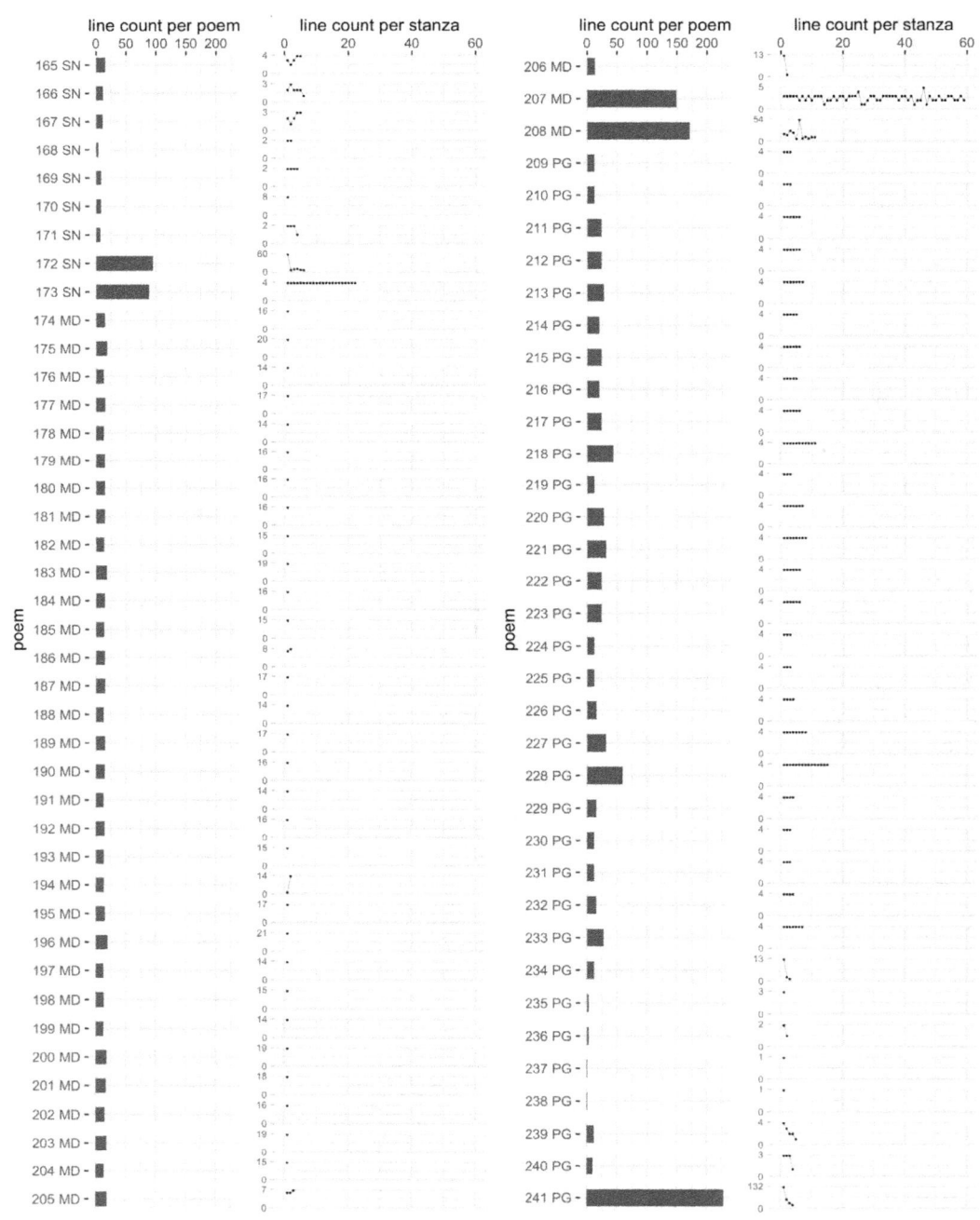

APPENDIX 171

FIG. A.2. Structure of poems in Barbara Pumhösel's *PN* (1). Column 1 (line count per poem) records the total number of lines in each poems. Column 2 (line count per stanza) indicates the number of stanzas in a poem (vertical axis) and the number of lines for each stanza (horizontal axis). Poems are identified by their number (in sequence) and the abbreviation of the section.

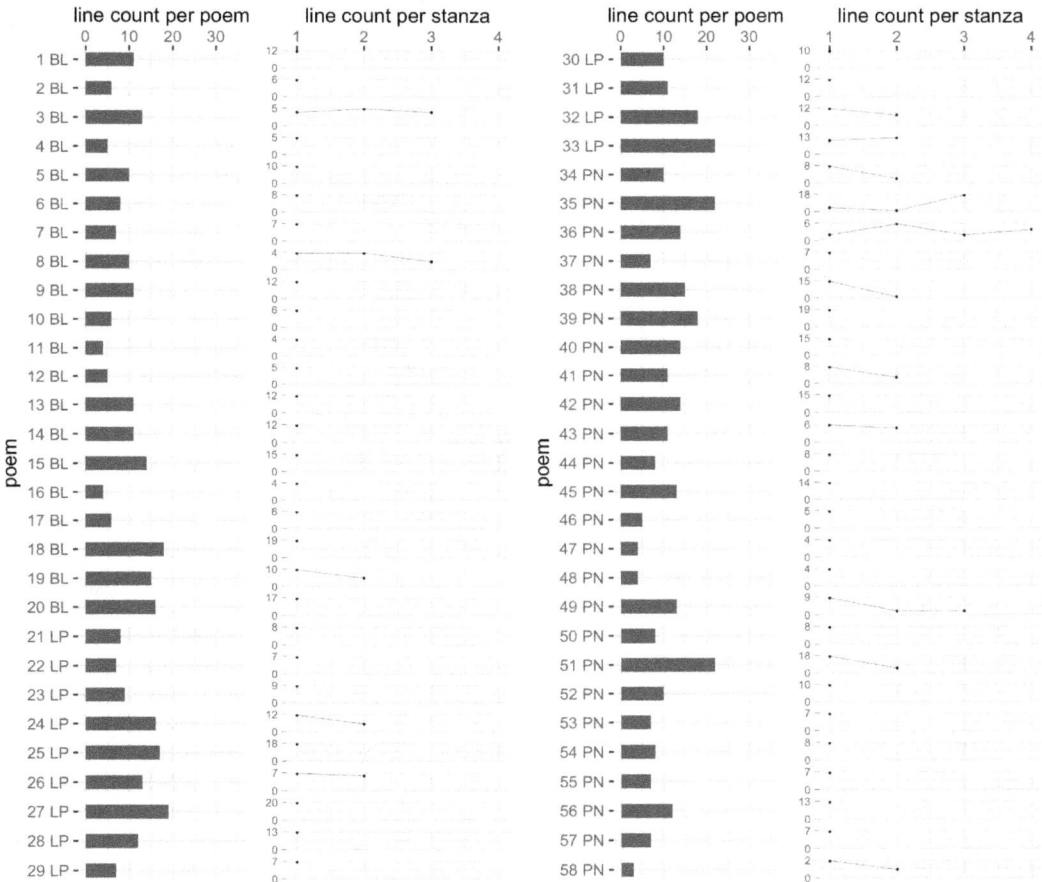

Appendix

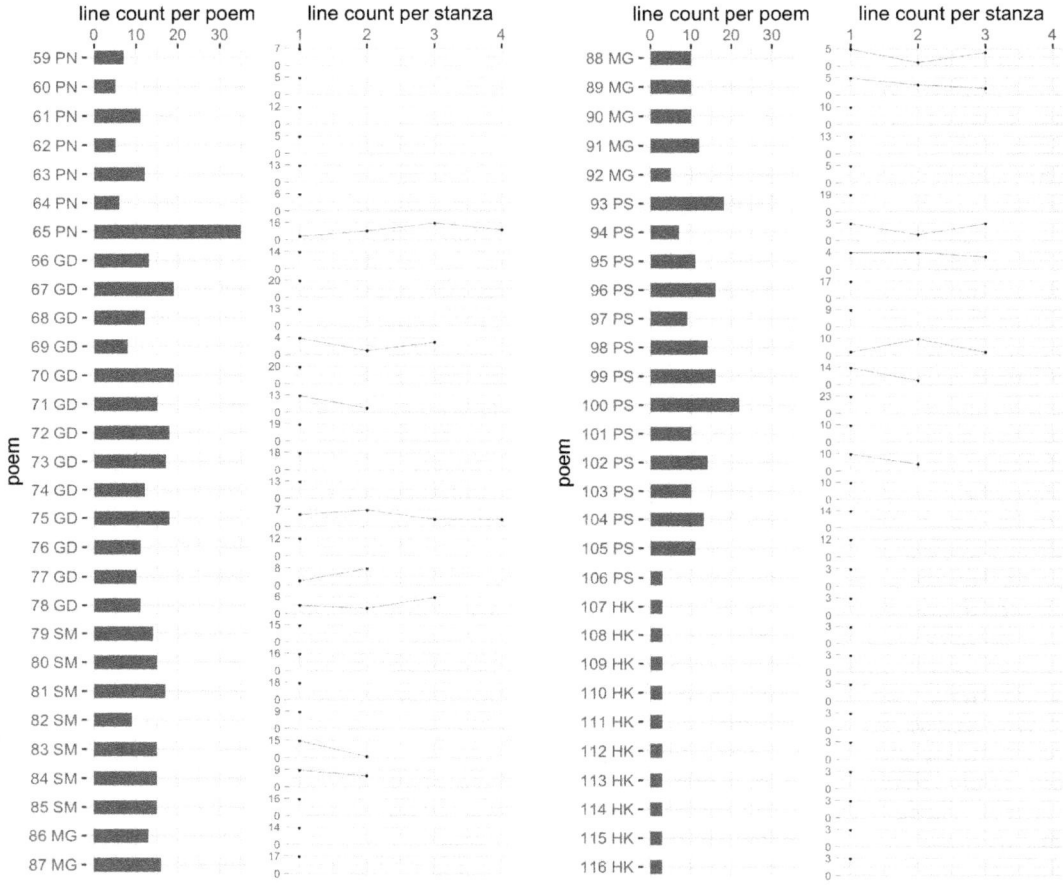

APPENDIX   173

FIG. A.3. Structure of poems in Hasan Al Nassar's RG. Column 1 (line count per poem) records the total number of lines in each poems. Column 2 (line count per stanza) indicates the number of stanzas in a poem (vertical axis) and the number of lines for each stanza (horizontal axis). Poems are identified by their number (in sequence).

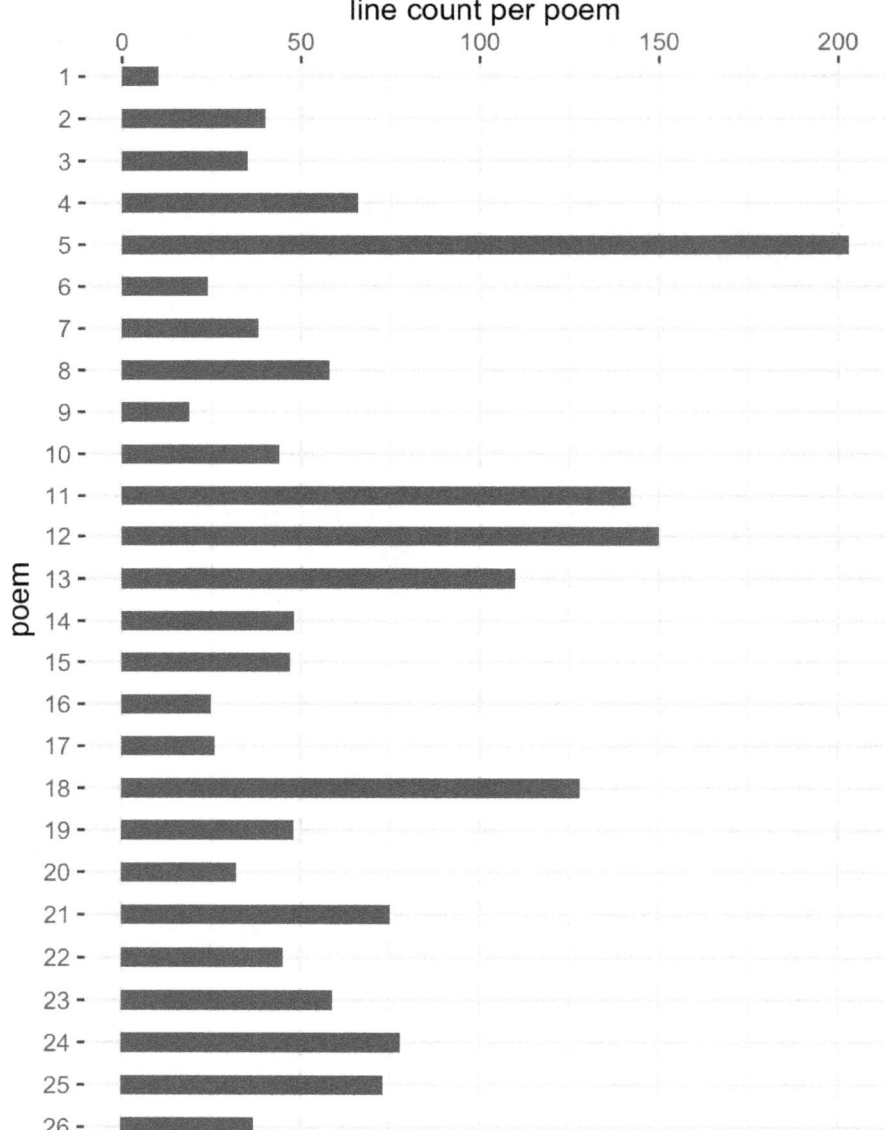

APPENDIX 175

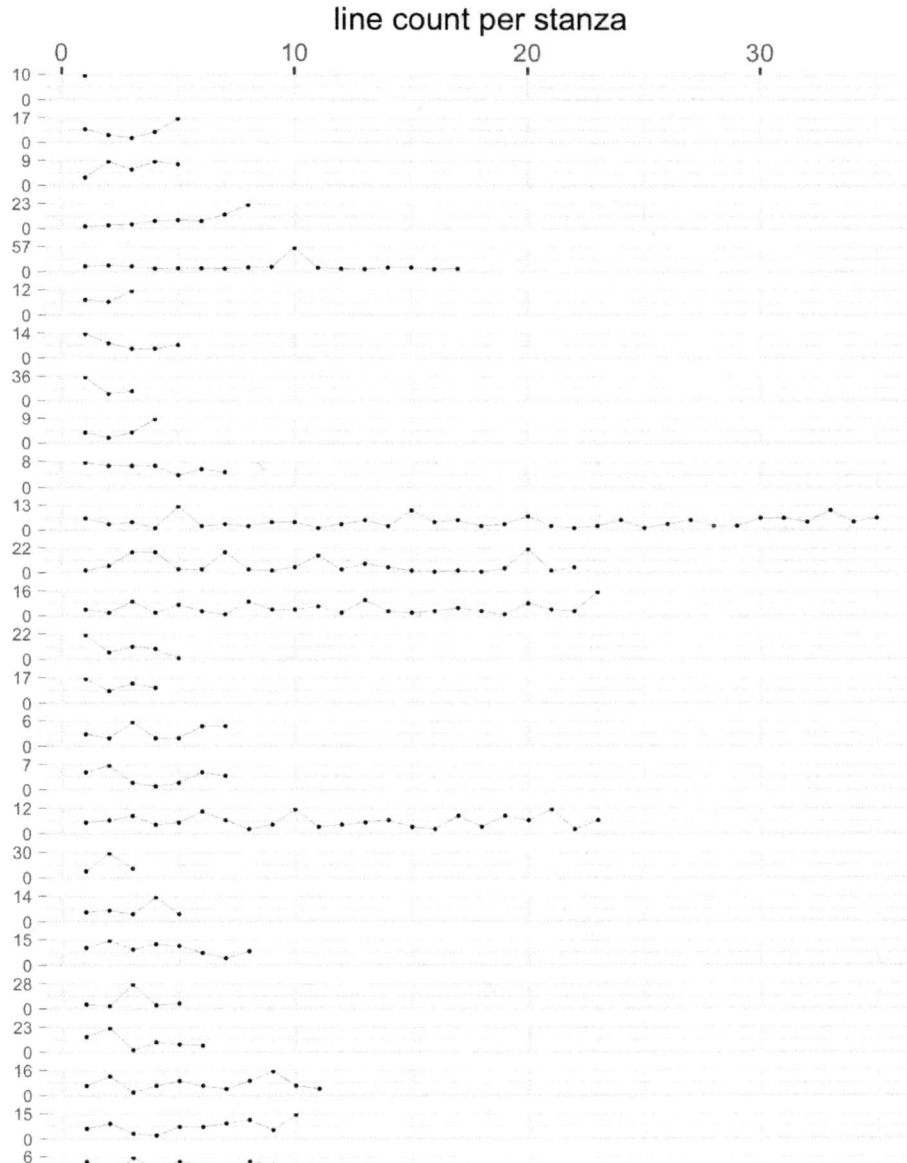

TABLE A.1 Most frequent words in Gëzim Hajdari's *PS*.

The frequency list indicates the part of speech (A = adjective, B = adverb, C = conjunction, P = pronoun, S = noun, V = verb, VA = auxiliary verb) and presents the absolute and relative frequency (AF and RF) of the hundred most frequently occurring words in *PS*.

			AF	RF				AF	RF
1	e	C	647	2.98%	51	buio	S	40	0.18%
2	mio	A	513	2.37%	52	verso	S	39	0.18%
3	tuo	A	343	1.58%	53	portare	V	39	0.18%
4	che	P	279	1.29%	54	mondo	S	38	0.18%
5	essere	V	249	1.15%	55	ma	C	38	0.18%
6	mi	P	233	1.07%	56	vedere	V	38	0.18%
7	non	B	227	1.05%	57	sentire	V	38	0.18%
8	avere	VA	186	0.85%	58	sapere	V	37	0.17%
9	essere	VA	130	0.56%	59	amare	V	37	0.17%
10	ti	P	119	0.55%	60	andare	V	36	0.17%
11	che	C	108	0.49%	61	luna	S	36	0.17%
12	notte	S	95	0.44%	62	volto	S	35	0.16%
13	giorno	S	90	0.42%	63	o	C	35	0.16%
14	si	P	88	0.41%	64	quando	C	35	0.16%
15	questo	A	81	0.37%	65	come	C	34	0.16%
16	ombra	S	75	0.35%	66	paese	S	34	0.16%
17	se	C	74	0.34%	67	mai	B	34	0.16%
18	tu	P	73	0.34%	68	cosa	S	33	0.15%
19	fare	V	69	0.32%	69	patria	S	33	0.15%
20	io	P	67	0.31%	70	canto	S	33	0.15%
21	corpo	S	66	0.30%	71	cercare	V	33	0.15%
22	me	P	64	0.30%	72	fuoco	S	32	0.15%
23	collina	S	64	0.30%	73	uccello	S	32	0.15%
24	tempo	S	61	0.28%	74	sera	S	31	0.14%
25	occhio	S	60	0.28%	75	acqua	S	30	0.14%
26	più	B	58	0.27%	76	albero	S	30	0.14%
27	anno	S	58	0.27%	77	nuovo	A	30	0.14%
28	dove	B	58	0.27%	78	fuggire	V	29	0.13%
29	pioggia	S	57	0.26%	79	volere	V	29	0.13%
30	pietra	S	56	0.26%	80	cadere	V	29	0.13%
31	suo	A	52	0.24%	81	né	C	29	0.13%
32	sangue	S	52	0.24%	82	vita	S	29	0.13%
33	nostro	A	51	0.24%	83	sogno	S	29	0.13%
34	voce	S	51	0.24%	84	nessuno	P	28	0.13%
35	venire	V	50	0.23%	85	uomo	S	28	0.13%
36	cielo	S	50	0.23%	86	primavera	S	28	0.13%
37	nero	A	49	0.23%	87	trovare	V	28	0.13%
38	te	P	48	0.22%	88	quello	P	27	0.12%
39	ci	P	48	0.22%	89	sasso	S	27	0.12%
40	campo	S	48	0.22%	90	volta	S	27	0.12%

41	ogni	A	46	0.21%	91	scrivere	V	27	0.12%
42	altro	A	46	0.21%	92	cenere	S	27	0.12%
43	avere	V	45	0.21%	93	stagione	S	27	0.12%
44	dire	V	45	0.21%	94	labbro	S	27	0.12%
45	anche	B	45	0.21%	95	città	S	26	0.12%
46	terra	S	43	0.20%	96	carne	S	26	0.12%
47	amore	S	42	0.19%	97	sempre	B	26	0.12%
48	nome	S	42	0.19%	98	mano	S	25	0.12%
49	quello	A	41	0.19%	99	destino	S	25	0.12%
50	chiamare	V	41	0.19%	100	crepuscolo	S	25	0.12%

TABLE A.2. Most frequent words in Barbara Pumhösel's *PN*.

The frequency list indicates the part of speech (A = adjective, B = adverb, C = conjunction, P = pronoun, S = noun, V = verb, VA = auxiliary verb) and presents the absolute and relative frequency (AF and RF) of the hundred most frequently occurring words in *PN*.

			AF	RF				AF	RF
1	e	C	222	3.39%	51	foglia	S	12	0.18%
2	essere	V	106	1.67%	52	volta	S	11	0.17%
3	non	B	94	1.44%	53	oggi	B	11	0.17%
4	si	P	67	1.02%	54	andare	V	11	0.17%
5	che	P	59	0.90%	55	aria	S	11	0.17%
6	avere	VA	53	0.81%	56	vita	S	11	0.17%
7	ma	C	41	0.63%	57	tornare	V	11	0.17%
8	fare	V	38	0.58%	58	la	P	10	0.15%
9	mi	P	35	0.53%	59	come	C	10	0.15%
10	anche	B	35	0.53%	60	anno	S	10	0.15%
11	che	C	34	0.52%	61	poesia	S	10	0.15%
12	essere	VA	31	0.49%	62	potere	V	10	0.15%
13	ancora	B	30	0.46%	63	ombra	S	10	0.15%
14	quello	A	29	0.44%	64	pietra	S	10	0.15%
15	io	P	28	0.43%	65	poi	B	10	0.15%
16	parola	S	27	0.41%	66	ed	C	9	0.14%
17	suo	A	26	0.40%	67	tutto	A	9	0.14%
18	più	B	23	0.35%	68	mano	S	9	0.14%
19	mio	A	21	0.32%	69	lei	P	9	0.14%
20	verso	S	20	0.31%	70	vetro	S	9	0.14%
21	volere	V	20	0.31%	71	specchio	S	9	0.14%
22	prugno	S	19	0.29%	72	prima	B	9	0.14%
23	forse	B	18	0.27%	73	dire	V	9	0.14%
24	se	C	18	0.27%	74	pioggia	S	9	0.14%
25	ora	B	18	0.27%	75	segno	S	9	0.14%
26	sapere	V	18	0.27%	76	sole	S	8	0.12%
27	stare	V	17	0.26%	77	mondo	S	8	0.12%
28	notte	S	17	0.26%	78	cadere	V	8	0.12%
29	sempre	B	17	0.26%	79	questo	A	8	0.12%
30	soltanto	B	17	0.26%	80	bianco	A	8	0.12%
31	ci	B	16	0.24%	81	chiedere	V	8	0.12%

32	avere	V	15	0.23%	82	loro	A	8	0.12%
33	ogni	A	15	0.23%	83	dovere	V	8	0.12%
34	quando	C	15	0.23%	84	voce	S	8	0.12%
35	mentre	C	15	0.23%	85	sentire	V	8	0.12%
36	me	P	14	0.21%	86	insieme	B	8	0.12%
37	quello	P	14	0.21%	87	passare	V	8	0.12%
38	prugna	S	14	0.21%	88	fermare	V	8	0.12%
39	terra	S	13	0.20%	89	pensiero	S	8	0.12%
40	altro	A	13	0.20%	90	solo	A	7	0.11%
41	vedere	V	13	0.20%	91	stesso	A	7	0.11%
42	o	C	13	0.20%	92	nuovo	A	7	0.11%
43	ramo	S	13	0.20%	93	continuare	V	7	0.11%
44	immagine	S	13	0.20%	94	rimanere	V	7	0.11%
45	lo	P	12	0.18%	95	ne	P	7	0.11%
46	vento	S	12	0.18%	96	pagina	S	7	0.11%
47	altro	P	15	0.23%	97	crescere	V	7	0.11%
48	cui	P	12	0.18%	98	aprire	V	7	0.11%
49	tempo	S	12	0.18%	99	tenere	V	7	0.11%
50	neve	S	12	0.18%	100	cercare	V	7	0.11%

TABLE A.3. Most frequent words in Hasan Al Nassar's *RG*.

The frequency list indicates the part of speech (A = adjective, B = adverb, C = conjunction, P = pronoun, S = noun, V = verb, VA = auxiliary verb) and presents the absolute and relative frequency (AF and RF) of the hundred most frequently occurring words in *RG*.

			AF	RF				AF	RF
1	e	C	231	2.63%	51	dire	V	17	0.19%
2	essere	V	216	2.46%	52	così	B	17	0.19%
3	che	P	145	1.65%	53	donna	S	17	0.19%
4	non	B	115	1.31%	54	ma	C	16	0.18%
5	nostro	A	86	0.98%	55	esilio	S	16	0.18%
6	avere	VA	73	0.83%	56	spada	S	16	0.18%
7	mio	A	68	0.77%	57	lei	P	16	0.18%
8	si	P	59	0.67%	58	luce	S	16	0.18%
9	suo	A	57	0.65%	59	adesso	B	15	0.17%
10	tuo	A	52	0.59%	60	volta	S	15	0.17%
11	guerra	S	51	0.58%	61	ogni	A	15	0.17%
12	acqua	S	46	0.52%	62	scrivere	V	15	0.17%
13	noi	P	38	0.43%	63	sogno	S	15	0.17%
14	amore	S	36	0.41%	64	sabbia	S	15	0.17%
15	mi	P	35	0.40%	65	forse	B	14	0.16%
16	vedere	V	35	0.40%	66	foresta	S	14	0.16%
17	notte	S	35	0.40%	67	ombra	S	14	0.16%
18	questo	A	34	0.39%	68	me	P	13	0.15%
19	che	C	32	0.36%	69	silenzio	S	13	0.15%
20	cuore	S	32	0.36%	70	morto	S	13	0.15%
21	essere	VA	32	0.36%	71	mattino	S	13	0.15%
22	terra	S	32	0.36%	72	strada	S	13	0.15%

23	fuoco	S	32	0.36%	73	paura	S	13	0.15%
24	avere	V	31	0.35%	74	pietra	S	13	0.15%
25	ci	B	31	0.35%	75	dormire	V	13	0.15%
26	città	S	30	0.34%	76	fare	V	12	0.14%
27	giorno	S	29	0.33%	77	erba	S	12	0.14%
28	chi	P	29	0.33%	78	uscire	V	12	0.14%
29	portare	V	27	0.31%	79	fiume	S	12	0.14%
30	casa	S	27	0.31%	80	potere	V	12	0.14%
31	ci	P	24	0.27%	81	estate	S	12	0.14%
32	entrare	V	24	0.27%	82	porta	S	12	0.14%
33	ed	C	23	0.26%	83	conoscere	V	12	0.14%
34	albero	S	21	0.24%	84	morte	S	12	0.14%
35	loro	A	21	0.24%	85	figlio	S	12	0.14%
36	tu	P	20	0.23%	86	cadere	V	11	0.13%
37	ti	P	20	0.23%	87	lontano	A	11	0.13%
38	questo	P	20	0.23%	88	altro	A	11	0.13%
39	ora	S	20	0.23%	89	occhio	S	11	0.13%
40	quello	A	19	0.22%	90	sangue	S	11	0.13%
41	mare	S	19	0.22%	91	testa	S	11	0.13%
42	corpo	S	19	0.22%	92	perché	C	11	0.13%
43	cielo	S	17	0.19%	93	sopra	B	11	0.13%
44	vento	S	17	0.19%	94	volere	V	10	0.11%
45	più	B	17	0.19%	95	campo	S	10	0.11%
46	io	P	17	0.19%	96	nascondere	V	10	0.11%
47	mano	S	17	0.19%	97	vetro	S	10	0.11%
48	anno	S	17	0.19%	98	nuvola	S	10	0.11%
49	nome	S	17	0.19%	99	sentiero	S	10	0.11%
50	o	C	17	0.19%	100	voce	S	10	0.11%

INDEX

Abate, Carmine 38
accentual verse 30, 35 n. 129
    accentual dynamics in Al Nassar 119, 133–38, 155
    accentual dynamics in Hajdari 60–72
    accentual dynamics in Pumhösel 100–05
Adonis 59, 118, 150 n. 5
Adorno, Theodor W. 19
Al Delmì, Fawzi 118–19, 150 n. 5
Al Nassar, Hasan Atiya:
    contexts 3, 6–7, 16, 20, 23, 26, 28, 119–21
    on displacement 117, 119
    Il labirinto 121, 151 n. 24
    Poesie dell'esilio 121, 122, 151 n. 24
    Roghi sull'acqua babilonese 6, 29, 121–50
        contrapuntality 123, 129, 144–45
        exile and displacement 119, 121–22, 131, 143–44
        elegy 123–24, 127–28
        language 145–50
        long lines 137–39
        long poems 122–24, 129–31, 137, 143
        metalanguage 145–46
        metaphors 148
        metre and rhythm 131–41
        multilingual inserts 146–47
        personification 125–26
        poetic forms (general) 123–31
        polyphony 139–41
        refrains 128
        space and movement 148–50
        function of stanzas 127–31
        structure 121–23
        use of repetition 141–45
        variants 122–23
    on translanguaging 120
Al Sayyàb, Badr Shakir 118
Albanian popular and epic poetry 42, 52, 54–59, 154–55
Ali Farah, Ubah Cristina 10, 14
Alighieri, Dante 14, 20, 54
Allen, Roger 124, 128
alliteration 99, 104
allocution 61–62, 128, 132, 144
alterity 2, 45–48, 51, 90
Amaruka 59
anaphora, *see* repetition
Arbëreshë 37–38
Arndt, Susan 22
assonance 46, 99

Bakhtin, Mikhail Mikhailovich 24–25
Bal, Mieke 4
Barthes, Roland 4, 7 n. 10, 12, 25
Basagoitia Dazza, Gladys 28
Baynham, Mike 18
Beckett, Samuel 16
Blasone, Pino 118
body:
    in Al Nassar 121, 125
    in Hajdari 39, 40, 50–52, 54, 57, 72, 77–79
    in Pumhösel 88, 91, 96, 108
    and rhythm in poetry 26
Boine, Giovanni 22
Bonaffini, Luigi 27
Bond, Emma 37–39
Bondarenko, Natalia 28
border 9, 37, 89, 110
Bouchane, Mohamed 13
Brioni, Simone 2, 12, 14, 17, 19, 40–41, 56, 74, 147
Brown, Charles Armitage 95–96
Bryson, Scott 85
Buell, Lawrence 84
Burns, Jennifer 9–12, 14

caesura 97, 105, 139
calque 30, 59, 74–75, 155
Canagarajah, Suresh 17
Carroll, Kevin 17
censorship 13, 45, 57, 119
chiasmus 144
Colangelo, Stefano 15, 97, 114 n. 56
Comberiati, Daniele 37–39
Compagnia delle poete 28, 35 n. 120, 83
concordance 72, 149
    see also lemmatization
Conrad, Joseph 16
consonance 46
Contini, Gianfranco 21–22, 30, 33 n. 88, 73, 149, 156
counterpoint 4, 14
Crecchia, Antonio 47
creolization 11, 28
crossing 12, 43, 77, 84, 85, 90, 110–11, 119, 156

D'Alessandro, Barbara 35 n. 124, 84, 111
Dante, *see* Alighieri, Dante
De Caldas Brito, Christiana 13
De Oliveira, Vera Lucia 28, 35 n. 120

De Vos, Arnold 28
Deleuze, Gilles 13, 32 n. 38
De Mauro, Tullio 20–21
deixis, *see* spatial deixis
Di Gianvito, Sara 35 n. 124, 48
dialogism 25, 41, 139
Dickinson, Emily 25
Dionisotti, Carlo 11
dislocation (of lines or stanzas) 95–97, 102, 128, 139
dissonance 64, 106, 126, 128
displacement 37–40, 117–20
distance (linguistic) 22–24
Dossi, Carlo 22
double language (Hajdari) 2, 6, 37, 40–43, 48, 57, 76, 79
double stresses 64, 66, 104–06
double verse 2, 4, 41–42, 48, 51, 56–57, 60, 64, 72–75
Dowling, Sarah 19

ecocriticism 84–86, 108, 113 n. 9
ecofeminism 6, 85–86
ecology 83–88
ecopoetics 84–85, 86
   see also translingualism and environment
Edwards, Natalie 5, 17–18
enjambment 54, 62, 91, 94–95, 100, 102, 124, 131, 133
exile 1–3, 6, 29, 39, 45–46, 48, 55, 79, 80 n. 12, 117–22, 143–44, 154
exophony 22–24, 33 n. 91, 73, 107

fluidity 5, 110, 122, 127, 153–54
Forster, Leonard 15
Fracassa, Ugo 14
free verse 30, 35 n. 128, 43, 60, 95, 121, 155

Gadda, Carlo Emilio 14, 16, 22
Gardini, Nicola 26
Garrard, Greg 87
Gazzoni, Andrea 39, 42, 48, 56, 80 n. 13, 154
ghazal 119, 124
Ghermandi, Gabriella 10, 14
Gibràn, Khalìl Gibràn 118
Glissant, Édouard 11
Gnisci, Armando 11, 27, 31 n. 18 & 19
Gramsci, Antonio 21
Grippi, Silvana 123, 151 n. 30
Guattari, Félix 13

haiku 95–98, 114 n. 56, 155
Hajdari, Gëzim:
   contexts 1–3, 16, 20, 23, 26–28, 30, 37–41
   on displacement 39–40
   on language, *see* double language
   Poesie scelte (1990–2007) 5, 29, 42–79
      Antologia della pioggia 43, 45–48, 62, 80 n. 28
      body and name 39–40, 50–52, 54, 57, 72, 77, 79

brevity 48
calques 59, 74–75
Corpo presente 43, 48–52, 62, 66, 69, 73, 75, 80 n. 28
epicization 52, 57, 64, 74
Erbamara 43, 45–48, 62, 64, 67, 69, 80 n. 28
exile and displacement 46, 48, 55, 74, 79
use of language 72–79
long poem 52, 54–55, 59–60, 66, 70
loss of words 48–52
Maldiluna 43, 52–54, 64, 69–70, 80 n. 28
matter 49, 62, 73, 75–76, 79
metalanguage 50, 76–77
metaphors 73
metre and rhythm 60–72
more-than-human 46–48, 52, 54, 59, 75–76
multilingual inserts 54–56, 74–75
neologisms 75
Ombra di cane 43, 48–50, 80 n. 28
Peligòrga 43, 56–59, 62, 64, 67, 69, 80 n. 28
poetic forms (general) 44–59
polyphony 52, 54, 56–59, 66–67, 70
quatrain 45–46, 48, 54, 57, 59–60, 66, 67, 69
Sassi contro vento 43, 48 –50, 51, 67, 80 n. 28
settenario 64, 66–67
space and movement 77–79
Spine nere 43, 52–56, 66, 70, 79, 80 n. 28
Stigmate 43, 52–56, 64, 69, 80 n. 28
structure 52–54
variants 43, 45, 47–48, 50, 56
Poema dell'esilio 38, 54
Poezi të zgjedhura (1990–2007) 44
self-translation 41, 43
Hanxhari, Anila 28
Haraway, Donna 85
hidden metre 25, 60, 64, 100, 123, 131, 141
Hikmet, Nâzım 59
hybridity 4, 6, 7 n. 9, 14, 30
hybridization 38, 40, 44, 59, 74, 86, 128
   see also metrical hybridization
Hussein, Saddam 117

immanence 50–51
in-betweenness 25, 52, 54, 109–10
indexicality 43–44, 47, 77, 91, 107, 111–12, 119, 148, 156
interspecies 86
intertextuality 54, 73–74, 87, 96, 114 n. 27, 154
Iovino, Serenella 85–86, 108
isochronism 60, 64, 72, 100, 138, 155
Italophone literature 13–15

Kafka, Franz 19
Kavafis, Konstantinos Petrou 59
Keats, John 96, 113 n. 26
Kellman, Steven G. 4, 15–17, 22–23
Khouma, Pap 13

Index

Kiemle, Christiane 12, 21
Kristeva, Julia 87, 114 n. 27

Laitef, Thea 118–20
Lakhous, Amara 27
language:
  in Al Nassar 145–50
  and animation 77, 85, 88, 107–08
  and childhood 23, 33 n. 96
  and deformation 30, 73, 125, 145
  in Hajdari 72–79
  and matter 3, 49, 73, 75, 102–03, 108, 144
  and movement 77, 111–12, 149–50
  and nature 75–76, 108–11, 148
  and space 77–79, 112, 148–50
  and pain 120, 123, 131, 145
  in Pumhösel 107–12
  see also double language
  see also translingualism
Lecomte, Mia 27–28, 34 n. 115, 35 n. 120, 118–20
Lee, Tong King 18
lemmatization 30, 35 n. 130
liberation 22–23, 89, 111, 154
Lidström, Susanna 87

Manzi, Luigi 50
maqamat 126, 151 n. 39
materialism 50, 72
Mattei, Alessandra 35 n. 124, 40
Mauceri, Maria Cristina 34, 151 n. 39
Mazak, Catherine 17, 32 n. 60
Mazzoni, Guido 12
Mengozzi, Chiara 10
Meschonnic, Henry 24–25, 41, 43
metalanguage 24, 50, 76–77, 79, 86, 107, 109, 145–46, 156
metamorphosis 52, 64, 77, 85–86, 108
metapoetic 77, 107, 145
metaphorical expressionism 22, 30, 73, 149, 156
Methnani, Salah 13
metres and rhythms:
  in Al Nassar 131–45
  in Hajdari 60–72
  in Pumhösel 100–07
metrical hybridization 4, 25, 123, 136, 139
migration 3, 11–12, 20, 23, 28–29, 72, 79, 83, 153–54
  see also migration literature
migration literature 9–12, 14, 17, 20–21, 26–27
minor literature 4, 7 n. 9, 13–14
mobility, see translingualism and mobility
monolingualism 15, 19
more-than-human, see translingualism and more-than-human
movement:
  and rhythm 24–26, 107
  see also language and movement

multilingualism:
  in Al Nassar 146–47
  definitions 4, 15, 19
  in Hajdari 55, 58–59, 74
  plurilingual effect 15
  in Pumhösel 87, 96, 110–11

Nabokov, Vladimir 16
Naguschewski, Dirk 22
Negro, Grazia 85, 87, 89, 111
neologisms:
  in Hajdari 46, 74–75
  in Pumhösel 110–11
Neruda, Pablo 59
Ngana Yogo, Ndjock 28

onomatopoeia 98
Oppermann, Serpil 108
Ortese, Anna Maria 85
Özdamar, Emine Sevgi 19

parallel texts 2, 29, 40–41, 74
Parati, Graziella 1, 10–11, 13
Pasolini, Pier Paolo 14
Perloff, Marjorie 23
personification 52, 85–86, 108–09, 125, 148
Petrarca, Francesco 16
Pisanelli, Flaviano 28, 35 n. 123, 117, 120–21
Plumwood, Val 85
poetic forms:
  in Al Nassar 123–31
  in Hajdari 44–59
  in Pumhösel 91–101
Polezzi, Loredana 9, 11, 17, 19, 40
polyphony 54–59, 122–24, 139–41
Poniatowska, Elena 16
postcolonial literature 40–41
post-monolingualism 5, 19–22, 27
Prévert, Jacques 59
prosimetrum 126, 151 n. 39
prosody 24–26, 30, 60, 86, 119–20, 139
Pumhösel, Barbara:
  on borders 84, 89, 110
  un confine in comune 113 n. 6
  contexts 3, 6, 10, 16, 20, 23–24, 26–28, 30, 35 n. 120, 83–88
  on language 86–87
  on linguistic distance 88, 107
  on migration 83
  prugni 6, 29, 89–91
    botanical vocabulary 111
    fording 93
    use of language 107–12
    matter 102–03, 108–09
    metalanguage 107–08
    metamorphosis 108–09

metaphor 108
metre and rhythm 100–07
more–than–human 88–91, 93–97, 108–09
multilingual inserts 110–11
neologisms 111
personification 108–09
poem–objects, poem–bodies, poem–worlds 91–100
poetic forms (general) 91–100
semantics of brevity 91–100
space and movement 111–12
stepped lines 91, 95, 101, 103
structure 88–91
synaesthesia 89, 95, 98, 107, 109, 111
transient rhythm 106–07
technical–scientific vocabulary 111
transitional imagery 107–08
variants 91
in transitu 113 n. 6
on translanguaging 86
see also language and animation

qasīda 6, 119, 123–24, 131, 155
qitah 124
Quaquarelli, Lucia 13
questione della lingua 14, 20

Ramzanali Fazel, Shirin 13
Rebora, Clemente 22
repetition:
  in Al Nassar 141–45
  in Hajdari 52, 66, 67
resistance 19–22
rhythm 24–26
Romain, Jules 22
Romeo, Caterina 13
Rosselli, Amelia 26
Rushdie, Salman 16

Said, Edward 7 n. 9, 119
Scego, Igiaba 10, 14, 27, 40–41
Scott, Clive 87
Segre, Cesare 21
self–anthology 29
self–translation, *see* translation
Serdakowski, Barbara 28, 35 n. 120
Shemtov, Vered 4, 25, 139, 155
Sibhatu, Ribka 13, 41
sonnet 96
spatial deixis 26, 30, 35 n. 131, 77–79, 112, 148–50
Spitzer, Leo 22
Stabreim 99
Stanišić, Božidar 28
Stella, Francesco 27, 118

step line 47, 91, 95, 101, 103
Stockhammer, Robert 22
synaesthesia 89, 109

Tawada, Yoko 19, 23–24, 88, 156
Tawfik, Younis 126, 151 n. 39
Taylor, Eva 28, 35 n. 120, 94, 115 n. 58
Toppan, Laura 28, 59, 117, 120–21
transhuman 72
translanguaging 16–17, 32 n. 60, 155
  in Al Nassar 119
  in Hajdari 60, 76, 77
  in Pumhösel 87, 110–11
  see also translingualism and translaguaging
translation 2, 4–5, 9, 11–15, 80 n. 27, 118
  as a metaphor 4, 9, 39
  of poetry 24–25, 87
  in postcolonial literature 2, 41, 74
  self–translation 4, 41, 43, 46, 120, 126, 154
  thick translation 40, 74
  see also translingualism and translation
translingualism:
  and childhood 23
  definitions 4–5, 15–18
  and environment 87
  and linguistic distance 22–24
  and migration 22–24
  and mobility 9, 14, 17
  and more–than–human 52, 88–91, 93–98, 148
  and multilingualism 15–18
  and poetry in Italy 26–28
  and post–monolingualism 19–22
  and rhythm 24–26
  and translanguaging 5, 16–18
  and translation 17–18, 40, 42
  from *within* and from *beyond* 5, 21–23
translocal 84, 113 n. 9
Triolet, Elsa 16
Tzara, Tristan 16

Ungaretti, Giuseppe 16, 114 n. 56

Venuti, Lawrence 40
Violi, Patrizia 25, 35 n. 131, 77, 149, 156
Vorpsi, Ornela 23

Wright, Chantal 23

Yildiz, Yasemin 5, 16, 19–20
Yûsuf, Sa'di 118

Zaimoğlu, Feridun 19
Ziarati, Hamid 27

www.ingramcontent.com/pod-product-compliance
Lightning Source LLC
Chambersburg PA
CBHW050454110426
42743CB00017B/3352